MW01096544

FIGHTING MAD

My Son's Wild Ride
Through the Mental Health System

by Ana Miranda

Copyright © 2011 Ana Miranda

All rights reserved.

ISBN: 1463579136
ISBN-13: 9781463579135

Photo on back cover, © John F. Rogers

For Patricia,
whose wisdom, support, and
compassion gave me
strength for the journey and
hope in the future

CONTENTS

ACKNOWLEDGMENTS

My husband and children stayed by Danny's side every step of his journey. Their support, encouragement, and prayers inspired me to share his story, in the hope that other families might feel less alone as they face their own hardships.

Our extended family and countless dear friends kept us going and gave us the courage to face each day with renewed hope and determination. I am especially grateful to my own parents and sisters, and to Carol, Teresa, Michael, and the members of my NAMI caring and sharing group and our parish's Caring for the Soul group for their empathy, encouragement, prayers, and support.

I am also deeply indebted to the many doctors, social workers, and other health professionals who went beyond the call of duty in order to help Danny stay on the road to recovery, or find it again when he had lost his way. Their selfless dedication to those under their care can be the difference between life and death.

While some people find their way through the maze of mental illness without relying on the resources of faith, I felt from the beginning that, as St. Theresa of Avila says, only God suffices. May all who call on him "out of the depths" find him.

PREFACE

It approaches like a gathering storm. In the beginning only the distant rumble of thunder, an almost imperceptible darkening of the sky, a subtle quickening of the breeze—then the first streak of lightning tears through the sky, triggering a deafening explosion, and the wild wind batters you with heavy rain. Mental illness creeps up on you that way. Before you know what to call it, something ominous darkens the horizon of a person's mind, and family and friends begin to wonder what it means. They attribute the changes to difficult circumstances, growing pains, adolescent angst, even drug or alcohol abuse—anything but mental illness. But inevitably there comes the time when, in a flash, the truth is undeniable . . . and the long journey begins.

At first it is a journey in the dark, with neither one's own experience nor that of others to draw on and no idea where to turn. People don't talk about mental illness the way they talk about heart attacks or diabetes or even cancer. Everyone is ready to recommend a pediatrician or orthopedist, but no one tells you where to find the best treatment for schizophrenia or what you need to do immediately if you want to find help for your child. (Perhaps even more critically, no one tells you what to avoid like the plague.) Blindsided by this sudden tsunami, plunged into overwhelming grief and confusion, you feel utterly alone.

In time you discover that there are medical and other resources for treating mental illness, but also that, initially at least, most of them are inaccessible to you. Countless obstacles stand between your loved one and the help they need, and even medical professionals and their teammates seem reluctant to relinquish the information that will help you navigate them. A diagnosis of mental illness is a living nightmare that almost always turns into a living hell before the first ray of hope appears on the horizon.

The first thing you learn is that mental illness is a chronic disease. No, really . . . *chronic*. As in *incurable*. So you have to begin to accept the unthinkable, a process that can take months and even years. How can I believe that my youngest son—this bright, compassionate, athletic, fun-loving seventeen-year-old, poised on the threshold of life's possibilities—is afflicted with an illness that carries a deep social stigma and from which he will never be free?

Psychiatrists sometimes try to soften the blow by comparing schizophrenia or bipolar disorder to diabetes and asthma. But the truth is that there's no comparison between a chronic physical condition and a mental illness. Nobody judges you because you have diabetes, and no one makes you feel ashamed because you're diabetic. People don't normally blame your parents for the fact that you're asthmatic or start avoiding you as though you might be contagious.

A person who develops diabetes or asthma or high blood pressure is essentially the same person he or she was before. Mental illness isn't like that. It changes everything, shattering every certitude that kept you anchored to the world, your

2

family, your faith, and even yourself. Descartes famously announced that nothing is more certain than "I think, therefore I am." But there are times when persons with auditory hallucinations don't know which of the thoughts or voices in their heads are their own.

It's tempting to describe this loss of one's identity as a "symptom." The term does have the advantage of making it sound more clinical, more like another medical condition—which, of course, it is. But the devastation caused by a mental illness is much more than a set of symptoms. It eats away at your personality and the talents and interests that made you who you were and shaped your plans for the future. In short, it blows your life to pieces.

No wonder, then, that it took my son and our family years to accept the reality and permanence of his illness. It was longer still before Danny would admit that he needed the psychiatric medications he was prescribed—and that he would probably need them every day for the rest of his life. Last to die was the illusion that "a little" alcohol or weed or Oxycontin couldn't really hurt; maybe it could even be a remedy for the effects of his illness—the anxiety and racing thoughts and anger and impulsiveness.

In this struggle to accept the unacceptable, I thought it was my duty to stay ahead of my son—to reconcile him to his new reality. But as the months and years passed, Danny often outpaced me in accepting the frustrations of his illness and its devastating impact on his life. I suppose the illusion hardest for me to surrender was that I knew what Danny needed. Well, not exactly it turns out. My certitudes are fewer these days.

1 Storm Clouds

How do you know that something is seriously wrong with your child? I wish I had a good answer to that question. It's something I've been asking myself ever since I learned my son was ill. Were there clues I overlooked, behaviors that should have tipped me off, incidents at school that went beyond the normal high-jinks of teenage boys? Perhaps there were, but I'm sorry to report that I still don't know what they were.

Danny was born in 1987 during a sweltering July in Washington, DC. He was greeted by big brothers Jose (Joey) and Alejandro (Alex). My husband Damian and I are college teachers, and Damian had just finished a fellowship year in DC, while I was recovering from a year of full-time teaching at a local university. Not long after Danny's arrival, we moved back to the Midwestern university where Damian held a permanent position. That next year was one of only two in my twenty-four year career when I didn't work at all—not even part-time—and I loved every minute of it.

As Danny grew old enough to play with his big brothers, he had to have the same Superman pajamas and big-boy swimming trunks, and insisted on a tricycle so he could follow them on their bikes, peddling furiously in order to keep up. In some ways, being the youngest of three boys defined Danny's early years. While he didn't have the quick verbal abilities of Joey and Alex, he made up for it in physical strength and athletic skills.

The boys certainly had their arguments and scuffles, but for the most part they got along remarkably well. I told my friends I was grateful (eventually) that they were born so close together, because they truly became each other's best friends. When Liliana joined this crew five years after Danny, she wanted to be part of the gang too, and Danny was the one who sympathized with her and tried to include her in whatever the guys were up to.

As Danny entered grade school, it was clear that he would be the entertainer of the family. His eyes sparkled with joy and adventure, and his dimpled smile was so disarming that often when I started to reprimand him I would end up laughing instead. He had a cheerful manner and bright expression that seemed to say, "How could you not love me?"

Danny was always ready for action and sometimes took the quest for excitement a bit too far, trying feats of daring (usually on an impulse) that might have led to disaster. He loved to be outdoors, and threw himself into games and sports with reckless abandon, always giving 100% to the cause. He seemed to thrive on physical contact and "mixing it up" with his brothers and friends, an enthusiasm that wasn't always shared by the others.

Hoping to channel Danny's rowdiness, I signed him up for PeeWee football at the age of seven, even though he was so much smaller than his teammates that I had to search far and wide for pants and shoulder pads to fit him. Still, his fierce tackles won him the nickname "Bone Crusher." He was so

5

proud of it that I tried to suppress my reservations about having signed him up in the first place. Football lasted off and on through Danny's freshman year in high school, but he was still so much smaller than the rest of the team that the coach called him "Little Man." I insisted that he finish that season, but we both knew organized football wasn't in his future.

Danny always did well in school, often bringing home straight A's, though comments from the teachers clearly indicated that he was suffering from ADHD. Damian and I were reluctant to seek a definitive diagnosis, however, and suspicious of the medication mania sweeping the country at the time. Some experts complained that medication was just a way of punishing boys for being boys. Besides, Danny kept his grades up and did well on standardized tests. He was smart and funny and popular with his peers, a leader rather than a follower. By seventh grade, he had a group of friends he called his "posse."

In spite of his general popularity, Danny always chose one friend as his true comrade and confidant. He was fiercely loyal to his friends and was always deeply hurt when it seemed they weren't there for him when he needed them most. But he also forgave easily, retaining the hope and optimism that were part of his nature from the beginning. Our family relocated many times over the years, but all four of the children seemed to adjust well to new situations.

We arrived in the Boston area in June of 1999, and Danny met Bobby, a boy his age in the next block who quickly became his best friend. They were both in seventh grade and, given their competitive natures, began to challenge each other for the highest GPA. For the next four years, Danny seemed to flourish in school, especially in math and science, and he had a positive attitude toward most of his teachers. His sense of humor was a bane or a blessing, depending on who you asked, and symptoms of ADHD continued to plague him into junior high and high school.

At the end of his sophomore year, we were forced out of our rented apartment in a close suburb of Boston. The landlord who had built our townhouse was dedicated to providing affordable housing in a city of affluence, but when he passed away, his heirs decided to sell. We were nowhere close to being able to buy the house, so we braced ourselves for another move. We hoped to remain in the same town for the sake of our children, but we found nothing in our price range that would accommodate the six of us. Ultimately, we decided to buy our first home, a unit in a newly-built condo in a neighboring suburb—a significantly less prestigious town, but one that was experiencing a recent influx of students and young families.

The most negative result of the move was that Danny had to transfer to a new school, leaving behind his friend Bobby and the school system he had known for years. Most of the kids he knew from junior high remained his classmates in the high school. Besides, both Joey and Alex were graduates of that school, and Danny and Bobby had already teamed up to try almost every sport the school offered (though Bobby wisely stayed away from football). Danny played drums in the pep band and jazz band, and was beginning to attract some attention from the girls.

For a time we considered letting Danny live at Bobby's house during the week so he could maintain a local address and continue to attend his familiar high school. But it seemed wrong to promote a deliberate deception to get around the rules—not exactly the lesson we wanted to teach our children. So we told our son he would have to try to adjust to a new school. Predictably, he was furious. When his life began to take a downward turn the following year, I assumed at first that it was a protest against our decision. Unfortunately, that turned out to be wishful thinking.

Damian and I thought Danny would do better in a smaller, more personal environment rather than starting over in a large public high school with several hundred students. So when we discovered a charter school in our neighborhood, and they bent their regulations to allow Danny to enroll as a junior, we thought it was the perfect solution. Lily was just starting seventh grade, and we were able to enroll her at the same school.

One of the few drawbacks was that the same building included students from seventh to twelfth grade. As a result, some of the school's rules and restrictions were more appropriate for 12-year-olds than for young adults of 17 and 18. A second problem was that, because of its innovative curriculum, the school attracted many young teachers, including some just out of college. This was, as you can imagine, a mixed blessing.

While Lily made a smooth transition and seemed to flourish in this new setting, Danny fought the school and every adult in it for the remainder of his time there. Before long, the head of school, the dean of students, and most of his teachers were exasperated with him. Detention nearly became part of his daily schedule, and it often involved arcane penalties like having to copy a sentence from the blackboard 100 times. Any absence from detention meant doing time on Saturday as well. Danny must have broken the bank on this front.

Of course I was called in for numerous consultations with various members of the administration. Often they would ask, "Is there something going on at home that we should be aware of?"—as though my husband, or I, or some dreadful

8

catastrophe in our family life, were the cause of our son's out-of-control behavior. They wanted a simple explanation too, I suppose—one that had nothing to do with them.

Looking back, I'm sure they must have been utterly frustrated with Danny. They would speak to him and to us about his intelligence and potential, hoping to find a way to motivate him to work harder and stop his destructive behavior. Sometimes they asked what I thought he needed, but I had no answers. It was a question I had asked myself many times over, always failing to find a satisfactory solution.

By October of his junior year, Danny was in real trouble. He sank into a deep depression, and nothing seemed to motivate him. He missed countless days of school, sleeping all day or wandering aimlessly around town, sorrowful and alone. He claimed that school had nothing more to offer him, and that the teachers targeted him for punishment even when he wasn't at fault. When I asked, "Not all of them, right? There must be some teachers who are kind to you," his response was unequivocal: "No, Mom; it's all of them. *They really hate me.*"

Perhaps I should have recognized this as a sign of growing paranoia, but that thought never entered my mind. After all, Danny had been so difficult to deal with that it wasn't hard to believe the teachers were fed up with his behavior.

I have a vivid memory of one of my conversations with Danny around this time. I was trying to motivate him by reminding him that his teachers thought he had enormous potential, but he blew up in my face. "I'm sick of hearing that, Mom. How do they know what potential I have? And what's potential anyway? Like I can do something someday? But what if I can't? Maybe I don't even care about potential; why would I want to spend four more years in school just so I can wind up like all of them?" Suffice it to say, I hadn't anticipated such a strongly negative response to what seemed like a positive observation. It made me wonder what was really going on with my son, this bright, capable, outgoing teenager who always had such high expectations for his future.

I held out hope that when basketball season started in late November, Danny would join the team as he had the previous year, getting some needed exercise and reconnecting with his teammates. When he decided not to play, my concern deepened. I considered trying to take him to a counselor, and eventually raised the topic with my husband. He was opposed to the idea, believing that what Danny needed was more discipline and a change of attitude. I wasn't so sure, wondering whether his troubling behaviors and emotions might come from something deeper than Danny's (by now) strongly oppositional stance toward authority figures.

I must add that even during this turbulent time, Danny's math teacher reached out to him, developing a friendship that has lasted for years. Math was always one of Danny's strengths, and Mr. Cole even encouraged him to consider a career in the field. On several occasions, when Danny was having a particularly bad day, Mr. Cole took him out for a cup of coffee at a local cafe, just to get away for a while and talk things over. Danny adopted this man as a role model and came to him often for fatherly advice and encouragement. Mr. Cole was the only adult outside Danny's family who truly believed in him, and he often kept Danny from the brink of despair. In fact, I believe he saved my son's life. A heart full of gratitude is all I have to offer in exchange for his extraordinary kindness to my son.

In spite of Mr. Cole's interventions, however, Danny continued to slide into deeper trouble at home and at school. At first, I chalked up his dark moods and absence of motivation to girlfriend problems or the early onset of senioritis, but by Christmas break it was clear that he was suffering from a deep and debilitating depression, and that our ordinary cheering-up strategies were not making a dent in it. I urged him to see a counselor or, failing that, to talk with someone in the guidance office or to one of his teachers. But Danny was reluctant to do any of these, and both he and Damian adamantly opposed seeking professional help.

So I began reading about depression on my own, and consulting the mental health professionals I knew about how to get help for Danny before it was too late. Their response was always the same: "Unless Danny recognizes that he needs help, nobody can help him." At the time, I just didn't believe them; or, to be honest, I couldn't believe them. How can you watch your own son sliding toward an abyss without believing there is something you can do to help? Even if they were right, I wondered how they could say it with such casualness, as though it were just another ho-hum truism about teenagers, when my world was flying apart at the seams. I felt I had to try every way I could think of to save my son. Then, even if I failed, there was a chance I could still live with myself.

During winter break, against Damian's advice and wishes, I prevailed on Danny to see a psychiatrist. "Just one appointment." I pleaded, "Just do it for me." While I knew Danny had no intention of receiving help from a "shrink," I naively believed that psychiatrists must have some way of winning people over and getting them to come back for more sessions. Not so. Danny cursed this dignified, mild-mannered physician up and down, storming out of his office amid a string of profanities well before the allotted fifty minutes. Given the spectacular failure of that attempt, my husband and son were doubly convinced that therapy was inherently worthless.

I asked at the charter school about the possibility of bringing Danny in for an evaluation, perhaps referring him to a counselor or a therapist or . . . well, *someone*. When they replied at all, it was to say that nothing like that was available. The only counselor at the school was there to help the students apply to college, not to address their personal problems.

It was sixteen months after the failed psychiatrist visit that Danny had his first psychotic break and received a diagnosis of schizoaffective disorder—sixteen months that seemed like decades. This was a season of unrelenting sadness for me, and for Danny as well, though sometimes he channeled his sorrow into anger or thoughts of revenge. During these months, Damian and I clashed strongly and constantly over what Danny needed, with Damian lobbying for stronger disciplinary measures and I pushing for encouragement, sympathy, and professional help.

Our other children were caught in the crossfire. I think it was an especially harrowing time for Liliana, who walked to school every day with an increasingly hostile and unpredictable brother—the sibling who used to be her best friend and loving confidant. I'm sure I made things even worse by asking her to overlook some of his behaviors and try to be understanding of him. Life was becoming unbearable for her, but at the time I was simply oblivious to it.

The older boys suffered in silence, rarely sharing what they thought or felt, about Danny or anything else. One of my deepest regrets about those months of dread and waiting, and many months afterward, is that I wasn't really there for my other children. I vaguely hoped they would be OK, but I didn't take time to listen to them or to give the events in their lives the attention they deserved. If I could have that time back, would I do any better? I hope so. But it's hard to know.

The most remarkable thing about the time just before the storm, however, wasn't the mounting problems or emotional turmoil. Rather, it was the strange fact that Danny and everyone around him continued to believe that things would be alright in the end, that somehow he would find his way out of the dark crevasse he had fallen into. Hope, it turns out, is incredibly resilient.

Timeout: Brain Science

For every person with a loved one suffering from a mental illness, and probably for the one who suffers as well, it is virtually impossible to know when the illness began. When I first learned that my son was seriously ill, I began to scrutinize every moment of his childhood, looking for telltale signs of what was to come. It seemed there should be someone or something to bear the blame.

Is it I? Every parent of a mentally ill child asks that question. Some never get past it, even though research overwhelmingly shows that a person's upbringing has absolutely nothing to do with the onset of a psychiatric disorder. Some children who develop a serious mental illness in their teens or twenties exhibited symptoms of impending problems from an early age. But, for most, the devastating blow that changes their world forever simply comes out of the blue. At 15 or 16 you're just a typical teenager, and then suddenly at 17 or 18 . . . you're not.

The only predictive factor for mental illness seems to be a genetic one. If there is mental illness in your family—siblings, parents, grandparents, uncles and aunts—there is a good

14

chance that you have at least a predisposition to mental illness as well.[1] I suppose I should have been better prepared, since both my brother and one of my husband's brothers were diagnosed with schizophrenia in their late teens, and many members of my family battled depression over the years— sometimes alcoholism as well. In fact, I was already taking several medications to offset depression, anxiety, fatigue, and post-traumatic stress, but that felt like my own isolated situation rather than a general trend.

Recently, the Boston Globe carried a story about a woman who confided that, since both she and her fiancé had a history of mental illness in their families, they had thought seriously about whether they were morally justified in getting married. This struck me as admirable in some ways, but also a little bizarre. Should I have walked away from the love of my life in order to spare our (theoretical) offspring a (potential) mental illness? Would my son be better off if he hadn't been born? What does that even mean? In any case, I have no regrets about marrying my husband of twenty-seven years, and certainly nothing but gratitude for each of my children. I can't imagine my life without them.

I gave up searching for causes of Danny's illness fairly quickly, having learned that there's a false security in believing mental illness makes sense. It's so tempting to think that if only you can figure out the cause or causes, you can regain some control. Perhaps you can intervene earlier with your other

---

[1] "Researchers . . . have pinpointed three genetic "hot spots" where deletions of big chunks of DNA appear to multiply a child's chances of developing schizophrenia up to tenfold." Carey Goldberg, "Genetic Hot Spots Tied to Schizophrenia," *The Boston Globe*, July 31, 2008, p. A2. It seems that, while some genetic patterns are inherited, others are the result of spontaneous mutations in the very early stages of fetal development.

children and avoid making the fatal mistakes (whatever they were) that affected this child. But, for better or worse, we live in a world where suffering is an equal-opportunity employer. It falls on the just and unjust—a fact we probably won't understand in this lifetime.

It may come as a surprise that I didn't seek detailed scientific information about schizophrenia until months, even years, after my son was diagnosed. I'm not sure if it was because I didn't want to know or because I thought I already knew so much that I couldn't bear to hear any more. Looking back, I realize it would have helped to have more information, both about the symptoms of this illness and the causes behind them.

One thing scientists know for sure is that schizophrenia is a disease of the brain.[2] While there are some who question this claim, it has been positively confirmed by recent technologies that allow detailed images of the brain, both when active and at rest.

In the rest of this section, I reproduce portions of an article published by two neuroscientists: Dr. Rashmi Namade, a PhD in Molecular Developmental Biology from the University of Cincinnati and postdoctoral fellow in the Laboratory of Genetics and Physiology at the National Institutes of Health, and Dr. Mark Dombeck, a PhD in Clinical Psychology from UC San Diego and postdoctoral fellow at Yale University School of Medicine. Their discussion of schizophrenia, especially in its

---

[2] According to the National Institute of Mental Health, "Schizophrenia is a chronic, severe, and disabling brain disorder that has affected people throughout history. About 1 percent of Americans have this illness." *www.nimh.nih.gov/health/publications/schizophrenia/what-is-schizophrenia.shtml.*

causes and symptoms, is one I found especially clear and accessible.

****

"Data from modern scientific research proves that schizophrenia is unequivocally a biological disease of the brain, just like Alzheimer's Disease and Bipolar Disorder. . . . Modern non-invasive brain imaging techniques such as Magnetic Resonance Imaging (MRI) and Computerized Tomography (CT), have documented *structural differences* between schizophrenic and normal brains.

[For example,] individuals with schizophrenia have up to 25% less volume of gray matter in their brains, especially in the temporal and frontal lobes (known to be important for coordination of thinking and judgment). Patients demonstrating the worst brain tissue losses also . . . show the worst symptoms. . . . Studies tend to show low levels of activation in schizophrenic patients' middle frontal cortex and inferior parietal cortex compared to normal people included as control subjects. . . .

In addition to structural differences, schizophrenic brains also show *neurochemical differences* when compared with normal brains. The brain uses a number of chemical messengers, called neurotransmitters, to communicate among its millions of individual neurons. At the most basic level, schizophrenic brains appear to be differentially sensitive to the neurotransmitter *dopamine* compared to normal brains. . . . [But] today, it appears more likely that other neurotransmitters are [also] involved in creating conditions for schizophrenia and psychosis, including *serotonin* (implicated in depression and anxiety), and *glutamate* (which is known to be implicated in the hallucinatory effects of the drug PCP ("angel dust"). . . .

17

Considered as a group and compared to normal people, schizophrenics show *observable functional deficits* as well. Functional deficits are problems people have in performing basic mental and physical tasks and activities such as remembering things, using executive functioning (being able to flexibly shift between various tasks, making judgments, etc.), intuiting rules from consequences, and hand grip strength.

On average, schizophrenic people show *reduced memory, attention span, executive functioning, and reaction time* compared to normal people. They have relatively more difficulty recalling things they learned five minutes before than normal people, for example, but are equally able to recall long-term memories. They tend to be more distractible and have a harder time engaging in problem solving and planning efforts than do normal people.

Abnormalities in sensory processing are also evident in schizophrenic patients. It is common for schizophrenic patients to show 'soft' neurological signs, meaning that they might have difficulty distinguishing between two simultaneous touches or in being able to identify numbers drawn on the palm of their hand. They also tend to confuse the right and left sides of their bodies more frequently than normal people. Such well documented observations of sensory processing problems suggest impairments or irregularities in the way that schizophrenics' brains are wired. . . . Considered as a whole, these numerous and methodologically distinct results suggest converging and compelling evidence for the idea that schizophrenia is basically a biologically-based brain disease."[3]

---

[3] Rashmi Nemade, Ph.D. & Mark Dombeck, Ph.D. "Evidence That Schizophrenia is a Brain Disease," at

****

New brain-imaging technologies are making the map of the
brain ever more detailed, offering hope for greater
understanding of mental illnesses and more effective
treatments for them. One team of researchers is perfecting a
"superscanner" which can produce high-resolution pictures that
capture the *connections* in the brain, not just its structure. The
scanner uses different colors to indicate the direction of brain
connections in three dimensions, like a DVD instead of just a
snapshot.

Dr. Bruce Rosen, director of the Martinos Center for Biomedical
Engineering at Massachusetts General Hospital, says that "the
connectome [the analogy here is with the human genome] is
the fundamental map of how the brain is wired and how these
parts work together. . . . Schizophrenia is thought by some
people to be disrupted connectivity. . . What we're looking to do
with this connectome project is fill in this crucial, but missing,
class of data."[4]

---

www.mentalhelp.net/poc/view_doc.php?type=doc&id=8812. Updated:
August 7, 2009.
[4] Carolyn Y. Johnson, "On a Quest to Map the Brain's Hidden Territory,"
The Boston Globe, October 11, 2010, B5, 7.

2 Off the Grid

Predictably, as his senior year wore on, Danny's fortunes continued to deteriorate. He passed his classes in the fall, some even with decent grades, but by the spring semester he had lost interest in everything related to school. My husband and I were both working full-time, so we weren't always aware of the many times Danny skipped classes, either failing to get out of bed or leaving school in the middle of the day.

As winter faded into spring, I became increasingly alarmed by Danny's lack of engagement in his life—he would sleep into the afternoon on weekends and, increasingly, even on school days, insisting that he didn't feel well or that he wasn't missing anything important. He was distant or sullen at home and would often disappear for hours at a time, returning in the wee hours of the morning or not at all.

We knew that alcohol and drugs had to be part of the equation, and Damian insisted that all Danny needed was to pull himself together and get serious about his studies, making whatever lifestyle adjustments were necessary. Teachers began contacting us to say that Danny was missing too many classes, failing to turn in assignments, and growing increasingly "oppositional" in his behavior. Getting him out of bed in the

20

morning turned into a daily power struggle. While Damian reproached Danny for his behavior, I became increasingly defensive for him, concerned that his depression would turn to despair—maybe even suicide.

In contrast to the downward roller-coaster plunge of Danny's senior year, there was one positive event that spring. Though he had been too jaded and depressed in the fall to finish any college applications, the guidance counselor (bless her!) had sent his application to the college where my husband and I teach—let's call it the University of Boston. One March day, out of the blue, Danny received an acceptance letter from U of B. Though he had pretended to have no interest in college, he was obviously delighted at the prospect of attending the school where both of his older brothers were already enrolled, and amazed that he was accepted. (So were we!) It was great to be able to celebrate with him.

In the next few weeks, we heard very little from Danny's teachers. I assumed this meant that he was doing better, perhaps motivated by his acceptance into college. But it could be that they had simply given up, and who could blame them? By the end of the third quarter, Danny was failing in every subject. A meeting was convened to see what might be done to get him through to graduation.

The pow-wow took place at the middle school, on neutral ground, and the school superintendent led the discussion. The rest of the group consisted of the head of school for the high school Mr. Luther, the dean of students, the guidance counselor, Danny, and me. Afterwards, I felt a small flame of hope in my heart, since it seemed that the superintendent both understood the situation and genuinely cared about Danny. He even had a plan to help him survive the rest of his senior year and receive his diploma. As we left his office, some of the details of the plan remained a little vague, but there was an atmosphere of goodwill all around and lots of hand-shaking.

In the weeks that followed, however, the rescue plan never materialized. I tried several times, by phone and email, to contact the superintendent who had pledged to oversee the operation. When these failed to produce a response, I showed up unannounced one day at the middle school, vowing to track the man down or die trying.

However, the receptionist informed me that the superintendent had recently accepted a job in New York City and, in fact, had already resigned and departed to get a head start on his new assignment. Since it was nearly April, the school apparently felt no urgency about appointing a replacement.

Distressed and desperate, I cast about for a backup strategy. It so happened that Mr. Cole, the one teacher who was pulling for Danny, had become head of curriculum for the math department, and I remembered that his new office was there at the middle school. I asked the receptionist where I might find him, and she pointed to an office just down the hallway.

Heartened by this prospect, I hurried down the hall, certain that he would be there in the middle of the school day like this. But the office was dark and the door firmly locked. Back once again at the reception desk, the secretary explained that Mr. Cole's wife had just given birth to their third son, and that he was in Children's Hospital Intensive Care Unit suffering from life-threatening medical complications. Given the situation, Mr. Cole was on an indefinite leave of absence.

My first reaction to this news was one of despair, followed immediately by anger. The only person I knew who might be able and willing to intervene in Danny's case was inaccessible to me. Naturally the anger was quickly replaced by guilt. After all, Mr. Cole was in circumstances not so different from mine, his son's life hanging in the balance while all he could do was wait and pray.

Actually, guilt was becoming a permanent state of mind for me. I kept asking myself questions with no answers: Why can't I figure out how to pull things together for my son? Why didn't I get on top of this earlier in the year? Why can't I motivate Danny to do the seemingly minor things that would keep him on track for graduation?

As the final quarter of school wore on, Damian put added pressure on Danny to get out of bed and get to school on time. I put added pressure on my husband to be more understanding, and to be firm without being caustic. Damian put added pressure on me to back him up and take a tougher stand on Danny's behavior. Both of us put added pressure on our daughter to keep her problems under the radar. Tensions in our home rose to a fever pitch.

At the beginning of May, I had a long talk with Danny about whether he had attended enough days of school to graduate. He assured me that, for seniors, excessive absences were not taken that seriously. As long as a student passed enough exams and completed enough assignments with passing grades, that would suffice. Having heard nothing from the school in several weeks, I assumed something like this must be right. Wouldn't they let me know if Danny was in danger of failing? Of course it was my responsibility, not theirs, to find out what the real policy was. I'm not sure why I didn't. I suspect it was because I really didn't want to know.

With graduation approaching, Danny somehow found enough energy to turn in some assignments and show up on time for his final exams. He received assurance from each of his teachers that he had passed the classes required for graduation—some with a D, but with no outright failures. I was relieved beyond measure that the protracted war between Danny and the charter school was finally coming to an end.

Since most members of my side of the family live on the west coast, we look for excuses to get together, and graduations have become one such excuse. So Danny's grandparents arrived near the end of May to attend his graduation, and his favorite cousin and her fiancé made the trip as well. We planned a party at our home after the ceremony, followed by a weekend getaway at a cabin in Maine that had been loaned to us by some friends.

The day before graduation, I suddenly realized I didn't know where it was being held. Come to think of it, I hadn't received any information at all—no invitations for Danny to send, no instructions about caps and gowns, no details about time and place. So Danny and I made a trip into the school office to find out what the arrangements were.

When we walked in, the secretary, normally cheerful and friendly, seemed strangely flustered and preoccupied. When we asked about the location for graduation and directions to the venue, she said that Mr. Luther would need to talk to us about that. Peculiar, I thought, but so be it.

Neither Danny nor I were prepared for what followed. Mr. Luther informed us, in oddly officious and indifferent tones, that Danny had missed so many classes during the year that, even though he had passing grades in the three subjects necessary for graduation, he had in fact officially failed every one of his courses. Therefore, he would not receive a diploma the next day. If he wished, he could still walk in the procession with the rest of his class.

What?!! We were dumbfounded, barely believing our ears! When I recovered from the initial shock, I became furious. Why hadn't Danny known about this? Or, if he did know, why didn't I? And how could they deliver this news the day before graduation? In fact, if we hadn't stopped by the office, I would have discovered it at the graduation ceremony itself. I was stunned into silence—not a familiar experience for me.

Mr. Luther insisted that Danny had known about this situation for a long time. In fact, he had sent several notices home with him in an effort to contact us. "Didn't you wonder why we never responded?" I asked. "Did you consider putting a letter in the regular mail? Calling? Sending an e-mail!?" None of it would have mattered anyway, I suppose. Danny had checked out of school a long time ago, and no one had been able to do anything about it.

Still, I walked out of the office seething with anger and resentment. (Mothers aren't required to stay rational, are they?) I just couldn't believe it. Danny's grandparents and his favorite cousin Rafaela, along with her fiancé, had traveled 3000 miles to see him graduate. His friend Bobby would be attending the graduation party at our house, which was meant to be a joint celebration with the two families. I felt poised on the deck of the Titanic.

Never have I seen Danny so angry—at the school, at himself, at everything and everyone. He spoke of revenge, and I began to fear he might actually harm someone or, more likely, harm himself. So we walked for two hours around the neighborhood in a misty rain while I tried to talk him down, to put a better face on things, to convince him (and myself) that it wasn't the end of the world.

Ultimately, Danny decided to walk through graduation with the rest of his classmates. At the ceremony, I could tell he was trying his best to be positive and cheerful for our sake. We all dressed up for the occasion, took pictures, enjoyed the cake, bid farewell to the teachers who were still speaking to us, and (mercifully) escaped to the cabin in Maine where we could forget about it all for a few blissful days.

The summer months only deepened my fears about Danny. He seemed excessively tired and listless, unmotivated to look for a job or finish his diploma. The charter school informed us that he had to pass three summer school courses, English, AP Spanish, and AP Calculus, in order to graduate. The other courses were considered a wash, since he could graduate without receiving credit for them. Summer session at the school would last just three weeks, running three periods back to back from nine until one, with three-minute breaks between them. One absence or two tardies from a given class would result in a failing grade.

Regrettably, Danny had taken up smoking during his senior year, and there was no way he was going to stick it out for four hours in a row without a smoke. He was allowed to leave the building, but required to be a block away from the school before lighting up. So, as you have probably already guessed, he failed all three summer courses.

I asked Mr. Luther if there were any alternatives. What about the summer courses at one of the local universities? No. They're not really graded and don't meet for enough total hours. What about night classes at the public high school? No.

They're not at a high enough level to match the courses Danny needs to pass.

I was growing more desperate by the day. The freshman dean at U of B had informed us that Danny's admission was contingent on having a high school diploma—the GED wouldn't suffice. But by now I had no idea how Danny could squeeze a diploma out of a school in which he had alienated nearly every adult. With September approaching, I dreaded the prospect of trying to keep him from sleeping another year away.

From mid-May through August, Joey and Alex were home from college, so all four of the children were crammed into our three-bedroom condo. Alex and Danny shared a room, and Lily slept in the study. The boys (really men by now) elbowed each other for space, both literally and figuratively.

A word about Danny's brothers. Like all of our children, Joey did well in school. As an incoming freshman at U of B, he had somehow persuaded the head of the chemistry department to hire him as a research assistant. But when he moved home that summer, he had barely survived his sophomore year, a period in which his lifestyle and study habits went rapidly south. Living in an on-campus "suite" with seven other adolescent males probably had something to do with it. (I use the term "adolescent" to refer to any male under 25. Females have to be assessed on a case-by-case basis.)

Alex had just finished his freshman year at U of B, more or less unscathed, but the university culture wasn't a good fit for him. He is the artist of the family—a writer, poet, and performer who was the first male at his high school to take four years of dance. In college he added voice lessons and worked on the literary magazine. However, in contrast to the North Face/Timberland/Juicy Couture fashion standards at U of B,

Alex tended to dress like an extra in *Oliver*, wandering around campus in a T-shirt and sandals even in the middle of winter. Still, given the free tuition (courtesy of Damian's teaching position), he expected that he would have to stay there until freed by a degree or by death, whichever came first.

Taking a sober look at our situation, Damian and I had to admit that our financial ship was taking on water—fast. So we informed our two oldest sons that we didn't have the resources to pay for another year of on-campus housing, but they were welcome to live at home and commute. Joey and Alex immediately sought summer jobs, hoping to make enough to allow them to rent rooms in an apartment for the coming year. When that didn't pan out, they each borrowed thousands of dollars in student loans instead; then spent most of that money on overpriced, state-of-the-art computers. The good life in a student apartment began to recede from their respective horizons.

We thus faced the unpleasant prospect of housing three large men with voracious appetites for the next several months, along with one seriously outnumbered eighth-grade girl. This at a time when Danny's sullen attitude and unpredictable moods were making our lives increasingly miserable.

A final note: At the beginning of that summer, just after the stomach-churning graduation fiasco and with our finances stretched to the breaking point, I chose to accept the long-term disability package from U of B rather than sign up for another year of full-time teaching. (More on this in the next chapter.) An immediate effect of my decision was that my salary was cut by a third. Damian was stunned, and deeply hurt that I hadn't even consulted him about it. But I had been equally hurt by his seeming indifference to the crushing fatigue, anxiety, depression, and mental mothballs that had made me a stranger to myself.

I expected him to protest the long-term leave, especially given our financial straits, but I felt I simply couldn't go back to the stress and exhaustion of full-time teaching. After two years of battling Damian over how to handle Danny and how to cope with my illness, I simply had no energy left for another campaign. I was utterly and definitively burned out.

3 Stress Test

Perhaps a brief chronicle of my physical decline will shed some light on our family dynamics during the years of Danny's growing troubles. I believe that my illness, in combination with Danny's, drove Damian and me farther and farther apart— almost to the point of no return.

My own physical problems began in September 1992. Our precious daughter Liliana had some breathing problems during labor, so she was delivered by an emergency C-section. I was warned that recovery would be longer and more difficult this time, but it seemed to me that I never fully recovered. I had been an avid athlete in high school and college, trying every sport there was and usually excelling at mediocrity.

This didn't dampen my enthusiasm though. I kept up jogging a few times a week and tried to get in some time at the college gym. I needed the exercise, but even more I needed some time alone—away from all my cares and burdens for a while. Best of all was when I could run outdoors, next to a lake or a river if possible, since then I was in my element. It felt like coming home.

But returning to my running schedule in the months after Lily's birth was much more difficult than it had been in the past. At first I attributed it to age, and to the difficulty of recovering from surgery. I assumed I would snap back eventually, and to some extent, I did. But I found everything in my life much harder to deal with.

During the next six years, Damian and I taught at a state university in New Jersey. I worked part-time, which meant working about as hard as a full-time professor for about a fourth of the salary. Lily was eight months old when we arrived in New Jersey, and her brothers were 9, 8, and 6. I tried hard to combine the soccer mom ideal with the academic expectations of the university and, somewhere in there, the role of a loving and attentive wife, knowing I couldn't keep it up forever but hoping I was wrong.

Just before leaving Jersey, my gynecologist prescribed progesterone and ordered a D&C, trying to locate the source of my increasing exhaustion. But everything seemed fairly normal. Once in Boston, I followed up with the OB/Gyn who had delivered Lily. She informed me that, barring a hysterectomy or standard birth control pills, I would bleed to death. I chose the pills. This had seemed a likely explanation for my constant weariness, but fixing my plumbing problems didn't seem to make much difference. Within two years I went into early menopause and off the pills, but the fatigue only worsened.

I also developed an allergic reaction of some kind that made my skin itch all over, especially when I got out of the shower. I worried that I would lose a layer of my hide by scrubbing it so hard with the towel. Seeking an explanation and (please!) a cure for this problem, I went to a dermatologist, who sent me on to an allergist.

Dr. Karpov, a congenial and confident Russian émigré, ran test after test after test, and concluded that I was allergic to shellfish. Then that I was just plain allergic, to something-we-know-not-what. He prescribed an antihistamine for "chronic urticaria," which sounds like a diagnosis but is actually just another phrase for "itch that won't go away."

At every appointment with Dr. Karpov, I sat for long periods in the waiting room with the rest of his longsuffering patients. Eventually, it dawned on me that everyone else was speaking Russian. In fact, every pamphlet, newspaper, and magazine in the room was in Russian. Given the variety of ailments presented by his patients, I surmised that Dr. Karpov was really a general practitioner for the Russian-speaking community.

That jack-of-all-trades mentality might explain why he considered himself something of a psychiatrist as well. When he learned that I was taking anti-depressants, he was horrified: "You don't need those pills! If you're sitting on a pin and you're in a lot of pain, you don't take a pill. *You get off the pin!*" So simple! Now if only I could figure out what the pin is, and how to get off it. Does running away count?

Still looking for a culprit, I made an appointment with a cardiologist to follow up on a heart murmur and irregular heartbeat. Two EKG's, one stress test, and a 24-hour Holter later, my heart was declared as sound as a dollar—maybe even a Euro. Blood tests ruled out thyroid problems, diabetes, hypoglycemia, Lyme disease, Lupus, and (for the most part) cancer. There seemed to be no physical explanation for my constant state of exhaustion. Even I began to wonder if it was all in my head.

In 2002, my routine physical revealed a small amount of blood in the urine sample, sending me on an unpleasant journey that began in the urology department and ended in a kidney biopsy. The urologist, another Russian émigré, though with the bedside manner of a prison guard, informed me that, since the "plumbing" checked out, "The problem must be in the meat." It took me several seconds to figure out that the "meat" was my kidneys. Were we holding a barbecue? I wrapped my paper sheet more tightly around my midsection, but Dr. Hyde left as abruptly as he had arrived.

My kidney malady turned out to be chronic but innocuous. I remember being almost disappointed by that result. I was desperate for a diagnosis—any explanation at all—something to show that my symptoms weren't imaginary.

The next chapter of my medical saga turned out to be the key to the mystery. Often when I was out jogging, especially in winter, I had difficulty swallowing. Sometimes it felt like I had a mouthful of rubber cement that I couldn't swallow and couldn't spit out. Since I was already deep in medical mode, I decided to consult an ear, nose and throat specialist to see if there was anything to be done about it.

The doctor announced almost immediately that my problem was not too much saliva but too little. He then proceeded, for reasons obscure to me at the time, to conduct a Schirmer test for dryness of the eyes. This procedure involves placing a strip of filter paper (aka sandpaper) in the corner of each eye for five minutes, then measuring how much of the strip has been soaked by the tears of the victim. My eyes were quite dry— hence the exquisite pain produced by the sandpaper.

ENT concluded, "I think you have Sjögren's Syndrome." Say what? Like many others, this illness is named for its discoverer, Swedish ophthalmologist Henrik Sjögren. It's an autoimmune disorder afflicting about four million people in the U.S., 90% of them women. Average age of onset? Late 40's. Bingo.

So in early 2002, I landed in the rheumatology department with a sympathetic and scholarly physician who painstakingly charted the course of my illness for three years. My relief at finding a cause for the fatigue was soon tempered by frustration over the failure of the attempted solutions. Dr. Heiland switched medications every couple of months, but my symptoms didn't improve—in fact, they seemed to be getting worse. Heiland wavered on the diagnosis, finding evidence for and against Sjögren's Syndrome, but nothing definitive. He ordered dozens of blood tests, repeated the sandpaper torture, and even set up a lip biopsy. Still no smoking gun.

By fall 2004, I was beginning to despair of finding any help for my constant fatigue. Dr. Heiland advised me to cut back on stress in my life. This in the middle of Danny's senior year when stress was *synonymous* with my life, and I was on the verge of a meltdown.

Damian grew increasingly frustrated, both with my persisting fatigue and the seeming futility of the endless parade of medical specialists and their time-consuming procedures. At one point, no doubt under significant stress of his own, he suggested that I wouldn't be so tired if I weren't constantly going to doctors. That stung. I assumed he knew me better than that—knew that I would stick it out to the last ounce of my strength. I was the last person who had time to hang out in clinics just for the "attention." I jumped to my defense (big surprise), explaining that my recent medical mania was motivated by a sense of urgency. I had to find out what was wrong with me and fix it, or I wasn't going to be there for him or anyone else.

34

The classes I was teaching at U of B that fall were starting to wear me out. I attributed it to the stress of dealing with Danny, but I had handled stress before without experiencing such overwhelming weakness. Late in the semester, I would sit in my office just before class, knowing I needed to leave immediately in order to be on time, but daunted by the prospect of getting out of my chair, finding the right books and notes, shoving them into my briefcase, pulling on my winter coat, hat, scarf, and gloves, and slogging through the snow and ice to the classroom building.

By the middle of the semester, I regularly arrived ten minutes late for class—even fifteen or twenty. I knew I was being incredibly irresponsible, and felt constantly guilty for wasting the students' time and short-changing them on the content of the course. But after a while, I found that nothing could motivate me to get up and get moving. Even the thought that the students might have decided to leave by the time I got there ceased to inspire me. "Oh well," I rationalized, "they'll probably be just as happy to have a day off."

Soon I couldn't even find the energy to prepare for my classes. So I developed the habit of asking the students to comment on the assignments, hoping to mask the fact that I hadn't read them myself. When the semester mercifully came to end, it took me so long to grade the final exams that I turned in the course grades two days past the absolutely final deadline. Against all my pride and stubbornness, I had to admit that I was no longer doing my job.

I decided to ask Dr. Heiland to sign the form that would grant me a six-month medical leave at full pay. The leave came through, but my sudden departure put an enormous burden on my colleagues, who had to take over my spring classes on top of their own. Over the next few months, the doctor suggested another possible diagnosis: Fibromyalgia. Not Sjögren's then? No, in addition to Sjögren's.

Fibromyalgia isn't an autoimmune disease, but it is chronic and its symptoms tend to be debilitating: fatigue and lots of it, along with muscle pain that is unpredictable in strength and location, varying from day to day and even hour to hour, depression, and impaired cognitive processes ("fibro-fog"). I thought I wanted an explanation for my symptoms, but this was more than I'd bargained for.

I decided to get a second opinion from a rheumatologist at Mass General Hospital who specializes in Fibromyalgia, Dr. Cushner. He confirmed the diagnosis with so much self-satisfied confidence that I wanted to slap him. He also took pains to impress on me that fibromyalgia is a chronic condition for which there is no cure. In fact, there aren't even any universally-accepted treatment strategies. "You have *got* to be kidding!" I thought. "How am I supposed to take care of my recalcitrant teenage son, a disgruntled husband, two adult sons, and a daughter on the brink of adolescence, while suffering from the illness from hell?"

Predictably, during the summer of 2005, with all our children living at home, every ship in the armada ran aground or sank. Tensions in and around us had built a wall of stone between Damian and me. Like a couple who loses a child, we found ways to blame each other for Danny's problems. In a way, we *were* losing our son, and neither of us could bear it.

At the time, Damian was treating all of our sons quite harshly, exaggerating their faults and overlooking their gifts, successes, and efforts to improve. I felt that if they had no way to gain his approval, no wonder they sank into indifference or despair. Damian thought I was the problem, coddling the boys, making excuses for their behavior, turning them against him, and refusing to acknowledge that they had any real character flaws.

The truth was no doubt somewhere in between, but we had pulled in opposite directions for so long that neither of us could see it any more. Familiar with the general script, our sons and daughter weighed in from time to time on one side or the other, gaining an advantage by playing us against each other. Sometimes they tried to understand what drove our mutual hostility, but mostly they kept to themselves, slowly dying inside from our pain and their own.

These problems added to my frustration and fatigue, and by the end of that summer, all I wanted was to escape. Life had become unbearable, and I had no answers to any of its problems. I was afraid that unless I found some solitude and peace, I would be tempted into the silence of no return. My husband seemed so angry—with Danny, and even more so with me. He still didn't quite believe I had a chronic and debilitating illness. That made me angry, but mostly it made me doubt his love.

Looking back, I have a better understanding of what it all meant to Damian. How could he really accept that I was falling apart at a time when our hope and sanity were already in shreds? He must have been terrified about what would happen to the broken pieces of our family if I wasn't at his side, trying to help him glue them back together.

I didn't think about any of this at the time. I only knew I was worn down to the last ounce of my strength, living in a state of constant dread, and losing badly on every one of life's battlefronts. I didn't feel Damian's fear and desperation, only his frustration and disapproval, and I came to believe I couldn't bear it any longer. I wondered if Damian was sorry he had married me, or just sorry he was married at all. He seemed disgusted with all of us, and spoke to me less and less. Maybe he just wanted out—out of everything, maybe even life itself. I know I did.

I began to think about finding a separate place to live, maybe renting an apartment where I could live for a few weeks or months until I knew what to think about my marriage, my children, my job, my illness. None of it was making any sense. I soon realized I could hardly move out of the house and leave Liliana to fend for herself. She was only thirteen and still trying to recover from the shock of her brother and best friend turning into a stoned and surly stranger.

So I let her in on my idea of a "vacation" from the source of our stress, and initially she was enthusiastic about the idea. I told her we would look for a two-bedroom apartment that we could afford on my salary alone, one that would let us have a dog (something Damian had always opposed). We could still spend time with Dad and the rest of the family and she could visit her friends every weekend. We talked about the colors we wanted for our bedrooms and the fun we would have in our imagined pool and fitness room.

Then reality began to set in. The only apartments I could afford were located miles outside the city, in towns with lagging economies and struggling schools. Still, I could count on having the car, since Damian doesn't drive, and we would just have to get used to a longer commute. OK, a *much* longer commute. Liliana began to worry about moving so far away from her friends and about whether her brothers would be all right. She even had the audacity to worry about her dad. "Won't he be lonely? Doesn't he love us anymore?" Suddenly the "plan" started looking less like an extended vacation from stress and more like a massive contribution to it. But I am nothing if not stubborn, and I was determined to see this through. What was the alternative after all?

One summer day when my husband was out of town, I told Liliana we would go for a drive to look at some apartments that seemed promising on paper. We liked them all; they were newly-built and freshly painted, and the appliances gleamed under the soft recessed lighting. There was internet and cable and a place to walk our imaginary dog. I was trying to think seriously about what it would be like to live in the area, so we drove past the local school and the town center. I nearly signed a lease for the last apartment we looked at, but decided that was too impulsive even for me.

Since the nearest mall was in New Hampshire, I wanted to drive by it before heading back home. Having consulted the map, I drove confidently along a two-lane highway that would take us north along the back roads. I mean, what can you tell about a place when you're flying past it on the freeway? "Let's just explore a little bit," I said, trying to sound cheerful. But Lily wanted to go home and I couldn't blame her. Even if this was a place to live, it would never be home.

Still, the apartment-and-dog-plan had been my lifeline for a few days now and I was loathe to give it up. So I told my daughter, "I just want to go a few more miles until we cross into New Hampshire to see if we can find the mall. Then we'll jump on the freeway and be home in no time, OK?" Liliana shrugged her shoulders, resigned to the inevitable.

The road wound back and forth past farms and cottages and roadside fruit stands, all charming in their own way but starting to look very much alike. After twenty minutes or so I began to wonder if we were still on the right road. I pulled over to look at the map again, with Liliana complaining that now we were lost and would take forever to find our way back. I was embarrassed about being lost and frustrated that the trip hadn't been anything like what I had hoped. Besides, I had always prided myself on my map-reading skills, but there was nothing rational about these rural roads. I couldn't even figure out where we were on the map. (GPS was still just a random group of letters for me.)

Suddenly, parked by the side of this road with no name, I realized how utterly drained I was. All the anxieties I thought I could leave behind came flooding back, pressing on my mind and heart more crushingly than before. This was never going to work. How stupid I had been, and how thoughtless. It was more than my own time and energies I had wasted on this plan. Now Liliana would have to pay too. No pool after all; no specially decorated new room; no puppy. Instead she must face the same sorrows and disappointments as before, but with the added pain of knowing her parents are falling apart.

By now I just wanted to get the hell out of there. I hoped that if I continued on the same road I would eventually come across some clue to where we were. Then I could use the map again to find the fastest route to the freeway. We drove for another twenty minutes without success. No other roads crossed our path, so there were no signs to use in figuring out where we might be. It began to feel like an episode of The Twilight Zone. I considered pulling over to ask for directions, but houses were few and far between and set well back from the road, and by now I was so lost I didn't even know what to ask. Anyway there were only two options—go on or go back—and the thought of driving back along this wretched road for another forty-five minutes was too much to bear. Besides, what if I failed to retrace my route exactly?

As we approached a farm stand on the left-hand side of the road, the SUV in front of us was cruising merrily along at 40 miles per hour and we were cruising along right behind it, if not exactly merrily. Suddenly, the driver in front of the SUV stomped on his brakes, trying for a last-minute U-ish left turn into the farm stand. My vision blocked by the monster SUV, I saw nothing of this. All I could see was the back of the SUV, which suddenly got much closer as it screeched to a halt on the strength of its anti-lock brakes. This took me completely by surprise, and I reacted too late to keep the front of our car from wrapping itself around the massive rear bumper and trailer hitch of the SUV.

We barely scratched that monstrosity, of course, and the owner never bothered to contact me about repairs. She was very angry, however, and refused even to get out of her car. When I went forward to see if she was OK, she kept telling me how stupid I was. "I never expected somebody to just slam into me from behind like that!" I wanted to say "Oh really? I do that all the time just for kicks," but thought better of it. Lily and I had our seat belts on, thank God, so we were not injured. But Lily was very upset. Traumatized even. Just before we hit, she was terrified that the airbag would smash into her face, and afterwards she was appalled that it hadn't deployed at all. It was a long time before she would ride in the front seat.

The sheriff was called and arrived in ten minutes or so. He wrote down our license and insurance information and told us we were free to go. Mrs. SUV hoisted herself back up into the driver's seat, shot me a final disgusted look, and sped off along . . . that road. Our ancient minivan looked like someone had socked it in the nose. The SUV won by a knockout—our car was totaled. I asked the sheriff what to do, and he suggested having the car towed to the nearest service station. So I had to explain that I didn't know where I was, didn't know the name of the road, didn't know whether I was in Massachusetts or New Hampshire, and had no idea where the nearest *town* was, much less the nearest service station. Also, my husband, who does not drive, was out of town, and I knew no one else I could ask to drive all the way up here to retrieve us.

The sheriff hesitated for a few minutes but eventually took pity on us. He called a towing company and told them to bring the car to the nearest service station, then brought us there in his cruiser. I negotiated briefly with the owner about leaving the car for a day or two until I could come and retrieve our belongings. Then he was free to sell it to the junkyard. Liliana and I found a place to order takeout, bought tickets for the commuter train, and spent an hour and a half getting home by rail, subway, and bus.

I spent a long day or two wondering how to explain to my husband that I had totaled our car on a country road in northern Massachusetts after a day of driving around with Liliana looking for an apartment there. In the end, I settled on telling part of the truth, leaving out certain key elements. But I hated myself for being so deceptive, and for dragging my daughter into both the disastrous expedition and the deception to mask it.

One might expect that this dreadful experience would be a wake-up call for me, but it wasn't. I was just as miserable as before, if not more so, and still desperate to change my life. There was no moving anywhere now, of course. That plan had crashed and burned—literally. Without a car, I felt trapped, with no way to escape the unbearable pain of losing both my son and my husband's love (as I thought at the time).

So I devised a new plan. I couldn't move out, but my husband could. He wouldn't have to take any of the kids with him, so he wouldn't need such a big apartment. And he could stay close to

42

town instead of moving into the sticks. Then we could both take time to think about where things stood and what we wanted to do. Damian had seemed so angry and hostile for so long that I was sure he would jump at the chance to be rid of us for a while. Maybe it was what he had wanted all along; probably he was only staying out of a sense of duty. Once I had thought I could make him happy, helping him to be at peace with himself and his life. But I had failed, and I was beginning to realize that it wasn't in my hands anyway.

Two weeks later, Damian and I drove (in a rented car) to Cape Cod to take Lily to camp. She would be gone for five days, and I hoped she would have a great time with the friends she had made in previous years. When we dropped her off, I spoke to the director of the camp, confiding that in all likelihood I would be separating from my husband soon. I asked her to try to give some extra TLC to Lily. Unfortunately, she had a miserable time at camp that year, but that's another story.

For some reason, I decided the trip back from the Cape was a good time to announce my plans to Damian. We were alone in the car and had traveled some distance in virtual silence. Finally I cleared my throat and informed him that I wanted him to move out of the house and into his own place for a while. I thought we needed some space from each other, not because I didn't love him, but because I couldn't carry his anger and disappointment any longer on top of my own burdens and sorrows. I was breaking.

Damian was completely blindsided. He begged me to pull over so we could talk for a while, and eventually I did. We both got out of the car and talked and paced for an hour or more, around and around the cracked and weed-infested pavement of a deserted parking lot. I remember thinking of it as a metaphor for our marriage. Damian was in a panic, utterly dumbfounded by what I had said. I hadn't expected that kind of vehement reaction. Wasn't this what he wanted? Well, no, it turned out. "What am I supposed to do?" he asked, with deep pain in his voice. "You're my family. You and the kids . . . you're all I have!"

Oh. Now I didn't know what to think. Will the real Damian please stand up? Maybe I didn't even know my own husband. Here I was, lost on a road in rural Massachusetts again, wondering whether to go forward or back. In typical fashion, I decided to go forward. "OK; well I still think it would be good to have at least some time apart. So I want you to find another place to live for a while." Here I stand. Maybe I would be standing there still, except for my beloved husband, who said, "Well, shouldn't we try something else first?" "Like what?" I shot back, "I've tried everything I can think of and nothing worked." "Ok, ok. Well, I don't know . . . couples counseling or something?" "*You* would go to couples counseling?" It was my turn to be dumbfounded. "Well, rather than this . . . yes!"

So, out of total desperation, we started marriage counseling, with a very wise and experienced psychiatrist who refused to charge us the co-payment for office visits, and was infinitely patient with our peculiar personalities. Over the years, Dr. Christianson became a dear and trusted friend. He was filled with wonderful advice, not just about human relationships, but about the best local car mechanic, the cheapest place to spend a weekend away, and the dozens of opportunities in the Boston area for free concerts, interesting museums, career options for our children—even affordable Christmas gifts. Oh, and he saved our marriage. But here I have to give an assist to my therapist, Dr. Hart, who undoubtedly saw before I did that the person I wanted most to escape from was me.

4 Chaos

As for our marriage, the item of first importance was forging an agreement about how to respond to our children, especially to Danny. Unless we could form a united front on this point, there was no hope of calming the chaos in our home. During the ill-fated summer of 2005, all three sons were having trouble finding full-time jobs. Nonetheless, Dr. Christianson insisted that unless we moved our adult children out of our home, our marriage didn't stand a chance. It was a strong statement, but since my own strategies for saving our marriage had an alarmingly poor track record, I decided to simply take it on faith.

Moving one's fledgling adults out on their own is a project fraught with emotional and logistical difficulties. Ultimately, we suggested that the three boys could rent an apartment together in the vicinity of the University of Boston. This would enable Joey and Alex to get to classes easily, and Danny could audit some courses—maybe even get advance reading done for freshman year. It all sounded so reasonable at the time. The boys found an available apartment and Damian and I co-signed the lease, coming up with the initial three months' rent required by the landlord. The plan was for the two older boys to work at least a few hours a week, making up the rest of their expenses with student loans, while Danny would find a full-time job to cover his third of the costs.

By mid-December this experiment had met with total disaster. None of the boys was meeting his share of the expenses, so the landlord was on the warpath. Danny had lost his job at a downtown Starbucks and was spending twenty-four hours a day locked in his room, hanging out with a friend he had met at U of B, the two of them chain-smoking pot and running a scam on an online poker site. The "friend," a senior at U of B, had devised a strategy for winning these games every time, at least in the long run, and had paid for both his college tuition and a Cadillac Escalade with the proceeds. Danny was dazzled by this sweat-free lifestyle—easy money, a steady supply of weed, and no responsibilities.

The only catch was that Danny developed a serious gambling addiction. Unlike his friend, he refused to stay with the reliable method, finding it tedious and unsatisfying. He loved the adrenaline rush of risk-taking, of losing big as well as winning big, relying on Lady Luck or the current tilt of the universe. A few days before Christmas, Danny called with the news that he had won $5,000 from online poker and was going to spend it on expensive Christmas gifts for everyone. Later that night, he called to say he had lost every penny.

One of the more sobering events during their sojourn in the apartment took place in October. Joey was invited to a party at a friend's apartment, and Danny tagged along. The scene was heavily oriented toward alcohol and drug use, and Danny took full advantage of it. At one point, he accepted the host's offer of "magic mushrooms." But instead of the euphoria he expected, he developed a severe headache and unsettling hallucinations, producing a level of anxiety that quickly turned to panic. Joey got him to the emergency room at the nearest hospital and called us around 11:00 pm to ask what he should do. Fearing the worst, my husband and I woke our daughter and the three of us rushed to the ER. Stories flashed through my mind of

young men who had died from an overdose or from tainted
street drugs.

As it turned out, Danny was not in any immediate danger. He
had made it into the inner sanctum of the ER, but there were
no rooms available, so he and some other unfortunates were
lined up along the wall across from the nurses' station like so
many dominoes. Except that none of them matched. Danny
seemed disoriented and extremely anxious about what was
happening to him. He was experiencing some visual
hallucinations that showed no signs of abating. He asked,
"Mom, do you think I'm going to have these for the rest of my
life?"

"No, I don't think so," I said, trying to sound like I knew what I
was talking about, "I'm sure they'll know what to do here, and
probably when the drugs wear off a little more, they'll just go
away." "But Mom, it's been hours since I took that drug; it
should have worn off by now." "Well, let's just see what the
doctors have to say, OK? It's probably not the same for every
person."

Minutes passed, then hours. Doctors and nurses brushed past
us, but no one stopped to ask if we needed anything, much
less to deal with Danny's symptoms or give us an idea of when
he would be seen. The stress of the day finally caught up with
me and I began to feel light-headed standing next to the
gurney. So I asked Danny to move over and climbed up beside
him. By the time the nurse came to take his vital signs, we
were both sound asleep. Her pursed lips suggested a distinct
lack of enthusiasm for visitors who sleep next to the patients.
Since I could think of no plausible excuse, I met her gaze with
what I hoped was a convincing expression of innocence.

FIGHTING MAD

The young physician who finally arrived listened to Danny's account of the evening's events and looked over the results of the blood and urine tests. He concluded that Danny's symptoms were due to the drugs he had been using and that they would probably fade over time, though they could last for several more days. This wasn't exactly what we wanted to hear.

The doctor didn't prescribe any medication or order any further tests, and his manner suggested that the symptoms were essentially no big deal. While signing the discharge papers, he told Danny to stay away from drugs: "They're bad for you, you know." No kidding. Many emergency room visits later, I detected a pattern of response from physicians who don't know what's wrong with you. "It's simple. Just stay away from drugs, and everything will be OK." Except when it isn't.

In late December, our sons' landlord notified us that we owed several hundred dollars in back rent. The boys told him they could not afford the apartment any longer and would move out by January 1st. The landlord replied that if he was unable to rent the apartment for the rest of the lease (that is, eight more months), we would be responsible for the rent that remained—approximately $10,000.

Of course we had nothing close to that amount, but there seemed to be no alternative. None of our sons had a job that provided enough income to float the apartment. They were behind in their payments, and Danny had so far contributed next to nothing to the total expenses. It was a somber Christmas that year, as each one considered his options for the coming months. We settled out of court with the landlord for two month's rent plus the difference between the rent he was able to charge from March to August and the rent he would have received had we not broken the lease. Not a small sum,

48

but significantly less than $10,000. We did take one valuable lesson away from this experience: *never, under any circumstances, co-sign a lease with your children.*

By the first of the year, the older boys had come up with a plan for the next few months. Joey opted to live at home for a while and find a full-time job to get back on his feet financially, using this break from school to decide what he wanted to major in. Alex found a room in a friend's apartment and borrowed additional student loans to cover his rent for the spring semester.

But Danny had no plan. We offered to let him move back home, provided he would accept the house rules we had put into place, but he was unwilling to commit to that kind of structured life. It gradually dawned on me what this meant. Unless Danny made arrangements to live someplace else, he would be homeless, unemployed, penniless, addicted to weed, and alienated from the only people who were able and willing to help him.

That was when I began to write Danny's story. It was my attempt to take some of the terror out of these events, as though recording them might help me to avoid constantly dwelling on each one and its unthinkable implications. Often I would experience agonizing losses for Danny that needed to be properly considered and assimilated, but other crises would follow so closely upon them that there was no opportunity to stop or to grieve. Writing about them means you can return to the place of those losses one day, when they are far enough in the past to be drained of some of their venom, and you can reflect on their significance and let yourself feel the sorrow they deserve.

The pages that follow are taken from that journal—my attempt to give words to my grief, and to tell my son's story when he was too confused, angry, terrified, or over-medicated to tell it himself.

****

January 7, 2006

Moving day. Danny sits in the apartment while boxes and furniture disappear around him. Finally, the couch he is sitting on has to go too. I ask, "What are you going to do?" No response. "Do you have someplace to go?" Again, no response. I repeat our offer for living at home, but he refuses it. In the end, I have to drive off with a car full of boxes, leaving my son on the sidewalk in temperatures below freezing. I'm not sure which of us is more miserable.

January 7-13, 2006

For the next few days, Danny survives on the goodwill of his brother Alex and some of his friends, but this strategy doesn't last long. At times he sleeps in the enclosures around ATM machines, at least until passing policemen kick him out. Sometimes he walks the city streets all night long, waiting for daylight when he can sleep in the back corners of a library or on a bench at the train station. By the middle of January I am desperate for a way to get him off the streets. So while I hate to ask, I call my parents on the west coast to see if they will consider letting Danny live with them for a few months, assuming he is able to find a job out there. To my eternal gratitude they are willing to give it a try.

January 13, 2006

Knowing Danny will never find a job on his own, I book a one-way flight for him and a round-trip for myself, planning to spend two weeks helping him get settled and, Lord willing, find a full-time job. Of course part of the strategy is to get Danny away from the drug trade in Boston and from the scene of so many bad memories, giving him a fresh start in Washington, in a small town nestled between the Columbia River and the Cascade Mountains. The day before the trip I take Danny to get his driver's license, since nearly every job he might have will require a commute.

The driving test in the nearest RMV office is given only by the state police. Danny fills out the requisite forms and he and I park in the assigned area while waiting for his turn at the wheel of fortune. When the state policeman walks toward the car, I recognize him immediately: Officer Stalin. He practiced his torture methods two years earlier on Alex, doing everything in his power to rattle and humiliate him. A man devoid of humor, he clearly sees it as his duty to defend the streets of Massachusetts against as many teenage drivers as possible.

As Trooper Stalin strides impatiently toward us, Danny is standing next to the car smoking a cigarette. "Why are you smoking?" he asks. "I guess because I'm a little nervous," Danny replies. "Well, if you know what you're doing, you shouldn't be nervous. Get in the car." Danny heads toward the driver's side of the car and makes the sign of the cross as he slides into his seat. "What's that for?" "I'm just saying a prayer that I pass the test." This provokes a grimace.

The officer takes the passenger seat and tells Danny to pull ahead a few feet, then stop. He starts to give further directions and then abruptly changes his mind. "Forget it. Just get out;

this test is over." "Why?" Danny asks. "What did I do wrong?" "I think you're too nervous and that counts against you on the test. So I'm failing you." We are told we can come back another day, but today is the last day before our flight. I appeal to the supervisor inside. He says I can register a complaint but there is nothing he can do for us today. I feel angry and frustrated, and guilty for putting Danny through this whole charade. All he needs is one more failure.

January 14-28, 2006

License or no, we fly westward to the Pacific coast, and several members of my family are there to greet us. My parents have knocked themselves out to make Danny feel at home, transforming a room of their house into a comfortable bedroom for him and even offering him the use of their second car. They do everything they can to encourage him and help him find leads for jobs in the area. He and I rise early every morning to look at help wanted ads online and in the newspaper, then set out for a day of tracking down the ones we can get to before 5:00 pm.

We find nothing. Usually Danny isn't even given the chance to fill out an application. Several jobs involve working in the fields for minimum wage and he won't even consider these. After a few days of this routine, Danny just gives up. I can't get him up in the morning and he has no interest in making a good impression on prospective employers. Our two weeks are almost up and I start to give up too. I can't fight Danny and the sluggish job market at the same time.

Though the odds are slim that this venture will succeed, my dad and I decide to take Danny to the DMV at a small town about 30 minutes away to let him try the driving test there. If he passes, he can transfer his license to Massachusetts when we return without having to face the officer from hell. My dad testifies that Danny is (for now, anyway) a resident of Washington, and the DMV officer agrees to give him the test. He passes on the first try, a great victory, and we celebrate by going out for lunch.

As we are leaving town, we pass a local lumber company and my father suggests they might be looking for help. So we pull into the gravel parking lot and Danny heads into the office to ask for a job. He is wearing his signature Yankees baseball cap, the one fixed item in his daily wardrobe. It turns out that the mill owner is also a big Yankees fan. (In small-town Washington? I consider this close to miraculous, and it fills me with hope.) After a brief interview, the owner decides to give Danny a chance, even though his work record for the last several months is porous at best. Danny returns to the car in triumph, application papers in hand, and we all rejoice at this promising turn of events.

It takes only a day for our joy to evaporate. One of the requirements for employment at the sawmill is a drug screen. Danny reports that it hasn't been that long since he's smoked marijuana, and it takes thirty days or more for traces of the drug to leave your system. Still, we turn in his application forms and I take him to the clinic for the lab work. Since it's a blood test, Danny is even more certain that it will be positive. His disappointment is almost too much to bear, for all of us.

Since my fourteen days are ending and Danny has no job, I decide to buy him a ticket to return to Massachusetts with me. I feel it wouldn't be fair to my parents to leave them with the task of getting Danny back out on the job-hunting trail. In fact, I'm pessimistic about Danny finding any job at all, since I assume most jobs will also require some kind of drug testing. It's hard to believe that the job at the lumber mill didn't work out. It seemed like such an answer to prayer and then it was just snatched away. I feel foolish for having spent all this time and money on a doomed project. My parents were so generous to make space for Danny in their lives, and I feel I've let them down too.

January 28, 2006, Sunday

It's a sad day. My parents drive us to the airport to return to Boston. When we land, Danny still has no place to go. I drop him off at Alex's apartment for now and wish him well. The temperatures are well below freezing. Danny spends a few days with his brother, leaving when the others leave in the early morning and returning late in the evening. On Wednesday night he can't sleep, and decides around 2:00 am to go out for a cigarette. Too late he realizes he's let the inner door to the apartment building close behind him. He leans on the buzzer for Alex's apartment *ad nauseum* without results, and eventually has to face the unpleasant fact that he will be spending the rest of the night outside in the frigid temperatures.

As Danny sits on the concrete wall in front of the apartment building, out of cigarettes and hope, he notices a man sauntering along the sidewalk—maybe one of the other residents? The guy sits down on the wall next to Danny and offers him a cigarette, one of his favorite brands. The two of them talk for a while, and Danny recounts his experiences of the past few days. He feels like his life has splattered against the wall.

The stranger tells him not to lose heart, that he's too young to give up on life. Their conversation lifts Danny's spirits. It's not that the advice is especially new or original, but it sounds like something you can rely on. Then, as mysteriously as he arrived, the stranger disappears into the night. A few minutes later, just as dawn is breaking, someone comes out of the building and Danny is able to grab the door and get back in. This is a short reprieve, however, since he has to leave the apartment when Alex and the rest depart for work or school.

February 2, 2006, Thursday

Since returning to Boston I've been in a state of confusion and despair. It seems impossible that the one hopeful job prospect for Danny could have just imploded. I know he can't stay with Alex for much longer—the arrangement is already wearing thin—and I dread what might happen to him on the streets in the Boston winter. Then today I receive a call from my father. He's heard from the lumber mill and they want Danny to start on Monday. "Wait . . . what did you say?" "Well, I don't know what you want to do about it, but I guess they gave Danny the job."

I'm not sure whether Danny passed the drug test or they just decided to overlook the results, but there it is—a genuine job offer! It seems surreal. We just spent a substantial sum to bring Danny back from the west coast on short notice. Does it even make sense to send him back? Will he be willing to go? I recall with a sinking sensation that Danny's cell phone isn't working, and I have no idea where to find him. Is this just some kind of cruel joke?

Not long after my dad's call, though, I receive a call from Danny. He is at a pay phone and wonders if I can come and get him something to eat. I'm relieved to know that he is OK and can't wait to tell him about this new turn of events. When I pick him up, Danny wants to talk first about his night in the cold and his conversation with the stranger. "Everything he said just made sense to me, Mom. Like it was obvious, somehow." I wonder if he was visited by his guardian angel. In any case, when I tell him about the call from the lumber company, he nearly chokes on his McMuffin.

Danny is doubtful that his grandparents will want him to come back at this point, however, and I doubt that we'll be able to find an affordable flight, but Danny says he wants to give the job a try if there is a way to work it out. When I call my parents they're excited for Danny too, and still want him to stay with them if he's interested in the job at the mill. So by evening I am online looking for any cheap flights to Oregon or Washington.

As it happens, the Super Bowl is scheduled for this coming Sunday, February 5th, and Southwest Airlines is running a $99 special into Seattle for that day only—I guess not many people travel during the Super Bowl. Still, Seattle is four hours away from my parents' home and I'm reluctant to ask them to make an eight-hour round trip on Super Bowl Sunday.

Amazingly, when I call to give them this information, they say they will actually be in Seattle that Sunday, since some of the family is getting together at my nephew's place for a Super Bowl party. I am speechless (a rare experience for me). A week ago the universe was pitted against us and now it's just the opposite. There must be some explanation, but I have no idea what it is. As time goes on I stop looking for explanations. The present moment is usually as much as I can handle.

5 Slip-sliding Away

February 5, 2006, Super Bowl Sunday

Danny and I drive to the Providence airport to catch the flight to Seattle. Both of us are excited and full of hope. Danny does live with my parents for the next two months, and is given a day shift at the lumber mill—unheard of for a newly-hired worker. He has to be at work by 5:00 am but is done by 2:00 and has the rest of the day free.

Every work day, my father rises at 4:00 am to make a big breakfast for him, then hands him the substantial lunch my mother put together the night before, and Danny drives to the mill in the car they've loaned him. My dad once worked in a lumber yard himself and knows how physically demanding it is, so he wants to give his grandson every chance to succeed. He's bought Danny an expensive pair of specialized leather work gloves so he'll be ready from the first day.

For a month or so, it all seems to be working. Danny finds life in a small town lonely at times, but he is getting physically conditioned and learning a lot about the lumber business. I send letters and photos from home and try to stay in touch as much as possible. But sometime around the beginning of March, Danny's life starts to unravel. By hanging around the local gas station and convenience store, he has finally made some friends. Unfortunately, the friends are other kids who hang around the gas station and convenience store. Their main occupation is drinking and drugging, and it isn't long before Danny is an all-too-willing co-conspirator with this group.

He starts disappearing on weekends, then on some weeknights too, and my parents often go to bed not knowing where he is or when (if?) he is coming home. Even when he is there, Danny sits in silence in the living room, staring glassy-eyed at the television or falling asleep on the couch. My dad tries to talk with him about the way things are going, but Danny is increasingly surly with both his grandparents and complains that they don't understand how things are for him. He blames everything and everyone except himself.

Though he is working full time, Danny never seems to have any money, and talks often about how hard it is for him there. I encourage him to attend the local high school basketball games, explore the beautiful lakes and mountains that are virtually in his back yard, go fishing with his grandfather, or get in touch with his cousins in the area. But he's not interested in any of these. I can sense that he is slipping away again.

I can't understand how life can be that difficult for Danny, especially since my parents are trying so hard to make it easy for him. But in my letters and phone calls I assure him that if he isn't able to keep things going there, he can always come back to Boston and (hopefully) find a job here that would allow him to rent a room in a shared apartment. Often when I call, Danny sounds distracted and far away. He says he is just tired, but I know that isn't the whole story. My parents confirm that he has come in drunk a few times, and they suspect he is also using drugs.

Danny starts missing days at work, jeopardizing his job and increasing the stress on my parents. Since he is often late leaving for work, he drives at high speeds along the winding two-lane highway to the mill. One day he takes a corner too fast and spins off the road. My parents' car suffers significant body damage, but since it's still drivable, they continue to allow Danny to use it for work. Their only stipulation is that he should avoid giving rides to others and should not take the car on long drives, especially not into the city.

One Friday night Danny is out late with his friends, and he has the car with him. When he returns in the wee hours of the morning, a window on the driver's side of the car has been smashed. Eventually it comes out that he took his friends into the most dangerous part of the city around midnight, presumably to visit one of their drug connections, and things took an unpleasant turn (I was never sure of the details).

By this time Danny has become an expert at giving each person the story most likely to evoke their sympathy, then revising it further to fit their reaction. In the end it's impossible to know whether it has any connection with the truth. The bottom line is that my parents are at their wits' end trying to keep Train Danny from running off the rails. By now their car has sustained $2000 worth of damage, Danny is treating them like the enemy, and they rarely see him when he isn't eating or sleeping.

April 7-9, 2009

This weekend Danny simply vanishes. He takes off with the car on Friday night and essentially disappears. Calls to his cell phone go unanswered, and by late on Saturday no one has seen or heard from him. My parents are frantic. Finally my mother decides to visit the houses of Danny's friends, looking for some sign of him. Eventually she finds him, holed up in a cellar with some of his drug buddies, the whole place reeking of pot and booze. I later learn that Danny has also tried crack cocaine for the first time, and it magnifies the symptoms that sent him to the emergency room in October.

More recently, Danny confided to me that crack will always be a temptation for him, since it produces such an intense and pleasurable high. As one crack addict told his psychiatrist, "The difference between you and me is that I've been to the Garden and tasted the forbidden fruit." I guess sacrificing your brain can seem like a small price to pay for utopia.

Confronted by his grandmother, Danny still refuses to come back to the house, insisting that even if he does, it will only be to move his things out. It's possible he plans to move in with one of his friends, though most of them still live with their parents. Not that the plan has to make any actual sense.

My husband and I receive a call early on Sunday morning telling us our son was in somebody's cellar stoned out of his mind all weekend and is refusing to stay with his grandparents any longer. They can't even get him to come back to their house. Clearly the mission has met with disaster and it's time to pull the plug. I tell my parents we will bring Danny home on the first flight we can find, and ask if they can send someone (preferably one of our stronger male relatives) over to get him and tell him to pack his bags.

At first I can't find any flights on the online search engines, but my hope is rekindled when I read that Air Tran has extended its flight patterns to include Seattle. Not only that, they are advertising an affordable introductory fare for the 11:00 pm red-eye flight from Seattle to Boston.

Will, one of our young nephews, has been visiting family members in my parents' town for the weekend, and plans to drive back to his Seattle apartment late Sunday afternoon.

We ask if he can give Danny a lift to the airport and he graciously agrees, even though the airport is significantly out of his way. Danny finally gets back to my parents' home around 2:00 pm and manages to stuff most of his gear into the bags he had brought with him. They will mail the rest of it later.

I know that the storm that has been gathering strength all these months is about to break all around us, and I am terrified. Fear and grief threaten to paralyze me. Now I write in this journal out of necessity, as my only defense against the whirlwind. Maybe turning these unbearable events into words can draw some of the poison out of my heart, transferring it onto the page . . . where it can't hurt anyone.

April 9, 2006

At 5:00 pm Danny climbs into Will's truck for the four-hour drive to Seattle. Before fifteen minutes pass, he tells Will to pull over so he can have a cigarette. Will refuses. He has another stop to make in about forty minutes and doesn't want to lose time by stopping twice. "You can have a smoke then, OK?" But Danny is already behaving erratically, talking to people who aren't there and twitching nervously in the passenger seat like a caged lion. Now he comes completely unglued, screaming and cursing at Will, even trying to grab the steering wheel.

Will is sufficiently rattled that he pulls off the road and lets Danny have his cigarette. The remainder of the trip seems like an eternity to Will, with Danny muttering under his breath and continuing to seethe over a perceived lack of respect from pretty much everyone he has recently dealt with. By the time

61

they arrive at the airport, Will is more than ready to be free of his disturbing passenger.

Meanwhile, I'm finding it impossible to finish booking the Air Tran flight from Seattle. Finally I call the airline's toll-free number. The woman who answers cheerfully informs me that although the web site did announce the new route to Seattle, they will not actually be flying from there until May 1st.

I can't believe my ears! Why do things like this keep happening? Are we wearing invisible signs that say "Please wreck my life"? Since Danny is already on the road to the Seattle airport, my only option is to try to find a flight on another airline that will leave that night or early the next morning. But it's already 9:30 pm on the west coast and there are no later flights coming to Boston . . . or Providence, or anywhere within 100 miles of us. The best I can do is an 8:00 am flight with a layover in Denver.

Will Danny be able to last the night at the Seattle airport? It doesn't seem likely. I try to reach him before he gets to the airport, hoping that Will might be able to let him crash at the apartment and then either bring him back to the airport in the morning or put him in a taxi. Of course I know nothing about the stress Will has been under for the past four and a half hours. Danny answers his cell phone on the first ring. I tell him there's just a small wrinkle in our plans; he won't be able to fly out until early the next morning.

Unfortunately, Will has just dropped Danny off in front of the airport and jumped hastily back into his truck, having left the engine running. Danny shouts at him to wait, but by this time Will is exhausted and a little afraid of Danny. He assumes he'll just be in for another passionate denunciation by a person who can't be reasoned with. I hear Danny cursing a blue streak, followed by a loud crash. "What was that?" "Oh, Will wouldn't stop the truck, so I threw my thermos at his back window." "Did it break?" "I don't know. Who gives a shit?"

I venture, "I take it the ride didn't go so well?" "Yeah. I guess he was pretty mad at me. But why would he just leave me here, Mom? We're family, right? You don't leave your own family standing on the sidewalk like that. He just grabbed my stuff out of the back of his truck and threw it down on the ground and didn't even say good-bye. Why'd he do that, Mom?" "Well, maybe he was in a hurry or something," I mumble. "Anyway it probably wouldn't have worked for you to stay overnight at his place, since you would need to be back at the airport by 6:30 or so." Danny is clearly upset, and I can tell he is close to tears. "What am I supposed to do now, Mom?"

My son sits on a curb outside a nearly-deserted airport, and I have no clue what he should do for the next eight hours. He seems confused and disoriented; I can hear the fear rising in his voice. Finally, I tell him to go inside and try to find a place where he can lie down, even if he has to stretch out on the floor. If anyone bothers him, he can explain that he missed his flight but he'll be flying out in the morning. There won't be any food service at this hour—by now it's after 10:00—but I tell him to find some vending machines and get something to eat. "You can call me any time if you need to talk."

April 10, 2006

Danny does call of course. At 1:00 am and again at 2:00 (4:00 and 5:00 in Boston). At 8:00 it's my turn to call. I tell him which airline counter to find and to let them know he has an e-ticket. He seems disoriented and asks how he is supposed to find the right counter. I try to sound nonchalant, but I'm starting to panic too. What if Danny is too impaired to go through the steps it takes to catch the right flight at the right time?

"If you don't see the airline's name, just ask a guard or a flight attendant or pretty much anyone in a uniform who looks official," I say. "They should be able to tell you where to go." Miraculously, Danny finds the right counter, checks his bags, and makes it through security. I call again to ask him for the gate number and to see whether he has found it. When at last he is on the plane to Denver, I collapse into bed, the night's vigil having caught up with me.

Danny calls again from the Denver airport. He thinks he might have missed his connecting flight. He wanted to smoke, so he had to go all the way outside the airport to the designated smoking area, and then back again through security where there was a long line. Once inside the departure area, he asked someone which gate he should go to and sat there for several minutes, but no flights to Boston were announced. He then asked a different person, who told him that the gate had been changed and his plane was about to take off. Danny raced to the new location as fast as he could, just in time to watch the plane pull away from the gate.

Again he is utterly devastated, hating himself for messing this up, and hating the person who sent him to the wrong gate. I try to sympathize without deepening his despair, and tell him we will just find him another flight—not to worry. Well, maybe just a little bit of worry. The only option the airline can come up with is an evening flight from Denver to Las Vegas, connecting to a red-eye from Vegas to Boston that arrives at 7:00 am Tuesday morning.

I phone Danny with this new agenda and find myself talking to a severely depressed traveler. His attention wanders frequently and sometimes I can't tell whether he is still on the line. He doesn't think he will be able to find all the right planes and make the right connections. "I'm really tired, Mom. And I don't feel good. Things aren't right. . . . I can't do all this. I don't want to, Mom. I don't think I even want to live any more. Everything is so messed up. . . . Do you think I will ever get home?"

Now I'm really worried. I shift my attention from helping Danny get through the hoops at the airport to convincing him that his life is still worth living. It's a hard sell. Everything he had going for him when he left on Super Bowl Sunday is buried somewhere in the crater left by his self-destruction. But I tell him over and over the only positive fact I know: "I love you, Son. I want you to live. I want you to come back home. I'm never giving up on you. We'll figure this out together, OK?"

Hours pass and Danny sometimes sounds as though he is hearing the plan for the first time. I tell him again that he should ask someone official to help him find the right gate. At last it is time for boarding and Danny makes it through one more leg of his journey.

In Las Vegas, Danny sounds a little more alert when he calls. Probably this is because slot machines are scattered here and there in the terminal. But there is another long wait before the next plane, and soon the darkness begins to descend again.

"I'm too tired to do this, Mom. I just want to stay here. I'll just stay here and sleep. I don't care what happens to me. . . I can't . . . I mean . . . what did you say?" Even 36 hours into this crisis, something ominous floats through the fog in my mind. Danny's thoughts are coming apart. It's as though his mind is fading in and out, like static on the dial near a radio station. At times it comes into focus and everything is clear, but some kind of interference keeps interrupting the signals. It is all I can do to persuade Danny to take this one last step.

"All you have to do is get on the plane, Danny. Just please get on the plane and come home. When you get here, Dad and I will be there to meet you, OK?" "Won't it be really early?" Danny asks. "Well, yes. But we've been waiting all this time and we really want to see you. We'll go and get some breakfast when you get here." After a lengthy discussion about the importance of making it back home, Danny finally agrees to find the right gate and make this last flight toward home. For a few hours, fatigue overcomes my fear and I sleep until it's time to leave for the airport.

April 11, 2006

My husband and I wait near the baggage claim, speaking very little, half-wondering if we will even recognize our son. As we've talked over the past hours and days, it's become clear to us that Danny is suffering from more than just a weekend drug and alcohol binge. There is some kind of psychiatric problem as well. We don't know what it is, and the truth is we don't want to know. Sufficient unto the day is the pain thereof.

When Danny arrives, we hug him close and tell him how glad we are that he's back with us again. His body is strong from weeks of hard work, but his face is pale and drawn and his eyes are oddly blank. Leaving the airport, we exit in East Boston and look for a place to have breakfast. Some local police officers give us a tip about a small cafe, and we are all grateful for a chance to focus on coffee, eggs and bacon. We ask Danny about his trip and about his job, but eventually we must turn the conversation to the subject no one wants to discuss.

"Danny," my husband begins, "I know you're very tired from your trip and you don't feel very well. But we're worried about you, and we'd like you to come with us to the hospital." Danny looks like someone just sent an arrow into his heart. "But I don't need to go to any hospital! I'm OK. I just need to sleep. Please . . . I've been awake for two days, and I've been cold and I haven't had anything to eat. I just want to go home."

Now it is up to me, since Danny always looks to me to take his side, to back him up, to show him mercy. "Danny, I know you're so tired. But you're also not doing very well, and we're pretty concerned about you. There were times on your way here when you felt that you might not be able to go on. So we'd like to go with you to the emergency room at MGH and see if they might be able to give you some help."

"But Mom, that's not what you said! You told me I could always come home—that's what you said in your letters. If I can't come home, why did you say that?" It's true. I did say that to him. And I meant it. Even now, all I want is to take him home and let him sleep, and believe that's all he needs. It takes all the reserves I have left to say, "I know, Danny. And I'm glad you're here with us again. But we really need to take you to the hospital."

Timeout: Saving our Children

An article in *The Boston Globe* on May 5, 2008 hit me like a sucker punch. It began: "The teenager spoke so eloquently about the wild cycles of bipolar disorder that she drew tears from a State House audience last May. Testifying about flaws she had seen in the mental health system, she wanted to show that one girl could make a difference. She signed her notes, 'Stay strong.' Sixteen-year-old Yolanda M. Torres of Plymouth was supposed to be a poster child for the proposal currently in the Legislature to improve mental health care for children. But not like this. In late January, in a violent impulse she left no note to explain, Yolanda committed suicide."[5]

Yolanda's illness grabbed hold of her life when she was only twelve years old, and loosened its grip only after many years of intermittent hospitalizations, medication trials and errors, and suffering the stigma of mental illness from her pre-teen peers. The article reports that she had waited as long as two days in

---

[5] Carey Goldberg, "In Teen's Memory, A Mental Health Push: Bill Would Alter Care for Youths," *The Boston Globe*, May 5, 2008, available online at *www.boston.com/news/local/massachusetts/articles/2008/05/05/in_tee ns_memory_a_mental_health_push/*.

hospital emergency rooms for a psychiatric bed to become available, watched at all times by security guards. Yolanda didn't want anyone else to undergo the indignities of this inhumane and dysfunctional system. Her mother said that "she talked about how hard it is to sit in an emergency room and you see the look in your parents' eyes; and they can't really help you go through it, but they're there for you."

The bill before the Legislature, sponsored by Senator Stephen A. Tolman, was named Yolanda's Law by a coalition of advocates for mentally ill children. It was signed into law by Massachusetts Governor Deval Patrick on September 24, 2008. In a speech announcing the passage of this legislation, Patrick said, "This bill provides some very important new tools in the network of support for young people—better screening, improved treatment options, closer coordination with educators, and people in public schools, and in public education generally. A way of lifting us all to a better place, in terms of the vigilance that we give to the emotional and intellectual and mental development of our young people."[6]

Reforms like these are long overdue, and it's heartening to see that the Legislature is capable of responding this quickly when a tragedy spurs them into action. If only they were moved in the same way by the less public tragedies that take place in our city every hour of every day.

Yolanda's mother, Mary Ann Tufts, wrote in a memorial essay: "There were many times her Dad and I lay with her as she cried, and promised that if we were able to take away her pain

---

[6] Available at the official website of the Governor of Massachusetts at *www.mass.gov/?pageID=gov3terminal&L=3&L0=Home&L1=Media+Ce nter&L2=Speeches&sid=Agov3&b=terminalcontent&f=text_2008-09- 24_child&csid=Agov3.*

and put it on ourselves, we would. Now, I think we have. . . No more meds, blood draws, voices, hallucinations, insinuations, or stigma. I envision her being kissed by the sun on white sandy beaches. Singing and laughing and always calm."

6 Drive-Through Service

April 9, 2006

I can tell that Danny has thoughts of running away, but he is so utterly exhausted from the ordeal of the past three days that he can't fight any more. The drive to MGH takes an eternity and no one knows what to say. At one point, Danny tells me he can see his thoughts; sometimes they travel down his leg and he can just shake them out at the bottom. My husband and I glance at each other, knowing what it means, and hating that we know.

The psychiatric emergency room at MGH is just beginning the day shift when we arrive. The rest of that morning is still a blur—most of it too painful to remain in one's memory for long. There are interviews with my husband and me, with Danny, with all of us together. Some tests, more interviews, a lot of waiting . . . and more waiting. I'm still numb from being punched in the face by reality.

My husband has to leave for work, so Danny and I are left to await the verdict from the MGH physicians. Taking pity on me as I sit weeping in the waiting room, a young resident, Dr. Jenkins, shows me a brochure about a new program they have

71

at MGH. It's called the FEPP program and it sounds wonderful. Dr. Jenkins explains that we will probably be eligible for it, though it will have to wait until Danny gets out of the hospital. I read the brochure again and again, feeling a sense of hope for the first time in months:

"The First-Episode and Early Psychosis Program (FEPP) of the Massachusetts General Hospital (MGH) was established to help patients and families around the time of a first episode of psychosis. FEPP is a research program that provides specialized evaluation, treatment, and education for people who are experiencing psychosis for the first time or who have been diagnosed with a psychotic disorder of recent onset (within one year). We offer the following services to eligible patients: Comprehensive medical and psychiatric evaluation, Second opinion evaluations, Medication treatment, Psychological treatment (cognitive behavioral treatment or "CBT"), Family education about psychosis and schizophrenia, Participation in research studies for interested patients, including state-of-the-art imaging projects."

Wow! This is so impressive—all these prestigious, Harvard-affiliated doctors and specialists working together with patients and their families to intervene before this illness takes over and destroys their lives. One section of the brochure asks "Why is Early Diagnosis Important?" Among other things, we learn that "often, untreated patients who have delusions and hallucinations lose their job, drop out of school, or alienate their friends and family. Sometimes, there are problems with the law. These consequences have been termed the 'social toxicity of psychosis.' However, if psychosis is treated early, these consequences may be prevented. There is also some research that suggests that the longer that patients wait to receive treatment for psychosis, the less complete their response to treatment because of changes in their brains."[7]

Exactly. It's a shame that I could never convince the MGH psychiatry department to let Danny into this program. Because of their refusal to help, he got to drink the cup of social toxicity right down to the dregs.

After a day-long sojourn in the Psych ER, as we learn to call it, the supervising psychiatrist decides that Danny should be hospitalized. We wait until they can find an open bed at McLean Hospital, and then wait some more until an ambulance is available to take Danny there. I'm not allowed to ride in the ambulance, so I bail my car out of the garage and try to find the hospital. It turns out to be a pretty elusive creature in the dark, and it's 10:00 pm when I arrive.

Apparently, there is no rest for the wicked, or in this case, the sick of mind and heart. I stay with Danny through the hour-long intake process, and begin my education on the Massachusetts mental health care bureaucracy (in fact, there are several poorly-coordinated bureaucracies) and the standard operating procedures of mental hospitals. Once past the locked doors to "the unit," there are no plastic bags allowed, no razors, glass containers, aluminum cans, aerosol cans, belts, shoelaces, cell phones, cameras, matches, or lighters. The doors to the patients' rooms have no locks, and they are given only markers or blunt pencils to write with. Directions posted in the elevator warn you to let the doors close before opening the door to the unit.

---

[7] See the web site for the FEPP program, *http://www2.massgeneral.org/schizophrenia/scz_care_treatment-1step.html.* Accessed on November 2, 2009.

Danny is in the AB unit, or maybe it's BA. Many labels in mental hospitals evoke a kind of secret code known only to the cognoscenti. Just one more thing to make you feel inept and overmatched from the start. There is a kind of paradox of respect in mental health units. What is normally a reciprocal attitude is already unbalanced by the doctor/patient relationship, and even by the custodial staff/patient relationship.

For the "clients" who live in the unlocked rooms with unlaced shoes, it's hard to command much self-respect, never mind respect from others. Although he is impaired, Danny is an intelligent and sensitive person, painfully aware of the attitudes of the staff toward him. It doesn't help that he is a young black male who is over six feet tall and angry about being there.

Over the next few days, I become more familiar with the vocabulary of mental health "providers" (one of my new words). Patients, I mean clients, are "compliant" or "non-compliant" with their medication and treatment plan, phrases that could be lifted from *One Flew over the Cuckoo's Nest*. We are told our son is "paranoid," "delusional," and "oppositional" (but not in what way or to whom). Given the seriousness of Danny's symptoms, I expect McLean to keep him as an in-patient for at least several weeks. But their ways are not our ways.

By 11:00 pm, the orderlies are finally ready to bring Danny upstairs and I have to say good-bye. I try to be reassuring. "These people can help you, Danny. You'll start to feel better, I'm sure. I love you, Son. I'll be back to visit, OK?" I go to my car and drive along the dark, deserted roads toward home. I have no tears; not yet. Mothers have hidden reserves of iron, I think, to draw on when those they love are in danger. The iron keeps them calm and focused and courageous for as long as they have to be. Even when the danger passes, it takes time

74

for the metal to yield to the gentleness and sensitivity one expects from motherly hearts. Maybe the iron and the gentleness are two sides of the same thing—a fierce love for our children.

April 12, 2006

Joey and Alex go to visit Danny at McLean. Everyone feels a little subdued today. I speak with Danny briefly on the phone. One minute he is angry and the next pitifully sad and hopeless. The day is cold for April. I am too exhausted to travel to McLean again, and I have an appointment for surgery on my left thumb—something called "trigger finger," though it's not a finger and has nothing to do with triggers. I consider cancelling, but I've waited for many weeks as it is, so I head to the hospital for what I'm told is a fairly low-key outpatient procedure.

Since only my arm is anesthetized, I'm awake during the operation. The surgeon knows me well, having operated on me twice before and treated three of my children for sports injuries. The nurse tries to make conversation, asking about my plans for the weekend. I tell her my son is in the hospital so I'll probably spend most of it visiting him. "Oh, which hospital is he in? Is he here?" "No, he's at McLean." The doctor knows McLean. He asks which son it is, and offers some comforting words. For the first time since Sunday, tears roll down my cheeks. Everyone falls silent. I wish they would have put me completely under. For a long, long time.

April 13, 2006

It's Friday the 13th. McLean calls to ask Damian and me to appear for a conference with Danny's "team" at 4:00. When we arrive, there is no private place available for the meeting. In the end, we sit on chairs at the end of the hallway near the kitchen and TV room. Patients walk back and forth past our huddled group. Some stare, others shuffle by as though we are invisible. The "team" is one doctor (not Danny's doctor, we're told, but a doctor), a case worker (who *is* Danny's case worker, but this is her last day on the job), and another case worker (the replacement for the first one). We've never met any of them.

The three providers mostly stand, facing the three of us— Danny and I sit on the one couch and Damian leans on the window sill. Someone begins, "We wanted to talk with you about a discharge plan for Danny." What?!! My husband and I exchange expressions of total shock. I manage some response: "Didn't he just get here?" "Well, yes." But Danny wants to leave and has signed a paper saying as much. Apparently they can only keep him for three business days after he signs the paper, and that means he will be discharged on Monday evening. They assume he'll come to live at home, of course—our home. "He is only 18 after all." It's hard to focus on their words . . .

We are completely stunned. Our marriage counselor virtually forbade us to have Danny live at home, warning that it would undo our marriage and destroy our family. We tell the "team" that Danny can't stay with us. They pressure us to change our minds, so we have to insist more strongly. Danny listens as long as he can bear it, growing more agitated by the minute. Finally he stands and stomps off, filled with hurt and anger. "You lied to me, Mom! You just betrayed me! How can I ever trust you again? You told me I could always come home! I believed you! It's the only thing that kept me going! And you, Dad . . . I don't even know what to say." After Danny leaves, we reiterate to the team that if he is discharged on Monday, he will have no place to live. They say (I think) that they will look into it.

April 14, 2006

Joey and Lily take the subway to visit their brother. Danny's friend Bobby and his older brother stop by as well. I speak to Danny briefly by phone, still unsure whether he wants to see me—today or ever.

April 15, 2006

It's a beautiful Sunday afternoon. Lily and I bring pizza and soda as a peace offering and go to visit Danny. He's glad for the pizza. We share some with his roommate, a teenager from New Hampshire who just attempted suicide. His mother and stepfather have driven down to see him. I try to talk a little with the other mother. She looks like I do—calm and pleasant and hopeful on the outside, and bleeding to death on the inside.

My daughter tries to find the brother she knew in this anxious, distracted, agitated boy with dark circles under his eyes. She is only 13, and I think she doesn't really recognize him. He is obviously desperate for her love and understanding, wanting her to accept him even though he barely knows who he is any more. Somehow, being together only makes them feel farther apart.

April 16, 2006, Monday

I visit McLean again and ask to speak with Danny's "case manager" (I'm beginning to learn the lingo). She is new—neither of those we spoke with on Friday. Danny's doctor isn't on duty today either. I ask about alternatives to living at home. "Aren't there group homes, half-way houses, or something for young people like Covenant House in New York?" No, I'm told—there's nothing. Even if there were, the waiting lists would be so long that it could take months or even years before a spot opened up. "Then can't you keep Danny here for a few more days? At least until we can find some place for him to go?"

No, I'm told, because Danny is not judged to be a clear and present danger to himself or others. "Really? He was suicidal a week ago when he was traveling here from the west coast." But that was then; now he is no longer suicidal, they assure me. How do they know? Because Danny tells them he isn't. "He's taking Risperdal, which is an antipsychotic medication, and he's very depressed. But smoking breaks are being banned at McLean and Danny wants out." They'll discharge him tomorrow afternoon. I never get to speak with a doctor.

April 17, 2006, Tuesday

Expecting Danny to be discharged late this afternoon, I start looking online for housing options. McLean calls at 11:00 am to say they're discharging him now. Now?! I lobby for a little more time, and they reluctantly agree to wait until 2:00. Again, I ask over the phone whether there's a place he can go. They're recommending a "partial hospitalization program" at the Arbour Hospital in Jamaica Plain.

I ask, "What's partial hospitalization?" though I'm sure I'm expected to know this already. "It's a program that runs from 9 to 3 on weekdays. There's a psychiatric nurse on duty who can prescribe medications, and several social workers who organize groups and so on." "Oh, OK. But where is Danny supposed to live?" The person on the other end of the line tells me that the Arbour runs a men's residence next door to the partial program, and it looks like Danny can stay there for the next few weeks. Wonderful! McLean actually came up with something!

I arrive at 2:00 to meet Danny and take the elevator up to his unit. An orderly brings out his belongings and tells us we can go. No one speaks to me. I don't know what Danny's medications are or whether there are any discharge instructions—I don't even know the address of the Arbour Hospital.

Eventually I track down one of the nurses and she explains that the residential program isn't going to work out after all. "What am I supposed to do, then?" "Well, Danny can probably stay at a shelter." "Do you have a recommendation of where to go?" She does not. "Oh. Well, do you have a list of shelters in the area?" No again. But she suggests that I look in the phone book. So I walk out of McLean with a phone number for Arbour's partial program and a very agitated, angry, and apprehensive "ex"- mental patient . . . my son.

I look at the page of numbers printed this morning from the online yellow pages, then at my cell phone, wondering where to start. Danny is beside himself for a smoke. We *must* stop for cigarettes, *right now*! He still resents his week in confinement and starts ordering me around, cursing me, the other drivers, and the world in general. Finally I find a convenience store and pull off the road. I give Danny money for cigarettes and he steals some candy and Red Bull to go with them. I am too distressed and exhausted to make him go back in and pay. I fervently wish the world would end. It stubbornly refuses to do so.

While Danny lights a cigarette, I start to call the shelters on my list. One is for pregnant women, another is a long-term program with a waiting list, a third has no beds left . . . We drive to some of the more promising sites only to be told there is no more room or we've missed the cutoff time, etc. It's beginning to get dark and Danny and I are at the end of our emotional ropes. I still can't believe I have to find a place for my son just to sleep, when this morning he was in a hospital where he could receive actual treatment.

Danny keeps begging me to let him stay at home, and I realize that I can't bear to leave him out on the street. Not today. So around 8:00 pm I bring Danny home, just to spend the night. Damian is opposed to the idea, but I explain that the housing plan McLean lined up has fallen through and I can't find anything else right now. Reluctantly, he agrees to let Danny stay with us for a few days while he gets started in the partial program at the Arbour Hospital.

7 Descent into Hell

April 18, 2006

Damian tries to get Danny up early, as the day program starts today at 9:00. I rise early as well, since Danny doesn't know how to get there on public transit and none of us has been to that part of the city. The hospital is supposed to be located on a side street just off the main avenue in Jamaica Plain. I drive up and down, searching in vain for the aforementioned side street. You would think a hospital would be hard to miss, but that thought only makes me feel even more directionally impaired.

Eventually I pull over to ask a passerby, and find that the hospital is on a narrow, winding street and that there is no sign for it on the main road. The glorified alley that leads to the hospital climbs steeply up a hill (I notice this because I'm driving a stick shift), then winds around to the entrance. In the year or so that Danny is in and out of that hospital, the street sign is never replaced, and there is no indication that a hospital is nearby. I learn to find it by the pizza shop on the corner.

Arriving late on this first day, we find one of the social workers and Danny joins a group meeting already in progress. I agree

81

to come back for him at 3:00 when the program ends. Over the next few days, Danny learns how to get to the hospital on the subway, and we encourage him to keep going. An RPN prescribes Risperdal for him, along with Klonopin, an anti-anxiety drug that can be addictive, but it does help him get to sleep at night.

By the following week, Danny is showing up later and leaving earlier, barely present for a program that is supposed to occupy him from 9 to 3. My husband is teaching and grading papers and traveling to conferences, so every day it's Danny and I, battling over whether he will attend the program that day. Every excuse gets trotted out—he feels sick, his head hurts, he's too anxious, the staff doesn't like him, he's not getting anything out of it.

Soon he tells the RPN that he doesn't need the program at all, just the medications. Astoundingly, she agrees with him! When I ask about ongoing psychiatric treatment for Danny, she says she will refer him to Dr. Umbridge, a psychiatrist at MGH. MGH! Hope leaps up in my heart as I remember the brochure about the FEPP program and the comprehensive treatment plan it described.

This could be our chance to begin something genuinely helpful at last! No more vague assurances or medical professionals washing their hands of responsibility for Danny and his health. MGH has the international reputation, the resources, and the cutting-edge research—surely we'll find help there and be able to make some real progress. Someone will help us all, not just Danny, to know what we need to do and where we can go with our questions. The appointment is two weeks away, though, so we have to hold out a while longer.

While we wait, Danny continues to spiral downward, making life at home increasingly difficult for the rest of the family. Desperate for some way to find help for him, I begin making inquiries among my friends, and someone comes up with a recommendation for a therapist. Dr. Ogunde is just setting up a private practice in Brookline and he specializes in child and adolescent psychology. He is relatively young and, like Danny, bi-racial.

I call to make an appointment and he agrees to see Danny within a few days. When I ask about fees, Dr. Ogunde is evasive. "We'll talk about that at some point," he says. Danny likes this man immediately and wants to continue seeing him. I see this as a real victory. Dr. Ogunde never sends us a bill and doesn't require Danny to pay anything, though eventually he says that Danny can pay what he can afford, even it's only five dollars.

The relationship with this therapist is, overall, a good thing for Danny, though my husband and I lose enthusiasm for it after a few months. Dr. Ogunde refuses to communicate with the rest of Danny's treatment providers and he often fails to return phone calls and emails. When he does speak with us, it's usually to tell us how unreasonable we are being with our son. He seems to buy into Danny's version of events wholeheartedly, which we find puzzling in a mental health professional, and presses hard to get us to lower our expectations and stop hassling Danny so much.

May 2006

Freed from the obligation to attend the day program, Danny turns increasingly to old habits and obsessions. We know nothing about this at the time, but it turns out that just before he left for the west coast, Danny and two of his friends pooled

83

their resources to buy several thousand dollars worth of cocaine from a connection in Boston. Or so the story goes. We've come to realize that Danny's memory often betrays him, especially when it involves something fraught with emotion. In any event, Danny explains that his friends were supposed to sell the drugs on the street for a significant profit, giving the drug lord his cut and then dividing the rest among themselves.

Unfortunately (or fortunately, depending on your point of view) the bottom dropped out of the cocaine market that spring, since the police had begun to target cocaine in their war on drugs. Sales were slow, and one of the partners, Rajib, eventually returned the unsold cocaine and what money they had to the drug lord. Total profit? Zero.

Just one catch—the drug dealer still wanted the money he would have made if they had "done the job right." So Danny sent as much money as he could spare from his paychecks at the mill, but they were still a long way from making up what they owed. The third partner, Caleb, was recalled to his home country for mandatory service in the army. This left Rajib and Danny holding the bag—literally.

Not long after Danny returned home, Rajib received a "visit" from the drug lord and his posse and was nearly beaten to death. He was thrown head first into the corner of the curb and spent several days in the hospital with a skull fracture. Now Danny is desperate to raise money, fearing for his friend and himself if the dealer returns.

So, though we don't know the reason, we notice large sums of money disappearing from our wallets and purses. Lily's savings somehow vanish, and other items of value go missing. Danny often leaves the house late at night and doesn't return until the wee hours of the morning. When questioned, he gives many different explanations, piling up so many lies that they start to collapse under the weight of reality. Over and over he violates the rules we had insisted on as a condition of his living at home.

June 2006

"Let your steadfast love become my comfort." Psalm 119: 76

The date for Danny's visit to the psychiatrist at MGH finally arrives. He and I go together to his appointment with Dr. Umbridge, and are directed to the 8th floor of the Wang Building. No other departments are located on that floor, so as soon as you push the button in the elevator everyone takes a second look at you. Oh, you're one of those people.

Once inside the doors to the psych unit, we sign in and take a seat. The others in the waiting room are mirror images of us. Patients fidget and mutter, looking nervously about and glancing away immediately if you catch their eye. Family members wait more calmly, with an expression of pained resignation, hope having drained from them long ago. The room is too small, not nearly space enough to hold all this fear and shame and despair.

Dr. Umbridge sees Danny alone and speaks to me only with Danny present. She is young for a psychiatrist, with blonde hair, piercing blue eyes, and long Barbie legs. She projects confidence and a definite air of superiority—always the professional, never just a person. She seems defensive for Danny. I'm clearly one of the enemy. I wonder if mental health professionals assume the worst about their clients' parents and families. Am I guilty of screwing up my son until proven innocent?

85

I want information. She doesn't want to give me any. I ask about the FEPP program. "Someone else handles that." "OK. Well, can we make an appointment with them?" "Oh, they'll give you a call." Dr. Umbridge jots a few notes in her book and gives Danny a prescription for more Risperdal but no Klonopin. "Come back in two weeks." Two weeks? That's it? But I'm still a believer. Surely they'll put some other things in place, won't they—the family counseling, the groups, the information about resources, the "team." There is a team, right? Maybe it just takes some time to get it all organized.

Soon Danny's appointments are a month apart. Dr. Umbridge adds Zyprexa to the Risperdal, but neither seems to be doing much good. I ask her again and again about the FEPP program. I'm told Danny isn't eligible for that program—something about his diagnosis, which they insist is bipolar disorder rather than schizophrenia. OK, maybe bipolar with psychotic symptoms. Eventually the diagnosis is changed to schizoaffective disorder, but by then it's too late. The "treatment system" seems to run at the pleasure of the doctors and researchers and their various minions. It was apparently more convenient to put Danny into the shorter CBT program, even though what he needed was the FEPP program.

To this day I have no idea why we weren't admitted to the program that might have spared us some of the agonies that lay in our future. CBT stands for Cognitive Behavioral Therapy, which sounds very helpful but actually consists of repeating the obvious to clients and their families until their eyes glaze over. There are many worksheets, in yellow, pink, or blue, with multiple choice questions like: "When I feel anxious and upset, I should: (a) have a beer to calm down, (b) take several sleeping pills, or (c) call a friend and talk about how I'm feeling."

The director of the CBT program is going on maternity leave, so we're assigned to a younger member of the staff, obviously new to the whole operation. She is nervous around Danny. He wears his baseball cap pulled low over his eyes and leans back in his chair, refusing even to glance at the many sheets of paper she hands out. I pretend to listen, but often lose patience with the pace of the conversation or the inane level of the materials.

After three meetings, I can't take it any more—"I thought we were going to find out about resources available in the community." "Yes, that's right, but that's not until the last session." Danny refuses to attend any more sessions, so I ask the teacher (guide? guru?) to skip to the last session so I can find out about the resources.

It turns out she doesn't know much about resources. She says it might be a good idea to apply to the Department of Mental Health. For what? Mental health? No, you just apply to be a *client* of the Department of Mental Health, DMH as it is known in psych lingo. And then what? "Then you'll be eligible for the services they offer." "Which are . . .?" "Well, they have their own treatment providers and social workers and so on, but mainly they provide housing options for those with mental illnesses."

Housing?! This bureaucracy holds the key to housing? Amazing! It has been over two months since Danny's stay in McLean, and this is the first time anyone has mentioned that he can apply somewhere for housing. "OK, so how do I go about applying?" "Um, I think you can find the application online. But it's better if someone helps you fill it out." "Can you do that?" "Not really. I'm not very familiar with the process. But there are probably social workers here at the hospital who can help you with it." "Social workers?" "Yes. They try to connect people with various social services. They might be willing to help with this."

"So where do I find them?" "I think they have an office on the ground floor of the hospital somewhere." OK. I don't know where the office is or how to recognize a social worker from an unsocial one, but maybe I'll give it a try. "One more thing," adds Ms. CBT, "Danny will have to sign several releases, for his medical records and so on."

Sure. I'll just ask him. "Danny, could you please sign these forms so I can convince DMH that you're mentally ill?" Between Her Highness Dr. Umbridge and the sweet but clueless CBT instructor, I despair of finding any effective help at MGH.

Strangely, the only follow-up to the CBT program is with a woman working for a research company in New Hampshire (or is it Vermont?). She calls to ask if she can interview Danny and me, separately, about our knowledge of the symptoms of bipolar disorder and the medications used to treat it. Also, about our experience with the mental health system. Danny agrees, but only because they offer to pay him $35 for each interview. I decide to go along with it for now—maybe Danny will get something out of it besides the money. Never mind that he doesn't actually *have* bipolar disorder. Whatever.

The interviewer sits across from me at our dining room table, laptop open and tape recorder at the ready. She grills me about every aspect of Danny's illness and its impact on him and on the rest of the family, especially on me. Do I resent Danny? Do I wish he "weren't here"? And so on. I submit to four such interrogations, six months apart. It is invariably devastating for me—emotionally draining, exhausting, and frustrating.

Danny's sometime therapist, Dr. Ogunde, tells me that he wasn't accepted to the FEPP program at MGH because he was assigned to the control group, though of course we were never apprised of that fact. The control group gets nothing—no family therapy, no special psychiatric interventions, no state of the art imaging techniques, no substance abuse counseling. It should be a criminal offense to do that to anyone. Eventually the issue becomes moot, since the FEPP program is available only to those who are within a year of their first diagnosis.

The interviewer interrupts this train of thought with another question. "How do you feel, on a scale of one to five, about how you've been treated by the mental health professionals you've encountered so far?" I choke on the reply. I hadn't realized how betrayed I feel by so many doctors and hospitals and indifferent social workers. Don't they know how helpless and vulnerable we are? I tell the interviewer I still don't understand why MGH couldn't do more for my son. She says she knows the director of the CBT program, Dr. Barker, who is back from maternity leave. "Would you like Dr. Barker to give you a call?" "Yes, I'd really appreciate that." I reiterate this request at every interview. The doctor never calls.

Some months later, I learn about a public lecture Dr. Barker is giving at MGH, so I make it a point to attend. Afterward I go up to the podium and wait for my turn to speak with her. She focuses on several other people on the other side of the podium, never turning to face me. As that group begins to disperse, Dr. Barker grabs her coat and briefcase and whisks out the door, surrounded by her colleagues—the worthy. I might as well be invisible.

Mid-July, 2006

I decide to take another shot at finding summer school classes that will enable Danny to meet the requirements for a diploma. Finally, a possibility occurs to me, and I call the head of the charter school to ask: "What about summer school at the high school in the next town? They offer some more advanced courses, so maybe Danny can finish up there."Well, yes, I guess that would be acceptable." That high school offers only two of the three courses Danny needs. Still, it makes sense to get those two out of the way, and maybe manage the third with some type of independent study.

Summer School II lasts for six weeks. Classes there are organized much more humanely than those at the charter school. One of Danny's classes even schedules some walking field trips to museums in the area. On the first of these outings, Danny decides to take a chance and light up a cigarette. This major violation of the school rules does not go unnoticed, and he is expelled from the program. Returning is not an option. Strike two. Game over.

July 21, 2006

"And the king was much moved, and went up to the chamber over the gate and wept. And as he went he said, "O my son Absalom, my son, my son Absalom! Would God I had died instead of thee, O Absalom, my son, my son!" (II Samuel 18:33)

Last night Danny didn't come home. He didn't answer his phone. My daughter is staying at a friend's house and my husband is out of town. As the day wears on, my fears multiply and my nerves become frayed. Finally, I reach Damian by phone and we agree that, with this umpteenth violation of the house rules (rules are definitely his nemesis), Danny cannot live at home any longer.

So I gather his clothes and shoes and some toiletries and pack them into a duffel bag. Then I leave the bag outside the back door, along with a brief note tucked into an envelope that tries to explain why Danny can't stay with us any longer. Finally, I take the car and drive away, hoping to avoid a direct confrontation, especially since Damian isn't here.

No such luck, it turns out. When I return around 10:30 pm, Danny is standing in the condo parking lot, arguing loudly with the downstairs neighbor Bob. He is too intoxicated to read the note I left, and insists that Bob read it to him. Bob isn't having it. Danny has been cursing at him, pounding on the outside door to the condo, and pressing our buzzer for the past thirty minutes. Bob is on the verge of calling the police.

I tell Danny he can't come into the house. He objects, offering several reasons why he deserves to stay. "Danny," I reply, "I don't want to discuss it right now. I'm exhausted, and you've had too much to drink. Let's talk about it when Dad gets home." Danny takes offense at this and walks up until he is standing directly over me, spewing obscenities and demanding proof for my evaluation of him.

It's the only time in the long months of Danny's illness that I've felt genuinely afraid of him. "Oh yeah, Mom!" he shouts in my face, "You know I'm drunk? How would you possibly know that? You don't have any proof. I'm *not* drunk, so why can't I stay at my own house, Mom? Come on! Just let me come in. I just need to sleep, I promise."

Suddenly, as if on cue, some of Danny's friends drive up and offer to take him with them. It's several minutes before they persuade him to go, but since Bob is still threatening to call the police, Danny finally picks up the duffel bag, gets into the car, and disappears down the street with his friends. I will never forget the look in his eyes.

Turning to go back into the house, I find the note I'd written blowing forlornly around the parking lot—the one where I assure Danny that we still love him, and that we're always ready to help him if he's willing to accept our help. I spend the rest of the night in tears.

Danny crashes at his friend Bobby's house, but within two days Bobby's family banishes him too, fed up with his stealing, drinking, and growing paranoia. He calls my cell phone, desperate for a place to stay. I tell him to find a shelter, but he seems too strung out to focus on anything I say. Finally I agree to help him find a shelter and, for the second time, we begin a long and futile search for a decent place to stay. Nothing is available. In the end, I have to ask him where he wants me to drop him off. He chooses a counter-culture hangout in the center of town, and sleeps in the nearby park for the next two nights.

July 23, 2006

Danny still has no place to live, and shows no interest in making significant changes in his life. He is deeply distressed about being banished from the house, though, and begins to talk again about not wanting to go on. He does meet with his therapist, who calls to tell me how heartless I am for failing to take care of my own son. "He just turned 19," Dr. Ogunde argues (as though I'm unaware of this fact). "He's too young to be living on the streets."

I try to explain the situation, but it's not clear whether Dr. Ogunde gets it. Finally, hoping to fend off his attacks, I ask if he knows of any place Danny could go that might be able to help him—maybe some kind of treatment or rehab facility. Dr. Ogunde doesn't know of any such places, but he consults a colleague who recommends a rehab facility in Connecticut called Silver Hill.

I'm skeptical about whether Danny will go to a rehab facility, and even more skeptical about whether we can afford it. But when I call, the center assures me that they accept many kinds of insurance, and they have a sliding scale for those with fewer resources. One catch is that Danny has to spend the weekend at McLean Hospital to receive a medical evaluation before he can be admitted. Amazingly he agrees to this, perhaps because even McLean looks better than spending another night on a park bench. Staff at McLean call Silver Hill and tell me that they have agreed to accept our insurance.

Danny is to be discharged from McLean late in the day on Sunday, and my plan is to pick him up at the hospital and head directly to Connecticut, spending Sunday night at a motel and checking into Silver Hill the following morning. Lily offers to come along so I'll have some company on the way back.

However, our car dies on Saturday, so my plan for Sunday is in shreds. Damian is adamant that Danny cannot stay at the house, even for one night, but I can't bear to tell him, for the second time in two days, that he can't come home. I'm desperate to find some kind of transportation that will take us to Connecticut, but the rehab facility is so remote that almost nothing goes there.

At 10:00 pm, it occurs to me that I can rent a car. Except that no rental companies are open at that hour. A woman who

answers one of the 800 numbers concludes that my only option
is the Enterprise office near the airport. Since it's not
accessible by public transportation, I call a friend to ask if she
can drive me there. She graciously agrees, saying that she's
happy to help. In a few minutes, she arrives at our house. Lily
and I grab our suitcases, and the three of us head to the airport
Enterprise office.

When we arrive, the car is ready to go. All I have to do is sign
the papers and produce a credit card. I hand over my Visa card
and the agent informs me that debit cards are no longer
accepted as up-front payments on car rentals. "But I just rented
a car from Enterprise a month ago and used this same card," I
object. "Right, but it's different here at the airport because
people come from so far away. So at these locations we only
accept credit cards." Of course you do. And of course I have no
such card.

My friend offers to let me use her credit card instead, since
when I return the car I can always pay with a different card.
Great! "Well, you can't do it that way," the salesman tells us,
"because the driver and the credit card owner have to be the
same person." My heart sinks. Damian is already unhappy that
I'm starting this trip so late at night, and now I've brought my
friend across town and all the way to the airport for nothing.
Worst of all, Danny has no place to stay tonight. My daughter
looks up expectantly, waiting for me to come up with some
solution. I hate to disappoint her, but my idea account is
already overdrawn.

Finally, my friend speaks up: "I know! I'll take the rental car for
now, and you can drive *my* car to Connecticut!" "You're kidding,
right? It's a long trip, and I would die if something happened to
your car." "Don't be silly. It will all work out fine. I really want
you to be able to go, and there aren't any other options, right?"

94

I will never be able to repay this dear friend for her kindness and generosity that night. Buoyed by her encouragement and hugs, Lily and I set out for McLean Hospital. We pick Danny up at midnight and head down the turnpike. By two in the morning, I can't stay awake any longer, so find a cheap motel and fall into bed exhausted.

Intake at Silver Hill is at 8:00 in the morning, so our motel stay is a short one. We arrive on time, but have to wait over an hour for someone to speak with us. We all feel a little sick from lack of sleep and no real breakfast. Glossy brochures in the waiting room describe the many wonderful programs and facilities offered here—dual diagnosis treatment for those with both substance abuse problems and a mental illness, DBT (Dialectical Behavioral Therapy, which means nothing to me), family support and counseling, and staff on call 24/7.

Strolling outside for a bit of fresh air, I begin to pay attention to the upscale environment. It looks like a country club, with perfectly manicured lawns and gracious Georgian buildings. More a retreat for celebrities than a refuge for the homeless. (In fact, I later read about an actor who spent time there following an arrest for drunk driving.)

At last, it's Danny's turn to enter the inner sanctum and speak with the director. By now he has filled out numerous forms, signed assorted releases, and surrendered his cell phone. (Cell phones with photo capabilities are not allowed in mental health settings, since they can compromise patient privacy. Unfortunately, this policy rules out 99% of cell phones.) The director makes a few calls and speaks to one of his assistants. Soon he comes back with the verdict: our insurance will not cover Danny's stay at after all.

So how much does it cost? "It's $40,000 per month, but sometimes we can give a discount based on financial need." "So with the discount, how much would it be." "Then it's only $35,000."[8] Wow! The teens on the front of the brochure look just like my son; who knew they were related to millionaires?

I try to persuade the director to let Danny stay out of the goodness of his heart, with predictable success. Reluctantly, we put Dan's gear back into my friend's car and begin the return trip to Boston. As I had promised Lily some swimming time, we stop for a while at a state park along the waterfront. But neither she nor Danny has much enthusiasm for skipping rocks and scanning tide pools. It's a cloudy day, and cool for July. After a few minutes, I decide to call it a wash. It's time to go home. Only there is no home for my son.

July 24 – August 17, 2006

For the next few weeks, Danny lives with friends or on the street. He doesn't appear for appointments at MGH and quits taking his medications. I'm increasingly worried about him, and frustrated that I haven't been able to find any housing we can afford. Danny occasionally visits his therapist Dr. Ogunde, who repeats his view that Damian and I are unkind and unreasonable. I don't understand why there's no one to help us take care of our son. Every day I make myself go through the motions of normal life, with my son hanging over an abyss.

At first I find support and comfort from my friends and neighbors, who witness some of what I am going through and try to understand and sympathize. Eventually, though, they

---

[8] "Forbes in 2003 indicated that the cost of a stay at Silver Hill is in the area of $1200/day." Taken from *http://www.nndb.com/detox/246/000043117/* on Nov. 18, 2009.

grow weary of listening. There is nothing they can do to solve this problem or make it go away, and they can't bear the thought that there is no cure for schizophrenia.

"Aren't there medications for that now?" they ask, looking for the kind of quick fix we've come to expect in this age of medical omnipotence, or "But eventually he'll get better, right?" or, most depressing of all, "I know a wonderful Chinese doctor with a secret remedy that worked wonders for my sister/friend/neighbor who was suffering from lupus/arthritis/fatigue!" Nobody wants to hear that you and your loved one will be suffering from the effects of this illness as long as you both shall live.

So friends call less and less often, or fail to return my calls and emails, protecting themselves from us and our pain. With the neighbors, there's the added factor that we (and hence our mentally ill child) live in close proximity to them, and they're nervous about what might happen to them or their children. They disappear just a little more quickly into their houses when they see us, keeping a safe distance, and no longer engage in the small talk that used to connect us to one another, however tenuously. When my son comes with us to church, people will often move further down the pew (much further), or shift uncomfortably in their seats, as if his illness is contagious or he might "go postal" at any moment.

The pain that these reactions cause me, though, is nothing compared to the rejection and humiliation that are part of my son's daily experience. For all its scientific sophistication, our society remains profoundly ignorant about the nature of mental illness. When you discuss it at all, you feel that you should speak in hushed tones. Most people, when pressed, acknowledge that schizophrenia is a disease of the brain, caused by some malfunction in the wiring or signals or what-have-you. For some reason, however, they don't go on to draw the conclusion that there is no shame in suffering from a mental illness.

Persons with schizophrenia or bipolar disorder or post-traumatic stress syndrome don't bring it on themselves. They have no secret character flaws that propelled them into psychosis. Whatever they did have, perhaps a genetic vulnerability combined with circumstances in their lives (or not—scientists don't really know), resulted in the onset of a debilitating, chronic, and heart-breaking medical condition. Prior to the illness, their lives, personalities, and family relationships are usually indistinguishable from those of people who never develop a psychiatric disorder.

One physician with many years of experience treating schizophrenia gets it exactly right: "People with schizophrenia and their families have to live with an extraordinary amount of stigma. Schizophrenia is the modern-day equivalent of leprosy."[9]

---

[9]E. Fuller Torrey, M.D. *Surviving Schizophrenia: A Manual for Families, Patients, and Providers*, 5th ed. (New York: HarperCollins, 2006), 394.

Timeout: Money in Mind

Below are some excerpts from the transcript of *Online Newshour*, a program on Boston's PBS channel, called "Homeless for the Holidays." It aired on December 23, 1997, and consists of interviews conducted by Paul Solman of the local PBS station with several health providers and administrators about the state of mental health care in Massachusetts.[10]

****

"During the holiday season, many donate time and money to the homeless . . . . Paul Solman, of WGBH-Boston, has been following what Massachusetts is doing to address the issue:

Solman: [Apparently,] death from homelessness in Boston is not just a matter of too little housing, but also too little care for the acutely mentally ill who make up so much of the chronically homeless population. By most estimates, some 75 to 90 percent of those who live on the streets are either poor mentally ill, poor substance abusers, or both. In Massachusetts, [these are] people for whom the Department of Mental Health is responsible. According to an internal department study, deaths of this population rose 79 percent from 1990 to 1994. The significance of that, says the department, is that in this period it began keeping better records. But to the critics who staged this event [a demonstration to protest inadequate care of the homeless], these were the years when the state was closing its mental hospitals and switching to private, managed care. . . .

---

[10] The transcript is available at *www.pbs.org/newshour/bb/welfare/july-dec97/homeless_12-23.html*. I have made some punctuation changes to allow for easier reading.

Solman: We've been on this story for two years now, following managed care of mental health for the poor here in Massachusetts, because this state's been in the forefront of the national move to privatize public services. It began in earnest in response to the taxpayer pressure of the 1980's, and by 1991, Massachusetts had begun to economize on its mental health care costs in several ways: by shutting down half of the state's eight public mental hospitals; by contracting with private hospitals, clinics, and day centers to assume a lot of its work, and by giving one company the job of managing all the private contractors. [That one company is the Massachusetts Behavioral Health Partnership.] As a result, costs have been held down but at a huge price, says psychiatrist Matthew Dumont, who we first interviewed in the fall of 1995.

Dr. Matthew Dumont, Psychiatrist: What we're having essentially is the devastation of a service system for very disorganized and chaotic people.

Solman: Dr. Dumont, a former assistant commissioner of mental health for Massachusetts, took us to a hospital he used to work at—Metropolitan State—former home to 500 patients, the kinds of people, he said, who had nowhere else to go.

Dumont: People who were sent to a state hospital like this were acutely psychotic; they were suicidal; they were generally people who were poor—you go to a state hospital when you don't have any insurance, or when your insurance runs out—or because they were the kinds of patients who were unacceptable to a private environment because they were too violent, or because they were too messy.

Solman: Dr. Dumont now works at one of the state's last public mental hospitals, places, he insists, that since the reforms of

100

the 60's, have been providing better care than you get with managed care.

Dumont: I have never been told that I can only have four sessions with an abused child or that this depressed person should be put on a drug and seen only three times. And I have never been told at the hospital I'm working in now that "I'm sorry, this patient's insurance has run out; the patient has to be discharged." . . .

Solman: In July of 1996, Massachusetts went further into privatization, contracting much its budget for the care of the indigent mentally ill to this man, Richard Sheola, whose private company, the Partnership, would manage the program by sending the business to places like the Deaconess. . . . The emphasis would be on efficiency, Sheola insisted, not arbitrary cost-cutting.

Richard Sheola, Massachusetts Behavioral Health Partnership: Less than a third of any earnings that can occur in this contract occur because of cost savings. Fully 2/3 of any potential earnings in the contract occur because we will hit performance standards, and there are 10 of them that have been established by the Commonwealth. If we hit all of those performance standards, we will earn a reasonable return on the investment. . . . [They include] timely admission to an out-patient setting within three days of a discharge. Timely decision-making in a crisis. Within two hours of getting a call, we have to make a disposition on the case and arrange for admission. . . .

Solman: Okay. It's now been more than a year since Sheola took over. What's happened? Well, the state has been saving money—almost $8 million this year—that's gone back into community care services, like this so-called clubhouse, a day rehab program in Boston. But Center House has been around for years. New community settings, a key promise of the Partnership, have yet to be established.

Partly as a result, perhaps, Boston's chronic homeless population hasn't dropped, which suggests the mental health system hasn't gotten its clients off the streets. In fact, on any given night, more of the poor mentally ill and/or substance abusers are now at Boston's main homeless shelter, the Pine Street Inn, than in all the state hospitals combined. There's also evidence that an increasing portion of the Commonwealth's prison population is made up of the mentally ill. Finally, there is that controversial study with which this piece began—that death rates have risen by 79 percent since the advent of managed care.

Dumont: Do we want to save money at a time of unprecedented wealth by allowing people to perish? They are perishing!

Solman: Dr. Dumont says that things have gotten worse, and replacing public institutions with free-market privatization is to blame. Even at one of the remaining state hospitals, Westborough, where Dumont now works, he emphasizes that a former halfway house for patients re-entering the community has just been turned into a lock-up facility for juvenile offenders. . . .

Dumont: I think the market has caused the mentally ill to be treated as if they were items of no importance. Their livelihood; their life; and, by the way, the life of the community in a very profound way has been seriously compromised.

Solman: Dr. Maryann Badaracco also sees her earlier fears coming true; that the state would cut back its services, hoping that private hospitals and clinics would simply pick up the slack.

Dr. Maryann Badaracco: And I think the state may also be thinking that this isn't going to become—isn't going to be very interesting to people because a group of people who are not going to be served have no advocates. . . .

Jean Bove, Alliance for the Mentally Ill: Many of the people who are in the program are going into emergency services; they're getting their few days of stabilization; they're being put out; they're going back; they're being put out; they're going back; they're being put out. . . .

Solman: But the state budget keeps getting cut for these kinds of services?

Sheola: Tough choices are being made, and that's not a population that has a great voice and a great constituency."

****

One would hope that, in the years since this program aired, most of the deep-seated problems that were being discussed have been addressed and at least partially resolved. In reality, the mental health system in Massachusetts has become even more dysfunctional. The web page for Massachusetts Behavioral Health Partnership describes its history as follows: "Established in 1996, the Massachusetts Behavioral Health Partnership (MBHP) was contracted by MassHealth to manage the mental health and substance abuse services for

MassHealth [i.e., Medicaid] Members who select the Primary Care Clinician (PCC) Plan."[11]

Select? There is no alternative to the PCC plan for Medicaid clients. However, in the opinion of MBHP (no support is offered for this claim), they have *improved both the delivery and quality of healthcare in the state.* "As a result of this success," the site reads, "MBHP was awarded a second five-year contract that began in October 2001." As of 2010, the Partnership continues to manage all mental health services in Massachusetts for those on Medicaid.

A *Q & A* page on the web site for Massachusetts Legal Help addresses this critically important question: "Who decides whether my mental health services are paid for?" The answer? "With the PCC program, you choose a primary care clinician (usually a doctor), who oversees your *physical health care.* A separate *private company,* the Massachusetts Behavioral Health Partnership (MBHP) manages your *mental health care* services."[12] In other words, it is neither your doctor nor the Department of Mental Health who decides whether your mental health services are paid for. Rather it is a private, that is, a *for-profit,* company, who decides. It's impossible to believe that those decisions are always made in the best interest of mental health clients and their caregivers.

---

[11] See *www.masspartnership.com/about/index.aspx*, emphasis mine.
[12] *www.masslegalhelp.org/mental-health/payment-decision*, emphasis mine.

8 Hell

August 2006

Damian participates each summer in a week-long seminar at a university in New Jersey, and I often take advantage of that time to spend a few days at a nearby campground. (My husband was raised in Manhattan and does not envy me these woodland adventures.) This summer Damian is away from August 13th to the 21st, and I am already desperate to escape the city with its unsolvable problems.

Taking only Lily along, I head for the campground on August 15th. By the 17th, she has had more than enough camping and misses her friends, so I head back into town to drop her off at one of their houses. Since Danny still has no place to sleep, I call and offer to bring him up to the campground for the next couple of nights. He has an appointment with Dr. Umbridge the following morning at 11:00, so one of my motives is to make sure he gets to that appointment and, Lord willing, back on some medication.

Danny welcomes the chance to go camping, but he's unimpressed with the plan to see the psychiatrist. He refuses to get out of bed the next morning, insisting that he despises Dr. Umbridge and doesn't want to see her again. *Ever*. It's already past the time of the appointment when I finally persuade him to get in the car for the trip to MGH.

We arrive over an hour late, and I worry that the doctor will refuse to see him. But soon she appears and brings a reluctant Danny into her office. He refuses to speak to her. She comes back to ask me to join them in her office. This has to be a bad sign. When Danny sticks to his vow of silence, Dr. Umbridge tells him he has to cooperate or she will send him down to the Psych ER.

At that point, Danny opens his mouth long enough to offer a string of obscenities, and becomes increasingly combative: "It's up to me whether I go there or not, and I'm not going!" Dr. Umbridge is not one to be contradicted. "Actually it *isn't* up to you. I can have you admitted involuntarily." "Oh, sure! *You're* going to make me go?" "No. We have security officers who will come and escort you." "Well, they better be ready for a fight."

Dr. Umbridge is more than happy to call security. Within seconds, two burly men in uniform appear with a wheelchair to bring Danny down to the ER. At first he refuses to sit in the chair, but is told that every patient being admitted involuntarily from another section of the hospital has to go by wheelchair. "So we can do this the easy way or the hard way—it's up to you." In the end, Danny gets into the chair and security exits with him in tow. The doctor says she will recommend that he be admitted to a hospital, which is likely to be McLean. I experience an unpleasant sense of *deja vu*.

I meet Danny downstairs at the Pscyh ER where we are brought just inside the locked door to a cramped waiting area that is feebly illuminated by fluorescent lights. We wait for over an hour, alone. No one comes to interrupt the silence. The room is very small. There is nothing on the walls (which are desperate for a new coat of paint) and almost nothing anywhere else—no coffee table, magazines, or even racks of brochures. Eight battered plastic chairs are the only furnishings. The room feels like an energy vacuum, as though the very air has lost its enthusiasm. I thought it strange that this area where psychiatric patients have to stay, sometimes for hours on end, should be so utterly dreary. It's enough by itself to send you into existential despair.

Once inside, patients are not allowed to leave, so you are stuck in this claustrophobic room with no windows, no distractions, and no human warmth. There is a sort of teller window (complete with bullet-proof glass) around the corner, where you can sometimes spot a nurse or receptionist. Their window-side manner usually leaves something to be desired, but I walk up anyway from time to time just to see another human being. Since I am not there to be evaluated, I'm allowed to escape occasionally to buy coffee and snacks for Danny. It's difficult to distract him from the fact that he hasn't had a cigarette for hours.

During our long wait, Danny continues to curse his fate and everyone connected with it. He blames me for forcing him to come to the appointment in the first place, and says he won't cooperate with the ER doctors either. Eventually a doctor appears to take Danny into a conference room. By now it is close to 3:00, and chronic fatigue is catching up with me.

I stretch across three chairs in the waiting room and try to rest. This is made difficult by the fact that all of the chairs have metal arms forming complete loops on both sides. But after numerous hours spent in hospital waiting rooms, I've devised a system. If I turn the first chair sideways to face the others, leave the next one facing forward, and turn the third one to face the first, I can lie with head and shoulders on #1, slide most of my body onto #2, and rest my legs on #3. It probably helps to be short.

When I wake up, it's 4:30. I begin to worry about being away from the campsite for so long, especially since we've heard that a major storm is heading our way. When we left this morning, there was no sign of bad weather ahead. Our tent and camping gear is in no shape to withstand even a light shower, so I need to get back there soon to break camp, take down the tent, and put everything in the trunk of the car before it's pouring rain and too dark to see.

Danny returns from his interview and I am called in to answer a few questions about his medical history and the circumstances of the ER visit. I explain to the social worker that Dr. Umbridge sent Danny here involuntarily, and that she expects him to be admitted to a hospital. What I don't know at the time is that the decision about whether to hospitalize Danny is no longer up to Dr. Umbridge, who has already left for the day, but to the head psychiatrist in the ER. The social worker sends me back to the waiting room, where Danny and I do another hour of penance.

At 6:00, I tell one of the nurses that I really can't stay any longer. Danny is sitting on the chair next to me, and when I stand up to go, he leans over and spits on the floor just as the nurse is walking by. It's not meant as an insult; Danny is just in the habit of spitting from time to time. But the nurse is furious. "Did you just spit on my floor? I'm not going to have that! That's just disgusting!" Again, orderlies appear to bring Danny back into the catacombs. I tell him I will see him the next day and hurry out to my car, confident that he will be OK at least for the next few days. Back at camp, it's a long and tiring job taking down the tent solo and getting the gear packed up. It's after 10:00 and very dark when I finally head toward home. The winds have picked up and it's starting to rain in earnest.

While I'm still on the highway, my cell phone rings. It's Danny. He says he's been discharged from the hospital and has no place to go. My heart sinks. "Why didn't they admit you to the hospital?" "Well, I wouldn't say anything, so they said they couldn't tell whether or not I was a danger to myself or others." "And since they didn't know, they just let you go?" "Yeah; I think they were glad to get rid of me." No doubt. But what could they possibly be thinking? If Danny's doctor thinks he is a danger both to himself *and* others, shouldn't the burden of proof be on the other side? I am stunned, and very, very angry. But the Psych ER is a court of no appeal.

I berate myself for not staying with Danny until their decision was made, camping gear be damned. I'm torn between guilt and outrage. Still, in spite of the wretched storm, I tell Danny he cannot come home. "Why not? Dad isn't even there right now. Why can't I stay just this one night?" But I know that if he comes home, I will never be able to send him away again—my heart is not nearly strong enough. Mustering every ounce of strength I have left, I tell Danny I cannot take him in; he has to find another place to stay.

Both of us know where it will be, of course, even in the howling wind and rain—somewhere under a tree in the nearest park. But we don't speak of it. Danny's voice is breaking when he says good-bye. Everything in me is screaming. It tears me apart not to seek him out and embrace him, like the father of the prodigal son. I want to bring him home where he can get a warm shower and a hot meal and a decent rest. Instead, I spend this darkest of all nights alone in an empty house, in the home that used to be Danny's refuge.

Fury at the staff at MGH gives way to a familiar mixture of desperation and helplessness. How am I to bear it? There is nowhere to hide from such overwhelming agony of heart. With

109

the slightest crack in my defenses, it all comes pouring in—not just my own pain, but the agony of my husband, my daughter, and my son. I feel them all. Ordinary suffering is different. It has an end; it can be healed, but this sorrow doesn't have a bottom. It goes all the way down.

August 19, 2006

It's Saturday morning and the sun has come out. I try to see this as a positive sign, though I'm becoming suspicious of signs these days. Damian is scheduled to return tomorrow and I look forward to having someone to share the burden of these past few days.

At around two in the afternoon, my phone rings. The number of the caller is unfamiliar, but when I answer, it's Danny's voice on the other end. He is calling from the county jail. "What?! Why are you there, Danny? What happened?" His story is brief and heart-breaking. At around eleven that morning, he woke up in the park feeling desperately hungry, as he hadn't eaten in over 24 hours. He had a small pocket knife he had borrowed from a friend as protection against the other guests in "Park Plaza Hotel."

For reasons obscure even to himself, he decided to hold up a small grocery store located just around the corner from where we used to live. Linda, a spunky, middle-aged clerk at the store, was always very kind to our family. She and I sometimes commiserated about the ups and downs of life and the challenges of raising kids, and she knew each of our children by name.

When Danny appeared that morning with pocket knife in hand, demanding that she open the till and give him some money, Linda recognized him immediately. She noticed he looked a little strung out—probably high on drugs or alcohol, she thought. Danny recognized her too, of course, and Linda was certain he wouldn't do anything to hurt her. So she simply told him, "No, Danny. I'm not giving you any money." Frustrated and confused, Danny moved to the next counter, which was staffed by a teenage boy Danny knew from high school. "Mike, give me some money. Come on, man!" But Linda called over, "Don't give him any money, Mike. He's not thinking straight."

Linda knew we would be mortified when we found out that Danny was acting like this, and she didn't want to involve the police. But customers who had witnessed the incident called 911 to report the attempted robbery, describing the assailant—my son—in painstaking detail. Danny fled the store and ran back toward the park, still focused on getting money somehow.

He later told me that the lyrics from "Change" by rapper Tupac Shakur were running through his head: "Come on, come on, I see no changes, wake up in the morning and I ask myself, Is life worth living, should I blast myself? I'm tired of bein' poor, and even worse, I'm black. My stomach hurts, so I'm lookin' for a purse to snatch." When Danny spots a woman walking along the sidewalk with a purse over her arm, he takes it as a sign. (See what I mean about signs?)

Grabbing her bag, he sprints across the park, which is fairly crowded in the middle of this sunny Saturday. The woman and some others begin shouting after him, and one gives chase, tackling Danny even before he makes it out of the park and pinning him down. Police officers are just leaving the grocery store, and they arrive on the scene in a matter of minutes to find Danny struggling against his captor and trying to reach the knife he still has in his pocket.

The police have nothing but contempt for this boy who has by now attacked two women. They kick him in the side a few times, badly bruising his ribs, before pulling him onto his feet. This elicits a string of curses, which are met in turn with a string of punches to his face. Danny says later that he was amazed at how hard they could hit. He felt betrayed by the one black officer who joined in the abuse with the other cops.

Eventually, one of the officers handcuffs Danny and throws him into the back of a paddy wagon that is already filled with the catch of the day. Danny sits next to a fiftyish black man who had spit at the cops when they arrested him. Now most of his front teeth are gone and, with his hands cuffed behind his back, the blood keeps running out of his mouth, soaking his T-shirt. Danny starts to feel almost lucky; at least he still has all his teeth.

Arriving at the county jail, Danny is marched with the rest of the prisoners into the holding jail and given his one phone call. On the other end of the line, I try to stay calm, but my heart is pounding. Oh my God! What could he have been thinking? My son, assaulting two helpless women just to get a few dollars? I feel like I don't even know him anymore. Suddenly I feel sick and dizzy, and have to sit down. "Why would you do something like that?" I manage eventually. "I don't know, Mom. I don't know."

I tell Danny that I'll talk with his dad and call back in a little while. Many years before, when such situations seemed remote, Damian and I decided we would not put up bail if any of our children committed a crime that injured others. When I call to explain the situation to Damian, he reminds me of our policy. It's probably the right decision, but I hate being the one who has to give the news to Danny. It feels like abandoning him all over again. Fortunately (I guess), the jail keeper says that nobody can be released on bail over the weekend, so the decision is out of my hands.

Danny spends Saturday afternoon to Monday morning in jail. We expect it to be a sobering experience for him, but find out later that treatment of prisoners in this facility borders on sadism. Though Danny is badly beaten and psychotic, he receives no medical attention. Instead, he is stripped of his clothes except for his boxer shorts and left shivering in a metal cell devoid of blankets. The only furnishings are a cot with no mattress and a latrine.

He is fed once a day, with a single McDonald's cheeseburger that is literally thrown through the slot in the door. He says it's difficult even to get that down because of the stench from the latrine. For two nights, he lies bruised, bleeding, and virtually naked on a barren cot. There is no hope of sleep, since one of the inmates protests his arrest by banging constantly on the bars of his cell. Danny's psychotic symptoms and paranoia increase in the absence of his medications. He is angry, but also anxious, confused, hungry, and full of sadness.

A thousand questions swirl in my mind. Why didn't MGH keep Danny in the hospital, at least for a few days? Though he's capable of putting up such a good show of sanity for the mental health providers, he must be very psychotic right now; couldn't they see that? Should I tell Danny what a horrible person he is for attacking these women—especially Linda, who was always a good friend to us?

How much control over his actions did he have when he walked into the store? When he grabbed the purse? Maybe they were partly free and partly driven by the symptoms of his illness, but what was the breakdown? It's virtually impossible to know the answers to these questions, which is one of the most maddening things about mental illness.

Danny sometimes does things that don't make sense to anyone but him, but could behavior this shocking be wholly caused by confused thought processes and the advice of his voices? It's hard to know for sure. But anyone who tries to rob a store full of people, where both clerks know you, in the middle of a busy Saturday morning, can't be thinking very clearly.

One of my friends, upon reading the first chapters of this book, told me that by this point she had no sympathy left for either Danny or me. "It seems like you're always looking for someone to blame—the school, the hospital, the police—but maybe no one is to blame. Maybe everybody did the best they could, and it just wasn't enough. I mean, Danny tried to rob a store and assaulted innocent women. He was dealing drugs, stealing from his family, strung out on weed and who knows what else, and treating everybody like shit. What were people supposed to do?"

She had a point. It's true that no one was responsible for Danny's illness or the suffering that came with it. On the other hand, the dreadful events of that Saturday would not have happened if the mental health system, in this case the staff at the Psych ER, had taken his illness more seriously and treated it more aggressively.

The point of writing Danny's story, though, is neither to justify his actions nor condemn those who, for whatever reason, failed to help him (including me). I assume it goes without saying that I was both appalled and deeply ashamed when I discovered that Danny had invested in a drug-selling scheme—with cocaine, no less. But by the time I learned of it, there was nothing to be done. Danny's psychotic symptoms were at their peak, the drugs were gone, the money was gone, and his friend Rajib was nearly gone. In fact, we feared that the drug lord might easily find out where Danny lived and put pressure on him by threatening his family. (While we did see a suspicious-looking car idling outside our home for a few hours one evening, nothing else seemed to come of it.) So we hardly took the news lightly.

I record these events because they happened. Some people with a mental illness may sometimes resort to violence in pursuit of purposes known only to them—or, more probably, known only to God. The vast majority are more likely to be victims than perpetrators of crime, but those events rarely make the headlines.

That Saturday, my son was arrested for his crimes and brought before the court. If found guilty, he would have served time in jail, most likely in a facility for the "criminally insane." Would justice be served by that outcome? I have no idea. The whole affair felt like a tragedy for everyone involved.

What I want to say to others who face a similar crisis is that, even when something this terrible happens, life does go on. There is no way either to predict or determine the outcome for persons with a mental illness who are not receiving treatment, no way to require them to accept treatment, and no way to require the mental health system to treat them. In time, whenever another crisis struck, I felt like saying, "Just tell me where to visit my son—ER, hospital, jail—wherever."

August 23, 2006

Monday morning insists on arriving. Damian is back, and he and I arrive promptly at 8:30 a.m. at the courthouse, a setting sadly familiar to us from a previous year-long ordeal involving Alex. We meet the public defender assigned to Danny, and hear the charges against him for the first time. They are serious—felony charges, in fact. The lawyer is confident that he can get them reduced to misdemeanors. We have no reason to believe him, but then again we have no reason not to believe him. I choose to believe.

The second floor cafeteria serves coffee, and I am in dire need of some. My husband and I pass a few moments with small talk, neither of us having the heart to talk about our son. Finally it's 9:00—time to find our place in the courtroom. A somber group files into the elevator with us for the ascent to the 13th floor. (Is the number intended as mockery?)

The tired, dimly lit courtroom hardly inspires confidence. A random collection of mismatched desks and chairs are strewn about behind the short wooden fence that separates the stars from the extras. After what seems an eternity, a world-weary, bespectacled judge enters to a standing non-ovation, then sits barricaded behind the enormous bulk of a dark wooden desk, elevated two feet above the muted buzz still going on among lawyers, police officers, and miscellaneous courtroom functionaries.

Once we are settled on the benches, Damian and I wait apprehensively for the moment when the prisoners will be brought in. Most of the defendants sit with their relatives or friends, waiting with us in the four long pews at the rear of the courtroom, forbidden to speak, read, write, slouch, nod off, drink, or chew gum. Even smiles are looked upon with suspicion. Attorneys pro and con exchange files and inside jokes, while the accused come forward one by one to stand alone at the microphone just outside the barricade, still a good twenty feet from the judge. For some, a relative or friend watches and prays from the back of the room.

The judge deals with the unincarcerated first—the litany of the sinners. Drunk driving and illegal possession of drugs top the list, followed closely by spousal abuse, fist-fights, and violations of restraining orders. After a few hours, the proceedings begin to resemble some kind of macabre dance—partners introduced at the microphone and spun this way and that by the practiced attorneys, until the judge cuts in and sends them to their fate. Those who enter in chains generally depart in chains. Most of the others are told to return next month, then the month after that, until they've practiced the dance to perfection. The principals—judges, attorneys, police, court recorders—all seem to know how it will end, though this is never leaked to the proletariat, huddled in the cheap seats and badgered into some semblance of respectful attention.

Finally, through a door to the right of the judge, the defendants in custody shuffle in with heads down, their shackled wrists and ankles clanking, providing a presumption of guilt more audible than any abstract presumption of innocence. Defeat is etched in their faces. I have seen it all before. But nothing could have prepared me for the sight of my son that morning.

His hair is wild and matted, his face is bruised, and there are dark circles under his eyes. He is dressed in a torn and stained pair of boxer shorts, their cheerful red-and-yellow poker theme (featuring a Joker card) on display for everyone in the room, creating a stark contrast to the shivering, sorrowful teenager wearing them. They are clearly visible below a thin, ill-fitting hospital smock which flaps open at the back with disconcerting regularity.

Danny has only socks on his feet, and his wrists and ankles are in chains. The other prisoners wear their own clothes; only Danny is singled out for the acute humiliation of appearing before the judge virtually naked, the very picture of a crazed mental patient. Still, when he scans the courtroom looking for us, I manage a weak smile of recognition and encouragement, battling against tears of anguish and indignation that I dare not show. My husband retreats into his impregnable stoic solitude, that by-now-familiar posture of unapproachable silence. I don't know what he is thinking, let alone feeling. I don't really want to know, fearing I will find it more than I can bear. Only my love for Danny keeps me there. Whatever happens, whatever he has done, he is still my son, my beloved son. I cannot leave him to face this ordeal alone.

All too soon it is Danny's turn to stand before the judge. He shuffles toward the microphone in the small steps allowed by the chains on his ankles, looking utterly forlorn in his brightly-colored boxers and the bizarre hospital gown. But the lawyer who stands beside him seems well-prepared for his role, convincing the judge that Danny is not a threat to the community and will surely appear for future court proceedings. Damian and I become exhibit A, proving that Danny has ties to the community and people who care about him—who will see that he does what he is supposed to do (more or less).

In the end, the judge releases him on his own recognizance and does not set bail, the best-case scenario. But Damian resents being used to lessen Danny's punishment and having his presence interpreted as a statement he never intended to make. He decides not to come to any more of Danny's court appearances. I wonder if he would make the same decision if he thought I wouldn't continue to come. In any event, Danny's handcuffs and ankle chains are unlocked by the officer in charge and he becomes a free man, for now . . . a free man dressed in Joker shorts and a tiny hospital gown. While I take a starving Danny to the cafeteria, my husband makes his way across the street to the mall to purchase sweats, a T-shirt, socks, sneakers, and clean boxer shorts for our son.

I want Danny to throw the ragged boxers in the garbage, but he refuses. I'm surprised at the intensity of his feelings about it. Maybe it's because they have been his only possession for two days, the only shred left of his dignity. For me, those ridiculous shorts represent all the trauma and humiliation of this day. I want to erase it completely from all of our lives, to make it disappear, to prove that nothing so horrifying could really have happened to us—to our son. But I've come to find that there is no erasing. There is only accepting what is, offering the pain and suffering to God, and looking for what can be learned from each experience. As I keep telling Danny, we have to live in reality. (Though I sometimes add under my breath that reality is *seriously* overrated.)

I ask Danny whether the jail has the rest of his things. He replies that, before he was arrested, he left his cargo bag under a bench at a nearby bus stop. So even though it's two days later, I drive by to look for it. Unsurprisingly, it has disappeared. I ask at nearby shops in case someone has turned it in and call the police to see if they had picked it up. But in the end I have to admit defeat.

For some reason, this relatively insignificant loss is the one that brings me to tears. In these past four months, the only shelter and care I've been able to provide for my son is in that bag—a warm coat, leather boots, a shaving kit, some granola bars, clothes that will make him look like his peers instead of a homeless person. I want him to be able to say—or maybe it's just that I want to say—that he's not one of them. Not really. He has a home, in some sense, right? You can tell someone loves him. Just look at what they've provided. He can look through his bag and remember when we shopped for these things, and how much it mattered to me that he have what he needs. Now even that has been stripped away. My son is finally, undeniably, utterly, homeless.

It is Danny who pulls me out of my despair. "Don't worry, Mom. It's going to be OK. I don't need very many things anyway." Gathering up the fragments of my heart, I turn to face the next crisis of the day. We need to find a place for him to stay. Damian is still of the opinion that Danny should suffer the consequences of his crimes, and upset that the lawyer didn't ask for a harsher punishment, or at least commitment to a hospital. But I suppose I would rather err on the side of mercy. Danny has already suffered in ways that make ordinary jail time sound almost attractive. (Would Martha Stewart change places with him?)

As we drive around Boston in search of a shelter with an open bed, Danny relates what he can remember about his failed assault on the grocery store and the disaster of the purse. He tells me about the Tupac lyrics that were playing in his mind. Pausing for a moment, he adds "I guess that's the last time I'll take advice from a rap song." Both of us laugh ourselves silly over this, and our mood lightens a bit.

When afternoon fades into evening without any success in finding a bed, we grow increasingly anxious. Our day ends at the shelters everyone dreads, Woods Mullen and Pine Street Inn, located south of downtown in one of those neighborhoods-in-mourning. Danny begs me to come in with him, and he seems so fragile and pitiful that I finally agree. After I drop him off at the door, it takes twenty minutes to find a parking spot. It's getting dark and cold now, and my head is pounding.

The shelter parking lot (authorized vehicles only) is fenced with barbed wire, and the building resembles an abandoned warehouse. It probably *is* an abandoned warehouse. Long lines of men and women with drawn faces and hollow eyes shuffle toward a fleet of waiting buses to be shipped to an overflow shelter on one of the Boston Harbor islands. My mind flashes to photos from World War II—lines of people, their shoulders bent by grief and exhaustion, lining up to be shoved into those hideous box cars. Thank God the destination of this crowd is nothing like that; though it's possible that, for some, this will be their last journey.

We find the shelter entrance off in a corner by what must have been the loading dock. Danny gets to the admitting desk and offers up his small backpack to be searched. He is told the unit is locked so he can't leave until the morning. Someone comes by and asks his age. "Nineteen? Better call Terri. . . . Hey, John! Find Terri, OK?" In a few minutes, we are ushered into a cramped office piled high with miscellaneous paperwork. Terri is a brusque middle-aged woman with graying hair and the arms of a wrestler, complete with tattoos. She is also an angel—the guardian of the weak. "Nineteen is too young," she insists. "This is no place for a teenager!"

Terri asks John to give Danny a tour of the "upstairs." His face is white when he returns, and he is close to tears. He whispers to me that one guy was sitting on a cot sharpening a knife, and another was shooting up heroin in the corner. There was one cop sitting near the door, watching TV, expected to provide security for the 200 men who will sleep there that night. Terri explains that this is a shelter of last resort—they don't turn anyone away, no matter what shape they're in.

But Terri knows of another place, one she helped found a few years ago. It's a group home for young adults under 21, and it's

121

located in our home town! She calls, and they agree to interview Danny that very night, as they expect to have an opening in the next few days. Terri even fills out a referral form for the program, and gives us her card and contact numbers. I am dumbfounded. At the lowest point in my life, when darkness and despair had destroyed all hope, God sent Terri.

That experience was one of many such paradoxes in Danny's journey—experiences that are deeply painful and desperate becoming the key to opportunities far better than we could have imagined.

Buoyed by this new prospect, Danny and I visit briefly with the case worker at the group home, and we are assured that a room will be available very soon. We celebrate over pancakes at IHOP and return home around 9:30. Damian is upset that I didn't leave Danny in the shelter, but even he is encouraged by this new possibility. Danny is just happy to be home. It's the first time he has slept in his own bed in weeks, and his relief is palpable. Both of us fight back tears and fall into a troubled sleep. But Terri has given us hope.

Timeout: Criminalizing Mental Illness

Most people have no idea what happens when a mentally ill person is accused of a crime, be it murder, robbery, trespassing, or urinating in public. As early as the arraignment, if the judge decides that a psychological evaluation is in order, the accused can be incarcerated for a minimum of thirty days while that evaluation is being made.

In Massachusetts, the prison of choice for those referred for a "psych-eval" is Bridgewater State Hospital, a wing of the Old Colony Correctional Center (CCC), a medium security prison housing those convicted of crimes ranging from petty larceny to murder. Though other facilities in the state also set aside a separate area for at-risk inmates, the state has plans to consolidate all such services at Bridgewater. Ideally, such a move would cut costs and improve the quality of care at the same time—a win-win situation.

When I first learned that Danny could be incarcerated for a month just to decide how sick he was, I was aghast. How could that be legal? Are people with mental illnesses guilty until proven innocent? I had assumed a psychological evaluation was a matter of hours, not days: pondering a few ink blots, penciling in responses to questions of dubious relevance, then maybe sinking into a soft chair to mull it all over with the sort of grave-but-gentle doctor you see on TV.

I'm embarrassed to say that my image of psych evaluations was based almost exclusively on *Miracle on 34th Street*, where Macy's house psychologist declares Mr. Claus "insane." In the movie, Claus only had to answer a few obvious questions ("What is your name?" "What day is this?") and demonstrate some basic motor skills, like touching his finger to his nose. The whole thing took less than two minutes.

The problem with the two-minute diagnosis, of course, is that most people who suffer from a mental illness aren't symptomatic at every moment. The real nature of their illness may show itself only after several days, once they've adjusted to a controlled environment and begun to trust the medical staff. Clients with enough insight to understand the stakes involved can often put on a pretty convincing show of normalcy, though only for a time. In fact, now that I know how hard it is to make a positive diagnosis, I marvel that psychiatrists are expected to render an opinion in only a month's time.

All of that being said, I can't imagine how distraught I would be if my son had to spend time in such a depressing place. I've been told that mental health care at Bridgewater is excellent these days, largely because of their determination to erase the embarrassment they suffered when Frederic Wiseman's documentary of daily life in that facility, *Titicut Follies*, was released in 1967.

At the time, Massachusetts officials immediately challenged Wiseman's film on legal grounds, arguing that it violated the privacy of the inmates, some of whom are shown naked. While there is merit to the privacy appeal, the real objection to Wiseman's movie was that it presented an unvarnished, unscripted, un-narrated, up-close vision of daily life in what was then a hospital of horrors. In fact, the documentary was a major influence on Ken Kesey's novel *One Flew Over the Cuckoo's Nest*.

Lawsuits succeeded in burying the documentary indefinitely, as the US Supreme Court twice refused to hear an appeal. In a 1968 review of the film, Roger Ebert commented, "*Titicut Follies* is one of the most despairing documentaries I have ever seen; more immediate than fiction because these people are real; more savage than satire because it seems to be neutral. We are literally taken into a madhouse. Inmates of varying degrees of mental illness are treated with the same casual inhumanity. . . . It appears that the inmates are deprived of clothing much of the time because that is cheaper and makes security easier. It is not explained how naked confinement in a barren cell cures mental illness, and indeed this hospital seems to come from the Middle Ages."[13]

In 1987, a special screening of the film took place at the University of Massachusetts Boston as part of a forum on patients' rights. An article in *The New York Times*, with the author's name withheld, reported that this was "a rare screening of the film that, under court guidelines, can be shown only to professionals in the legal, human services, mental health and related fields." (Now, however, I'm able to borrow the film from the university library.)

Though by 1987 the mental health wing of the prison was housed in a new building, and more training was mandated for

---

[13] Roger Ebert, "Titicut Follies," *Chicago Sun-Times*, October 8, 1968, available at *rogerebert.suntimes.com/apps/pbcs.dll/article?AID=/19681008/REVIE WS/810080301/1023*.

prison guards and support personnel, the article continues:
"But the hospital is still surrounded by barbed wire, staffed by
220 prison guards who receive about 40 hours a year of
training in mental health care. All patients are subject to the
rules of the Corrections Department concerning dress, canteen
privileges, and visitors. There are 25 nurses and 49
psychiatrists, psychologists and social workers for 436 patients,
according to Mary McGeown, a spokeswoman for the
Corrections Department."[14]

Today, more than 20 years after the UMass forum and 40
years after Wiseman's film appeared, Bridgewater continues to
work at restoring confidence in the quality of care it provides.
The web site lists numerous programs offered to inmates—
everything from art therapy and music theory to
communications skills and computer training. One of the more
baffling programs is listed as "The Jericho Circle Project," a
"volunteer-facilitated group that targets a variety of
criminogenic risk factors that are pre-cursors to criminal
behavior."[15] Criminogenic factors? Does mangling the English
language count?

---

[14] "Film on State Hospital Provocative after 20 Years," *The New York
Times*, May 17, 1987, available at
*www.nytimes.com/1987/05/17/us/film-on-state-hospital-provocative-
after-20-years.html*. This article was published on my 4th wedding
anniversary, when I was seven months pregnant with Danny. I blush to
think how little it would have mattered to me then. How can I ask others
to pay attention to the travails of my son and others like him when I
simply passed these people by, ignoring them until I realized, belatedly,
that they are my neighbors and I might at least learn to greet them by
name.
[15] These programs are described at:
*www.mass.gov/?pageID=eopsterminal&L=5&L0=Home&L1=Law+Enfor
cement+%26+Criminal+Justice&L2=Prisons&L3=Offender+Programs&*

Sadly, as a recent front-page story in *The Boston Phoenix* illustrates, major flaws continue to plague Bridgewater. The *Phoenix* declares that "in a state where convicts reportedly kill themselves at more than three times the national rate, in 2010 CCC is the facility where prisoners are most likely to commit suicide. Attorneys for a recently deceased prisoner who hung himself there say the inmate complained up until his death about being denied his anti-psychotic drug regimen as retribution."[16]

The sad fact is that it doesn't take any ill-will on the part of prison guards to deprive a prisoner of anti-psychotic medications; some things just fall through the cracks. Suppose Jim is taken into custody on Friday night for a relatively minor matter, and held in a city jail over the weekend, pending a Monday morning court appearance. A case worker appears on Saturday with Jim's medications, and the officers agree to administer the medications while Jim is in their custody. By Monday, however, a different set of officers bring Jim to court early in the morning—hopefully remembering to bring his medications along.

At the second courthouse, Jim is transferred to the custody of officers of the court and placed in a holding cell. If all goes well, Jim's meds are transferred too. When he appears before the judge, she rules that Jim's case should be decided by a different court, and orders him held overnight awaiting an appearance at that court on Tuesday morning. The day wears on, and officers of the morning are replaced by officers of the evening.

L4=Programs+Offered+at+Each+Institution&sid=Eeops&b=terminalcontent&f=doc_inmate_programs_institution_specific_programs_statehospital&csid=Eeops.
[16] Chris Faraone, "Troubled Over Bridgewater," *The Boston Phoenix*, September 10, 2010, pp. 10-12.

The night shift gives way to Tuesday's day shift, so officers new to Jim's situation will transport him (and others) to the next court, bringing along whatever personal effects (including medications) belong to each of the prisoners. There Jim is handed over to officers of *this* court (along with personal effects) and placed in a holding cell until his case is heard. If everything has gone according to plan, Jim's medications will have changed hands eight times by now. But whatever the outcome of his hearing, it should come as no surprise that Jim exits Court #2 sans watch, wallet, cell phone, and, yes, medications.

Should the officers involved in transporting prisoners be more vigilant about guarding their personal effects along with their persons? Probably. Should there be a better system for ensuring that a person who is incarcerated (who may not even have committed a crime) receives his or her psychiatric medications? Certainly. We should treat these illnesses as seriously as we do diabetes or heart disease. We don't often hear of a prisoner dying in a diabetic coma because the prison guards lost her medication. Why aren't mental illnesses treated at least that seriously?

Clearly more education about mental illness should be mandatory for police officers, prison guards, lawyers, and judges. There should be clear protocols for handling prescription medications that are reviewed often and enforced always. This is a gap in the system that we could actually do something about, and it's just possible that someone in the labyrinth will insist that we do.

Without systematic reforms in hospitals like Bridgewater, young men and women will continue to be driven to despair and even suicide. We call them the *criminally insane*, as though insanity itself were a crime. And as long as we drive the lepers of our day into concrete blocks behind razor-wire fences, we pound that message home to them every day—whether they are inside or outside the walls.

9 No Direction Home

September 1, 2006

After what seems like *quite* a few days, the youth center finally calls. They have a room! Jubilation prevails in our whole family. We move Danny's things to his new room at a large house that is home to sixteen young adults, and celebrate with pizza and cake. The fee is only $20 a month for rent, and the case workers initiate an application for food stamps for Danny. They will help him finish high school, they say, and assist him in finding a job. We are thrilled! It sounds very promising. There are early curfews and drug testing and group meetings, and the staff will help residents with organizational skills and social skills. There is a TV, a computer, and a place to wash your clothes for free. Bless Terri! What a dramatic change from the barbed-wire shelter to this!

October 16, 2006

As the weeks pass at the youth home, Danny finds ways to alienate staff and residents alike. He refuses to take the job his case worker finds for him, sweeping and cleaning at the very shelter from which he was saved. On the other hand, he is never offered any help toward getting his high school diploma.

The staff and some of the other residents complain that Danny is often hostile and verbally abusive. He sometimes smokes in his room at night, since the last smoking break of the day is at ten and Danny is usually awake until one or two in the morning. One day, Danny is in an especially foul mood and curses at one of the staff members. Later that evening, there is a fire drill and everyone files outside to wait out the mandatory few minutes. When it's time to go back in, Danny refuses, wanting to finish a cigarette. But the staff give him no choice, so he stomps back inside and punches the fire alarm (punishing it, I guess?). The alarm goes off, and the fire department arrives to find no emergency. The program gets a $200 fine for the false alarm, and Danny gets the door. He has lived there just six weeks.

October 18, 2006

I go to help Danny move his things. The floor of his room has the same stains that were there when he moved in. We leave some things for the next resident and take the rest in the giant black trash bags provided by the staff. Over the coming months, those bags become emblematic for me. When your time is up, your housemates or the staff throw everything you own into large black garbage bags. Sometimes things get broken or go missing; sometimes a sock or sweater turns up that isn't yours. There is no sympathy for the banished; your things don't even qualify as garbage. "Here's your shit," they say. Why not another bag for my son, then? In fact, make it two.

Again there is no housing for Danny. I offer to keep his things at our house for a few days while he figures out where to go next, and drop him off at the city park of his choice. Later that evening, Danny calls. It's hard to make out what he is saying. He's at a train stop just a mile from our house, and he is beside

himself. "I don't feel good, Mom. I can't really think right now."
"Well, can you catch the bus and come on home so we can
talk?" "I don't think so, Mom. I feel really bad. My symptoms
are coming back, and I feel sick . . .Um, what did you say? .
What? . . long pause." "Are you still there, Danny?" "Yeah.
Mom, can you please just come and get me? I feel really bad. I
always f*** everything up. My head isn't right. I don't want to
live like this anymore. It's not worth it." These words set off a
siren in my head. I jump in the car and race to the train stop
faster than prudence would dictate.

Danny sits on the concrete wall outside the station, his long
curly hair blowing wildly in wind, chain-smoking cigarettes and
muttering to himself. It's obvious at once that his psychotic
symptoms have returned. He wants me to take him home, but I
suggest going back to the MGH Psych ER. "I know you're not
feeling right, Danny, but I really don't know how to help you. At
the hospital they have people who can actually make you feel
better. Maybe they can give you some better medications.
Plus, it's a safe place to stay."

Danny is adamant that he will not return to MGH. In my
desperation, I suddenly remember someone saying that the
Cambridge Hospital also has a psychiatric emergency center.
"What about going to Cambridge Hospital then?" I ask. "You've
never been there, and maybe it will be a better experience. I
think they can really help you, Danny. I will stay with you the
whole time, and you don't have to accept treatment if you don't
want to." After several more rounds, Danny finally agrees to get
in the car and go to the hospital.

October 17-24, 2006

The doctors at Cambridge Hospital decide to admit Danny
because of his suicidal thoughts, but he signs a three-day

request for release as soon as he arrives, since the hospital doesn't allow smoking. The staff buy some time by persuading him to withdraw that request, but he signs another one the next day. The psychiatric staff will release any patient who does not want to stay there and is not certifiably dangerous to himself or others. The emphasis is on "certifiably" (that is, the person has tried to commit suicide or homicide and has immediate plans to finish the job).

Massachusetts law on "involuntary hospitalization" is meant to protect individuals from being coerced into mental institutions by friends or relatives or health care providers when they are not truly ill. Sadly, it errs on the other side by making it nearly impossible to get medical help for a person who clearly needs it. Psychotic symptoms are not enough. Running around the house naked is not enough.

It is exceedingly difficult to *prove* that a person will immediately harm himself or others if discharged from the hospital. But I give it my best shot: "Doesn't it count that a person is likely to *be harmed* by others, taken advantage of, or convinced by the voices to attack someone or to 'fly' off a bridge?" "I'm sorry, but no. There has to be a credible threat of physical harm the patient would cause or suffer."

After six days, Danny's physicians discharge him "to" their partial program, the by-now-familiar 9-to-3 round of group meetings, with occasional brief one-on-one chats with a doctor or social worker. The groups don't always operate as advertised. During one of his later hospital stays, Danny laughed about a group in which the social worker spent most of each meeting trying to prove to "Barry" that he wasn't George Washington. As a rule, however, the groups focus on their goals and can help patients learn from one another as well as from the staff.

133

The groups at this day program seem well-organized and are staffed by experienced case workers. But Danny soon alienates the people around him, mocking some of the other clients and making rude remarks to the staff. One day, in a private conversation with a social worker, Danny admits that he's thought about taking his life. "Have you thought about how you would do that?" "Yeah. I'd probably shoot myself." "Oh. Do you have access to a gun?" "Sure." "Where is it?" "At my house. Sometimes I keep it in my bedroom."

"Well, I'm going to have to notify the authorities about that," the case worker explains. "Whenever there's a weapon involved, we're required to let them know." "What will they do? Arrest me?" "Probably not. But they'll go and search your house for the gun." "Actually, it might not be there right now," hedges Danny. "Where else would it be?" "Um, maybe at my friend's house." "Which friend?" Danny gives her a name and address, and is required to wait in her office until the situation is resolved.

I'm shopping for groceries when I receive a call from the police informing me that some officers are on the way to my house. "What for?" "They're looking for a gun." "What?! We don't *have* any guns!" "Well, your son mentioned to someone at the Cambridge Hospital that he was keeping a gun in the house. There will just be two officers and they won't stay long. It's just a quick look around." This doesn't put me at ease.

I hurry home, but of course the police are at the door before I have a chance to warn my daughter. She looks terrified. I invite the officers in and ask where they would like to start. They head upstairs to Danny's bedroom while I try to pretend to my daughter that police searches are pretty ho-hum for me. True to their word, they don't spend long going over the room. "We're not convinced he really has a gun here anyway," they say, "but we have to check these things out just in case." I don't know what to say. What is the protocol for hosting police officers? Should I offer them coffee? Where *is* Martha Stewart when I need her?

When I question Danny later that day, he admits that he sometimes did have a gun at our house, but only briefly. (Oh—no problem then.) The gun belongs to Rajib, the one with a metal plate in his head. "But why would you have the gun, Danny? What did you need it for?"

It comes out that during the previous summer, when Danny was gone from home for long periods in the middle of the night, he was sitting on the front steps of Rajib's house with a handgun. Rajib wanted backup in case the drug lord or his henchmen showed up again. Suddenly I feel nauseous, imagining what would have happened to Danny and Rajib had they gone up against experienced gang-bangers and their automatic weapons with a hand gun that neither of them knew how to use. For the first time, I truly fear for his life.

"So did you tell your case worker who had the gun?" "No. I gave her Bobby's name." "Why would you do that, Son?" "Because I thought if the police asked about Bobby, you would cover for him—I mean, he's like one of your own sons." (Well, the last part is certainly true.) "But I knew you wouldn't cover for Rajib." (Also true.)

Danny is irate at the social worker for calling the police, especially since officers also appear at Bobby's house, causing major confusion and consternation all around. He decides he has had it with the partial program, case workers and all, and stops attending. This time, however, the hospital staff actually come up with a place for him to live. We're told it's a sober house, a residence for men with a history of substance abuse, or who are in between jobs, or maybe just passing through.

What they don't mention is that a number of the residents are ex-cons, and these residences function as half-way houses for them. There is some meager staff support, though not on-site, along with random drug testing and encouragement to attend twelve-step meetings. They have a curfew and a limit on the number of nights residents can spend away from the house each week. The conditions are Spartan, however, and each resident has to buy and fix his own food. The cost is $520 a month, payable only by weekly money orders of $130, due precisely on the Friday of each week.

Damian and I deliberate briefly. We can't afford this expense, but there seems to be no alternative other than the downtown shelters or the street. So we agree to pay the rent, and Danny moves into a three-story house on the southern end of Boston Harbor, close to a subway stop. He shares a room with two other men, at least for now—residents seem to come and go from the sober house like so many pawns on a chess board. We're told we must pay a deposit of $260 on top of the initial $130. If Danny finds another place to live and gives two weeks' notice, he can use the deposit to pay for those two weeks. If he gets expelled from the house, the deposit is forfeited. Over the next eight months, Danny lives in three different sober houses. We never recover a deposit.

October 24-December 31, 2006

Danny's room at the sober house has three twin beds and three dressers, with barely enough space to squeeze around them. The air is thick with dust and the stale smell of old clothes and discarded food. Danny refuses to use the shower, since mold and scum are so thick on the floor and walls that the residents have to wear shoes when showering. But the kitchen is relatively clean and organized, and the living room is furnished with older but fairly presentable couches, a large glass coffee table, and some upholstered chairs. There is cable TV, a staple in the lives of men with no jobs and few prospects. Off the living room is a large covered porch that serves as the smoking area.

It's late October when Danny moves in and things seem fairly stable for a while. In December, a decorated Christmas tree appears in the corner of the living room. Not long afterward, however, the glass coffee table is shattered during a fight between two of the residents that sends one of them to the hospital and does significant damage to the tree.

The sober house promotes the more reliable residents to positions as house managers, authorized to collect the weekly rent and "enforce" the house rules. At this sober house most of the residents range in age from 30 to 67; Danny is by far the youngest. Some of the older guys try to look out for him, but sober house culture doesn't lend itself to genuine friendships. Those recently released from prison still operate out of a guarded hostility. Danny tries to watch what he says to the other residents, but once a newcomer to the residence grabs him by the throat and holds up his fist, ready to smash Danny's face in. "You motherf***er! I'll f***in' *kill* you!"

One day Bill, the house manager, gets into a fight with a much heavier man who tries to choke him to death. Bill spends the next several weeks in the hospital. Months later, long after Danny has moved away, he learns that Bill survived the choking incident only to die a few weeks later from a heroin overdose. Danny wept, filled with regret over his last words to Bill—a string of curses ending with "F*** you, Bill!"

Given the constant friction between them, I was surprised at Danny's sorrow over Bill's death. Maybe it's just that, whatever the tensions among the hard-luck crowd in the city's shelters and sober houses, underneath there is a shared experience of suffering, failure, and rejection that binds them together. That and the knowledge that they live every day in the valley of the shadow of death.

Just after Christmas, Danny gets expelled from the sober house for breaking a mirror in the weight room and punching a vending machine. This living arrangement has lasted over nine weeks, a new record. But now it's the middle of winter, and I fear Danny will end up downtown after all, at the shelter of Our Lady of Sorrows. However, it turns out that there is a network of sober houses around the Boston area. You can be expelled from one and move to another, shuffling around the city like peas in a shell game. I suppose that, like the staff at the downtown shelters, the program director knows that the vast majority of his charges have nowhere else to go.

January 1- February 20, 2007

Danny's next residence is north of Boston, in a spacious three-story home across the street from a boardwalk along the harbor. It's called "Ocean View."[17] I don't think the previous house had a name. (Gates of Hell?) This one has been recently painted and re-decorated, and the furniture is relatively new. The kitchen is large and clean and, unlike the last house, doesn't smell continually of gas. There is enough space so Danny has a room of his own on the second floor, with windows and an actual lock on the door.

----

[17] The name has been altered.

At the front of the house, on every floor, is a large deck overlooking the ocean. Since Ocean View is located on a peninsula, you can look toward the west and watch the sun set over the water with the city skyline in the background. It is one of the most beautiful places I have ever seen, and I almost envy Danny the opportunity to live there. The boardwalk is filled with walkers and bicyclists and pets with their owners. A wide jetty leads out a hundred yards or so into the bay. It seems like a place where a person could find healing and peace. I am full of hope that Danny will get out in the fresh air here and be motivated to make a new start.

As it turns out, Ocean View is a disaster. The nearest bus stop is several blocks away and the bus drops you off at a subway station that requires two more transfers in order to reach the heart of the city. Danny doesn't find the remote setting at all consoling. He feels lonely and isolated and abandoned. I try to visit him as often as I can, but it's a forty-five minute commute each way—even longer during rush hour. The local population resents the presence of the sober house in their upscale neighborhood, and view its occupants with undisguised contempt.

Worst of all, it turns out that almost all the home's residents, including the manager, are heroin addicts. It's incredible to me that this has escaped the attention of the powers that be. But I suppose a large enough joint conspiracy can work the system with surprising facility. Danny gets many invitations to come and "party" with the gang, but heroin scares him. So he ends up avoiding the others as much as possible, deepening his sense of alienation.

This house is co-ed, and altercations between the residents tend to end badly for the women. One day, Dick, the most feared thug in the house, begins tormenting one of the women, and no one is feeling courageous (or stupid) enough to intervene. So Danny takes him on, receiving as a reward some serious injuries and the eternal wrath of Big Dick. A few days later, someone brings donuts for breakfast and puts them down on the dining room table to share with the other residents. When Danny reaches for one, Dick tells him he can't have any—they're not for him. Danny assumes it's just Dick's usual way of hassling people. But when he reaches again for a donut, Dick stabs him in the hand with a fork. He still has the scars—a perfectly straight row of punctuation marks.

January 4, 2007

Danny needs a new psychiatrist to prescribe his medications. One of my friends is a psychiatrist, and she recommends a doctor at the Arbour Counseling Center, located next to Arbour Hospital of Mystery Road. We contact the center for an appointment with Dr. Gomez, and today is the big day.

Danny's appointment is at 9:00 am, so I drive to the sober house to pick him up and then try to find my way back to Jamaica Plain—from one unfamiliar neighborhood to another. We arrive late and are told we have to return at 3:30 pm if we want to see the doctor. So now this "brief appointment" will take up the entire day.

It doesn't make sense to make the round trip twice, so we decide to kill some time along Main Street in this hipster neighborhood, grabbing lunch at a vegetarian café and wandering past the used-clothing shops and organic food stores. We return to the counseling center at 3:30 and take a seat in the crowded waiting room.

Several people are called in to Dr. Gomez' office, until finally we are the only ones left in the room. It's 4:30. I approach the window to ask when Danny is going to be seen. "Oh, well you have to take a number. Didn't you take a number when you came in?" "No. We weren't told anything about numbers." "Well, that's the way it works. Let me see if Dr. Gomez is still willing to see you." *Willing* to? It's fortunate that he agrees to see us—especially for him!

This first appointment is barely five minutes long. Dr. Gomez writes a prescription for Zyprexa along with the other meds Danny is taking. He complains that the Zyprexa doesn't seem to be working, but Dr. Gomez is not about to take time to discuss the issue. When we call for Danny's next appointment, we learn that Dr. Gomez is in the process of moving to a more prestigious position in another hospital, so his attention is clearly elsewhere.

A month after Danny's first visit, he needs refills for his medications, but it's impossible to make an appointment with Dr. Gomez. Emails, voicemails, and messages left with the secretaries go unanswered. On Friday, I pull out all the stops, since Danny's medication will run out on Saturday. Again I come up empty. I am frantic.

On Saturday morning I happen to run into the friend who had recommended the elusive Gomez, and explain our dire situation. She offers to call Dr. Gomez herself—in fact, she will call from her office so he knows it's another doctor. I doubt this will do any good; surely the man is in Australia or something. But behold! He answers right away and says it will be no trouble at all to call the pharmacy with my son's prescriptions. How kind of him to take time out during his trip to Australia. Maybe I was wrong about him.

January 15, 2007

Danny wants to keep working toward his high school diploma, so Damian and I decide to allow him to enroll in two courses at the Harvard Extension School. Cost: $1200 for tuition and $300 for books. When Danny is forced to drop out (to be explained), we receive a refund of $900 for tuition and nothing for books, thus losing $600 on that experiment.

January 19, 2007

Damian and I finally have to admit that our finances are a mess, and though we've been making the $520 payments for just three months, we lost the $260 additional deposit from the first sober house and still had to make the same up-front payment of $390 for the next one. So, over Thanksgiving, Christmas, and New Year's, we had $2,060 of expenses that we hadn't anticipated. Worse, the strain on our budget shows no sign of letting up. As far as we know, we'll be paying $520 a month in perpetuity, as well as providing cigarettes, food, and transportation for our son.

In desperation, I contact our pastor to see if he knows of any charitable organizations that might be able to help us. He refers me to the parish chapter of the Salvation Army, as they raise funds every year to help those in the parish with special needs. "Oh . . . ok . . . thanks." Sure. As if I'm a person with "special needs." Come on. I'm not one of "those" people, right? I'm respectable. I put money in the offering every week. I buy tickets to the Christmas choir concert, for Pete's sake. I'm the one who *gives* to charities. And, yes, I'm the one who can't pay my bills.

So, swallowing my pride, I appear before the Salvation Army committee to make my request. Some of them are people I

142

know, fellow parishioners I see every week. I know my situation isn't as dire as most of those presented to this group, and I feel guilty asking for funds that could go to someone in greater need. But I opt to leave that up to the committee. They say they will let me know of their decision in a few days. In the end, they give us $1500 to defray the cost of Danny's rent for the next three months. I'm so relieved and grateful, I cry.

I'm beginning to realize that the journey with mental illness is, among other things, a lifelong lesson in humility. It's been humbling even to realize how little humility I have. There are groups of people I see very differently now—rather, people I didn't see at all, but now I do. They have many names, names that distance us from them, with connotations of our presumed superiority. They are the "needy," "homeless," "addicted," "bums," "crazies," "welfare cases," "social parasites."

Yes, we are. And it looks really different from the inside. Not because you pity them (or yourself), but because you start to know them—their personal gifts and talents, their needs, their courage, and their capacity for hope and generosity and compassion. I used to hurry past so many people that disturbed my peace, ignoring them as though they were unworthy even of a kind glance or a smile. Now, in their faces, I see my son.

Timeout: Drug Dealers[18]

A front-page story in *The Boston Globe* on October 19, 2010 reported that in 2009 and the first three months of 2010, doctors and researchers affiliated with Harvard Medical School were paid 45% of the $6.3 million given to Massachusetts doctors by seven major pharmaceutical companies that disclosed payment information for at least parts of those years. In other words, roughly $2,835,000 in speaking fees or other benefits went to Harvard-affiliated doctors, whose professional prestige makes them prized spokespersons for the medications being promoted by the large drug companies.[19]

Some physicians claim that they only recommend drugs they have found effective in their own practice, and that may be true of many physicians. But control over the content of presentations is tilting toward the companies themselves. The *Globe* reports: "Most doctors say they were approached by the

---

[18] The information in this section, unless otherwise noted, is drawn from Liz Kowalczyk, "Prescription for Prestige," *The Boston Globe*, October 19, 2010, pp. A1, 8.

[19] The article states: "This project was produced in partnership with *ProPublica*, a nonprofit investigative journalism organization, *NPR*, *PBS Nightly Business Report*, *The Chicago Tribune*, and *Consumer Reports*."

companies, usually by sales representatives, to join speaker's bureaus. At first, doctors said they created their own presentations. Now, companies generally make them, and they are reviewed by the US Food and Drug Administration [FDA]."

Unfortunately, leaving physicians and drug companies to draw the moral boundaries of this cozy arrangement has resulted in some truly outrageous conflicts of interest at the heart of the nation's premier health care system. According to press reports, more than two dozen Massachusetts psychiatrists, endocrinologists, and other specialists who gave frequent talks for drug companies made anywhere from $40,000 to $100,000 a year in speaking fees.[20]

An essay in the *The New York Review of Books* describes an especially egregious example of the cozy relationship between doctors and drug companies. "Take the case of Dr. Joseph L. Biederman, professor of psychiatry at Harvard Medical School and chief of pediatric psychopharmacology at Harvard's Massachusetts General Hospital. . . . In June, Senator Grassley revealed that drug companies, including those that make drugs he advocates for childhood bipolar disorder, had paid Biederman $1.6 million in consulting and speaking fees between 2000 and 2007. . . . After the revelation, the president of the Massachusetts General Hospital and the chairman of its physician organization sent a letter to the hospital's physicians expressing, not shock over the enormity of the conflicts of interest, but sympathy for the beneficiaries: 'We know this is an

---

[20] The *Globe* article reports: "The data on physicians payments was compiled from the websites of Eli Lilly, Pfizer, Astra-Zeneca, GlaxoSmithKline, Merck & Co., Cephalon, and the Johnson & Johnson companies by ProPublica and analyzed for Massachusetts by the Globe."

incredibly painful time for these doctors and their families, and our hearts go out to them.'"[21]

As this practice has become more widespread, some medical organizations are responding with new policies designed to prevent their employees from profiting from such speaking engagements. Partners HealthCare, an alliance that includes the Harvard-affiliated Brigham, Massachusetts General, and McLean Hospitals, has banned promotional speaking appearances by its doctors, because of the temptation for doctors both to overstate the benefits of particular medications and to press for the use of more expensive drugs, whether or not they are more effective.

However, this ban was not implemented until January 2010, the same month in which Eli Lilly accepted a settlement that amounted to the largest criminal fine in United States history. According to the story in the New York Times, "Lilly paid a $515 million criminal fine as part of a broader $1.4 billion settlement with the government."[22] Lilly was outdone only by Pfizer, makers of Geodon, who paid a $1.3 billion criminal fine as part of a broader $2.3 billion settlement.

The Times reports that "the Lilly case focused entirely on its antipsychotic drug Zyprexa," and quotes John C. Lechleiter, Eli Lilly's chief executive, as responding to the Zyprexa scandal with the comment, "That was a blemish for us." Only in a market where psychiatric pharmaceuticals generate revenues of $14.6 billion a year could a $2.3 billion fine be dismissed as a "blemish."

---

[21] Duff Wilson, Side Effects May Include Lawsuits," The New York Times, October 2, 2010.
[22] Gardiner Harris and Alex Berenson, "Lilly Said to Be Near $1.4 Billion U.S. Settlement," The New York Times, January 14, 2009.

Times reporter Duff Wilson lists some of the actions that brought on these unprecedented penalties: "According to the Justice Department, drug companies trained sales reps to rebut valid medical concerns about unproved uses of antipsychotics. For example, the department says, Lilly produced a video called 'The Myth of Diabetes' to sell Zyprexa, which became its all-time best-selling drug, even though evidence showed that Zyprexa could cause diabetes [what?!], as well as other metabolic problems.

Lilly salespeople also promoted a '5 at 5' drug regimen in nursing homes—5 milligrams of Zyprexa at 5 p.m. to sedate agitated [problematic?] older patients for the night. . . . In 2005, after a new analysis of 15 previous studies, the FDA issued a public health advisory saying the use of antipsychotics to calm older dementia patients would increase risk of death from heart failure or pneumonia. The FDA asked drug makers to add a special warning about that on packaging."[23]

Here is a puzzle in itself. If a pharmaceutical company recommends prescribing a drug to thousands of dementia patients that *can't* help them but *can* kill them, why is the FDA's only response a request to add a note to the label? Do dementia patients even read labels? But I digress.

The *Boston Globe* reveals that, prior to the ban on speaking fees, Dr. Brent Forester, a geriatric psychiatrist at McLean Hospital, was one of the biggest earners in Massachusetts in 2009. Dr. Forester "made $73,110 for giving nearly 40 talks for Eli Lilly to colleagues about the anti-psychotic Zyprexa and the anti-depressant Cymbalta over dinners in restaurants and in doctors' offices. He has resigned from speakers bureaus to

---

[23] Wilson, "Side Effects."

comply with the new rules, but said he 'never felt like a spokesperson for the company at all. It was an opportunity to educate primary-care doctors about the treatment of psychiatric conditions.'"[24] (And, incidentally, the opportunity to collect $73,000.)

Dr. Forester's presentations to primary-care physicians take on a different light in the context of the Eli Lilly report issued by the Justice Department: "The information[25] also alleges that, building on its unlawful promotion and success in the long-term care market, Eli Lilly executives decided to market Zyprexa to primary-care physicians. In Oct. 2000, Eli Lilly began this off-label marketing campaign targeting primary-care physicians, even though the company knew that there was virtually no approved use for Zyprexa in the primary-care market. Eli Lilly trained its primary-care physician sales representatives to promote Zyprexa by focusing on symptoms, rather than Zyprexa's FDA-approved indications."[26]

The *Globe* reports that Eli Lilly spent 50% of its speaker dollars on Harvard doctors in 2009, pulling back to 33% in the first three months of 2010. Perhaps this indicates a shift in strategy, but it might be nothing more than a temporary reshuffling of the speaker's bureaus. Drug companies are not required by law to

[24] Liz Kowalczyk, "Prescription for Prestige," *The Boston Globe*, October 19, 2010.
[25] This refers to a report filed by Assistant Attorney General for the Civil Division, Gregory G. Katsaas, and acting U.S. Attorney for the Eastern District of Pennsylvania, Laurie Magid in presenting the case against Eli Lilly and Pfizer.
[26] U.S. Department of Justice, "Eli Lilly and Company Agrees to Pay $1.415 Billion to Resolve Allegations of Off-label Promotion of Zyprexa," Press Release, Thursday, January 15, 2009. Available online at *www.justice.gov/civil/ocl/cases/Cases/Eli_Lilly/Lilly Press Release Final 09-civ-038.pdf.*

report the names and earnings of those who pitch their products, and very few choose to do so.

Even though the recent media spotlight on their morally dubious sales methods casts drug companies in a nefarious role, it's clear that they have no intention of going slumming in the speaker market. Hence, it is up to Harvard-affiliated hospitals, clinics, and medical schools to develop their own standards and effective means to enforce them.

Physicians who want to stay on the gravy train have ways of circumventing the system of course. According to the *Globe*, Dr. Lawrence DuBuske, an allergy specialist at Brigham Hospital, earned more money than any other speaker in Massachusetts, hauling in a whopping $219,775 in speaking fees for 2009. When the hospital announced a speaking ban, he promptly resigned. "DuBuske said he is still packing them in, even after leaving the Brigham and Harvard. 'It's not like after being there for 30 years I suddenly got stupid,' he said."

We also learn that the State of Massachusetts in 2009 banned doctors from accepting free dinners paid for by drug companies who were sponsoring a presentation. What was the effect of the ban? These cozy dinner-and-drug soirees simply relocated to neighboring states, giving new meaning to the phrase "doctors without borders."

I was pleased to find that none of Danny's physicians appeared on the list of offenders published online by the Globe. But this sorry episode may have damaged the reputation of the medical profession beyond repair. Professionals, whose work is often unsupervised and not easily evaluated by others, are assumed to be committed to conducting themselves with the utmost diligence and integrity, knowing they are entrusted, not only with the dignity of the profession, but also with the welfare of those affected by their work. Traditionally, professionals are expected to hold themselves to high standards of moral excellence without the need for external pressures or penalties.

Often our health, our fortunes, and our very lives depend on the professional integrity of doctors, lawyers, judges, and businessmen. While lawyers are routinely mocked for (reputedly) lacking principles and bankers are caricatured as greedy and deceptive, doctors have retained something of the aura of respect once accorded to all the professions.

The scandal of the drug companies is also a scandal of the medical profession, of physicians willingly bought and trained to dupe their peers and the general public into accepting false claims, sometimes with fatal consequences. While individual doctors and hospitals will recover from this disgrace, the honor of the medical profession may not.

10 Losing Ground

February 20, 2007

"Oh that I had wings like a dove! For then would I fly away, and be at rest."[27]

Just two months after moving to the new sober house, Danny calls at 7:30 this morning in great distress. He has gone on a binge and been expelled from Ocean View. Literally. He's standing on a corner with all of his belongings in a duffle bag—cold, sick, hungry, frightened, and penniless. My son, on the road from Jerusalem to Jericho. Damian is again out of town, and I have agreed to proctor an exam for his 10:00 class.

I hesitate. In rush hour, it will take forty-five minutes to reach Danny and at least an hour to get from there to the university. But he sounds completely disoriented, and seems to have no clue about what to do. He's been told to wait at a nearby diner until a van from AdCare, a rehab program located in Worcester

_____

[27] Psalm 55:6.

(an hour away), comes to pick him up. He can't remember when the van is supposed to arrive. Maybe 10:00? So I tell Danny I'll meet him at the diner, praying that I'll get back to the university in time to give the exam.

When I arrive, Danny is standing on the corner outside the diner, smoking and shivering. He looks very anxious and badly disheveled. We go inside and get some hot coffee. I try to get some information from him about the events of last night and this morning. But he can barely hold a conversation, staring at the floor for long periods and muttering inaudibly under his breath. I order breakfast, hoping the protein and coffee will revive him a little.

Since I cannot stay until ten, I hope Danny can wait inside the diner for another hour or so. Given his confused state, I wonder whether he's even tuned in enough to remember that he has to stay put until the van arrives. I ponder this problem for a few minutes, but no enlightenment is forthcoming. Finally, I settle on asking one of the waitresses if Danny can stay at the table until his ride comes. I give her a large tip, and ask her to keep him supplied with coffee.

As it turns out, the van doesn't show up until eleven. Danny must have been well-caffeinated, if nothing else. By the time he arrives at AdCare, his psychotic symptoms have returned in force. AdCare is unprepared to deal with the mentally ill, it seems—they are a detox center only. Hence, they call an ambulance and ship Danny to St. Vincent Hospital in downtown Worcester.

Meanwhile, back at home after a long and trying day, I know nothing about the deepening crisis. I'm relieved to return to a familiar setting where there is a measure of peace and predictability. By 8:00 pm, I'm already in bed and Lily is asleep upstairs, exhausted from the stress of this latest crisis with her brother.

At 8:30, the phone rings. It's one of the doctors at the emergency room in St. Vincent's, informing me that they have my son and haven't been able to get any coherent information from him. Alarms go off in my mind. What could have happened? Overdose? Injury? Suicide attempt? "Why isn't he at AdCare?" I manage at last. "Well, he was taken there initially but they weren't able to handle him, so he was brought here. Can you come down to the hospital by any chance?"

"Now?" "Well, yes. We haven't been able to figure out Danny's last name or anything about his prescriptions or medical history. He just keeps asking for you." Apparently they found my number on Danny's cell phone. I explain that my husband is out of town and my teenage daughter will be home alone if I leave. Also, that I suffer from chronic fatigue, so I'm not sure I can even make the hour-long drive to Worcester and back this late in the evening and in the dark (and on a day like this, I add silently.)

"I know it's an imposition, ma'am, but we've had to put Danny in restraints, since he doesn't know where he is and keeps trying to go outside for a cigarette." My son in restraints? Visions of straitjackets and shock therapy flash through my mind. "OK," I reply as calmly as I can. "I'll be there in an hour."

I pull on sweats and a T-shirt, remembering at the last minute to grab a warm jacket. Hurrying upstairs, I try to rouse Lily enough to explain that I need to go to Worcester to help the hospital decide how to take care of her brother. She looks worried, and a pang of guilt makes me hesitate; she knows of the crisis this morning, of course, and has no way to put it into perspective. If only we had family here in Boston—even closer friends. But I assure her that I will lock all the doors and be home when she wakes up in the morning. "Call my cell phone if you're worried or if you need anything, OK?" "Sure, Mom. Be careful driving." I know she's trying to be brave for my sake, and I love her for it.

By 8:45, I'm speeding along the Mass Pike toward Worcester as fast as I dare, wishing I had a cup of coffee to keep me alert. For some reason, knowing what lies ahead makes it harder, not easier, to stay awake. The hospital looms above the freeway, lit up like the Lincoln Memorial, so finding the right exit is no problem. But the signs for the ER are confusing and it feels like I've circled the hospital at least twice before I find the parking lot and hurry inside. A nurse takes me behind the locked doors to Danny's "room"—essentially part of a large space divided by white curtains, so there isn't much privacy.

Danny is awake but drowsy when I arrive at his bedside. His arms and legs are pinned to the gurney with large Velcro straps of some kind. "Hi, Mom . . . thanks for coming. I don't feel very good." I give him a hug and try to be as reassuring as I can. "I can't move, Mom. Why can't I move?" "Well, I guess you're not supposed to go outside and maybe that's kind of confusing. They want you to just stay in bed and rest for a while." "Oh," he sighs, lying back on the pillow. I stroke his head, trying to get him to fall asleep, but every few minutes he startles again and his eyes open wide with anxiety. "It's OK, Danny; I'm right here. You're safe now. Just try to rest."

I stay by his bedside for what seems like an eternity, weeping as I try to comfort him. I pray to Mary, my Mother, and feel her presence, standing with me by the cross of my son. Though in a lesser way, I feel that my own heart has been pierced with a sword. When I have no more prayers, I ask her to pray for both of us—for me and my weary son.

Eventually the nurses and doctors in the ER decide that Danny is calm enough in my presence that they can remove the restraints. As the hours wear on, Danny gets off the gurney over and over, trying to go outside for a smoke. I run after him each time, explaining all over again why he's not allowed to go out. Finally, in one of the few violations of the rules I have ever seen at a hospital, they allow the orderlies and me to watch over Danny while he goes just outside the sliding glass doors for a long-awaited cigarette. Back inside, he seems much calmer and at last begins to fall asleep.

A social worker comes in to tell me he's trying to find an inpatient psychiatric hospital that has a bed for Danny. He's hoping for the Arbour Hospital in Jamaica Plain, since they are the only mental health care facility that allows smoking breaks, and it's obvious by now that Danny won't do well if he's not allowed to smoke. This longsuffering man works the phones until 2:00 am, haggling with the hospital staff and the insurance company. When it begins to look as though the Arbour will work out for Danny, he comes to let me know and urges me to go back home. "There's really nothing more you can do at this point," he says. "In a few hours, Danny will be taken by ambulance to Arbour Hospital. They'll call when he arrives."

Reluctantly, I leave the side of my sleeping son, who is now so exhausted and medicated that he doesn't hear me say good-bye. I give him a kiss on the cheek, wondering that my 6'4" son with his size thirteen shoes sticking over the end of the bed should look so much like the sweet little boy I used to sing to sleep every night.

February 21, 2007

Danny is admitted to Arbour Hospital at 6:00 in the morning. It is Ash Wednesday.

155

February 22, 2007

Today is Damian's birthday. As we had planned, we eat out at
a nice restaurant and attend a play at a newly-opened theater.
We try not to think about the last two days, but there is no real
escape from the sorrow, the muted chaconne that plays
beneath the melody of our lives.

February 23, 2007

"They will walk with me dressed in white, because they are
worthy." Revelation 3:4

St. John, recording his visions in the last book of the New
Testament writes that, at the final judgment, the faithful will
receive their wedding garments. Then, dressed in white, they
will follow the Lamb wherever he goes. Will my son be there
too? Is he able to follow? How does God speak to those whose
minds are clouded and confused?

I am on a retreat this weekend, trying to reflect on the topics of
the meditations, but my heart is not in it. One of the women has
her six-month-old son with her. He is always happy and
smiling, busy and playful—all boy, like Danny as a baby. It was
so easy then to keep him safe, to make him laugh, to keep him
close, to show him how much I loved him. Now my love looks
like indifference, my help looks like harm, and my friendship
looks like betrayal.

February 21 – March 12, 2007

Danny spends three weeks in Arbour Hospital, his longest stay
to date, since both McLean and Cambridge Hospitals
discharged him in less than a week. His physician, Dr. Adams,
is a wonderful man. I've never had an opportunity to discuss

Danny's illness with any of the professionals we've dealt with so far, and I am amazed at Dr. Adam's willingness to respond to my questions and concerns. If I leave a phone message during the day, he will call me back even at 8:30 in the evening and stay on the line until I have no more questions. At times we talk for an hour or more.

One of Danny's case workers at Arbour finds that I'm having trouble applying to DMH and MassHealth (Medicaid) for Danny, so she continues the applications herself, getting Danny's signature on the relevant documents and tracking down medical records from his previous physicians. In order to qualify for MassHealth, Danny has to be removed from our health insurance plan.

It's counterintuitive that you have to take your child off an insurance plan that is supposed to be one of the best in the state so he can receive state-funded insurance that will cover a stay in the hospital for as long as necessary. Still, for the first time in the year since Danny returned from the west coast, I begin to believe there may actually be some help for my son.

Since Danny is still covered by our health plan, however, he can only stay at the Arbour Hospital for three weeks, the maximum allowed by most private insurance companies. Given this much time, I'm hopeful that they'll been able to find a better living situation for him, one with more supervision and treatment providers nearby. Alas, all such housing arrangements are available only to the very wealthy (who can afford to pay for private care) or to clients of the Department of Mental Health, and Danny's application to DMH is still pending. So he is discharged to yet another sober house, this time in a suburb about a half-hour north of us.

FIGHTING MAD

March 13, 2007

Danny's court case has been continued month by month until today, when it will at last be decided by a judge. We let him stay at our house last night, since he has to appear at 9:00 am and I want to make sure he's on time. Damian declines to attend, so I bring Danny to the courthouse and meet with Mason, the public defender who has represented him from the start.

Mason is a native of Texas with a law degree from Georgetown. He seems genuinely concerned about the fate of young men like my son, struggling with a mental illness, who are so easily swept onto the distressing merry-go-round of prison—state mental hospital—street—shelter—prison . . . while their mental and physical illnesses gnaw away at their lives.

Though he can't be more than 35, Mason handles the courtroom scene like a veteran, wearing his signature cowboy boots below the mandatory suit and tie. Over time, he develops a close friendship with Danny, appearing at his side at every court date, regardless of where and when. I am deeply grateful to him for his amazing kindness to my son, and for being the kind of man Danny can look up to and strive to emulate.

At the side of my son, I've encountered dozens of people who have dedicated their lives to those suffering from the effects of mental illness. While it's true that some have seemed indifferent or distracted, the vast majority amaze and humble me by their kindness, generosity, and dedication. As this story testifies, I've visited my son in many different hospitals, shelters, clinics, and sober houses. Every time, I marvel at the ability of the staff to remain calm, to persevere, to defuse tension and anxiety, and somehow, through it all, to preserve a sense of humor and an attitude of hope.

I would not last a day in their shoes, yet they spend weeks and months and years caring for men and women who rarely thank them and may even view them as the enemy. Watching them serve the needs of others so willingly and effectively is a privilege and a grace. Though I wouldn't have chosen the circumstances, I'm grateful for the opportunity to know some truly remarkable people. Mason is one of them.

On the 13th floor of the courthouse, we wait for Danny's case to be called. I remember from Alex's hearing in this same court that his lawyer (whom we paid several thousand dollars) worked hard to make sure his case would be heard by a specific judge, one who is sympathetic to young men with borderline psychological problems. (Alex suffers from chronic depression, among other things.)

Alex's lawyer also wanted his case to be the last one called, so the courtroom would be empty of onlookers whom the judge might be tempted to impress with a "tough-on-crime" ruling. Making use of his many connections in the multi-layered courtroom culture, that lawyer had a brief word with the bailiff, who moved Alex's file to the bottom of the stack, instead of leaving it in alphabetical order with the others. Just like that. It made me wonder what happens to defendants who have no one to massage the system for them.

When Danny, Mason, and I arrive at the assigned courtroom that morning, I am astonished to see the very same judge presiding, especially since Mason tells me that judge is now an infrequent presence at this court. It also happens that Danny's file is on the bottom of the pile, so we've somehow stumbled into the very conditions that our highly-paid, much-acclaimed attorney spent months trying to put into place. It's hard to see it as a coincidence.

To our collective relief, the judge orders Danny's case continued without a finding (CWAF for short), assigning two and a half years of probation, during which Danny must stay out of trouble and comply with his treatment plan. It's the best outcome we could have hoped for. One unsettling condition of accepting a CWAF is that you must give up your right to a trial. This is in exchange for probation instead of jail time, plus the chance to erase the charges from your record.

If you comply with the conditions of your probation for its duration, you receive this coveted outcome. If you violate those conditions, you are brought before a judge who will decide how to "dispose of" your case. I've always hated that phrase. Disposing of a case sounds too much like disposing of a person. In any event, in order to verify that you are "in compliance" with the terms of probation, you must appear before your probation officer (assigned by the court) approximately once a month, with documents supporting your place of residence, employment, and so forth.

The condition of Danny's probation is just one: cooperating with his treatment plan. This plan has three parts: regular visits to a psychiatrist, taking his prescribed psychiatric medications, and "staying clean and sober." It turns out that even receiving drug counseling satisfies the last condition. I worry—in fact I know— that Danny's compliance with these conditions will be inconsistent at best. Still, I'm relieved beyond measure. I steeled myself as much as I could, but I wasn't sure I could have survived watching my son be led out of the courtroom in handcuffs.

The plan is for Danny to move to the new sober house that very afternoon, but it's late by the time we leave the courthouse, and residents aren't allowed to move in after 3:00 pm. So he spends one more night at our house. He is always so grateful to be back home. Like any nineteen-year-old, he still thinks of it as *his* home. On the countless heart-breaking occasions when he asks why he can't come back, I say, "Well, soon you'll have your own home, Danny. Now that you're an adult, you'll want to have your own place and set it up the way you like. You can have your friends over or watch TV or rest as long as you need to. No one wants to live with their parents forever, right?"

But even I don't find it very convincing. I would give everything I have to be able to bring him home where I still feel he belongs. Yes, Danny, it *is* your home; but we can't take care of you here. How cruel life is sometimes.

The following morning, we move Danny to Sober House III. There he shares a room with five other men, so there's no privacy but many opportunities to practice social skills with people that have even fewer such skills than he does.

March 16, 2007

It's been four days since Danny moved to the sober house. It's a quiet Friday night and I am alone, if anyone is ever completely alone. I'm reflecting on a homily I heard when my husband and I were spending a weekend near the ocean last January. The pastor challenged us to consider making this "a year of favor from the Lord"—for our family members, friends, colleagues, even enemies. Let them all go free.

May God teach my heart and soul to love, and leave the judging to him.

161

Timeout: How to Wash Your Hands

Distressingly, many mental health facilities are beginning to style themselves as rehab-only centers, which enables them to refuse to treat the vast majority of those with substance disorders, most of whom also suffer from mental illness. Unfortunately, facilities that wish to focus on one of these problems in isolation from the other don't always make their intentions clear in their advertising and application materials.

I know a father of a mentally ill son who placed him at Wild Acres (where do they get these names?), a privately-owned treatment center in Boston, for three months, at a cost of $11,000 a month. Seemingly out of the blue, the clinic staff declared that they could not help this young man after all, since he had a mental illness as well as a substance problem. Surely his father could have been notified of this policy before he wasted three months and $33,000 on what he thought would be first-rate treatment for his son.

The attempt to separate mental illness from substance abuse also works the opposite way. One of the most affordable private agencies in the Boston area is Wellmet, an organization that runs group homes for the mentally ill. Oddly enough, however, many of the most common symptoms of mental illness are grounds for dismissal from the program. Wellmet's web site states: "Issues of *drinking, drugging, violence* (including acts of self-harm), or *suicidality* will be reviewed on a case by case basis. We do not allow these behaviors, as they are beyond the scope of our program and are "triggering" to others struggling with the same issues."[28]

At the top of the economic scale, the Taj Mahal of treatment facilities, located in Monterey, Massachusetts, stipulates: "Gould Farm cannot serve those with: a history of arson, sexual offense, characterological or sociopathic disorders, violence, unresolved legal entanglements, mental retardation, severe developmental disorders, *active substance disorders*, a refractory constellation of disorders, complications including but not limited to pregnancy, or those wholly dependent upon state-supported services."[29]

In other words, those with Medicaid, Medicare, food stamps, or SSI benefits need not apply. Further, since nobody knows what is meant by "characterological disorders" or "a refractory constellation of disorders" (if anything, they sound like definitions of mental illness), this statement gives the impression that the farm simply refuses admission to any client they don't want to deal with.

Of course there are still many clinics who accept the "unwashed" recipients of state-supported services. One of the most prestigious is the Freedom Trail Clinic, affiliated with Harvard Medical School and Massachusetts General Hospital. Their materials boast of their innovative *holistic* approach: "Continuing care is provided under the supervision of faculty members at the Freedom Trail Clinic, because optimal

---

[28] *www.wellmetproject.com/requirements.html*, emphasis mine.
[29] *www.gouldfarm.org/admission.html*, emphasis mine.

treatment for individuals with schizophrenia requires a community-based team approach, which integrates many services, including case management, outreach, emergency services, day treatment, substance abuse treatment, social clubs, residential programs, and vocational services."[30]

Wonderful! Yet my son was denied services at this clinic in April 2010 because he had substance abuse issues as well as schizoaffective disorder. They would know, I suppose, since Danny's first out-patient treatment was at the MGH psychiatric department with Dr. Umbridge.

On the positive side, there are agencies and legislative groups committed to overcoming the bifurcation of mental health and substance abuse services. One such organization is the Association for Behavioral Healthcare based in Natick, Massachusetts. Their description of "Who We Are" reads:

"For over 30 years, the Association for Behavioral Healthcare (ABH) has been the leading advocacy organization in Massachusetts' mental health and substance abuse arena. Fighting for high-quality, community-based care for families and individuals with mental illness, addiction and substance-use disorders, ABH provides leadership and statewide coordination on important public policy, financing, preferred clinical models, and quality assurance issues."[31]

Organizations like ABH give hope to those of us who wonder whether the many hands of the agencies that work with the mentally ill—the State Department of Mental Health, the Federal Department of Health and Human Services, the

---

[30] *www2.massgeneral.org/schizophrenia/scz_care_treatment.html*, emphasis mine.
[31] *www.abhmass.org/site/about-us/who-we-are.html*.

Department of Transitional Assistance, the public housing offices in every municipality, schools, training programs, hospitals, and clinics—will ever know what the others are doing.

At present, "the system" (an appropriately Orwellian phrase) is broken. It is a vast jungle of intertwined and overlapping agencies that mostly operate in ignorance of the others, like a collection of windowless monads. With hard work, determination, and a spirit of cooperation, this situation can change. Better coordination among agencies serving the mentally ill is imperative, since it is one of the few ways to reduce the cost of staffing and management without making cuts in the social services that are already inadequately funded.

11 Running on Empty

March 19, 2007

Tonight I attended my first meeting of a NAMI support group for relatives of those who suffer with a mental illness (NAMI stands for National Alliance on Mental Illness). Several people recommended this organization and I got as far as looking up their web site, and even paying for a membership so I could read the message boards. But I've never gone to any kind of support group, preferring to think of myself as the Lone Ranger, soldiering on through hell and high water with no need for the advice or support of others.

One of my dear friends invited me to this meeting, though, and it seemed impolite to refuse—also a little presumptuous, since her daughter has suffered with a serious mental illness for ten years now. The Caring and Sharing Group meets in the basement of a hospital, in a large room devoid of furnishings except for a large conference table in the center that is flanked by non-matching plastic chairs.

As soon as I walk through the door, I feel immediately at home. There are about a dozen people around the table, mostly women but also a few men. In spite of the dreary setting, the group creates an atmosphere of warmth and acceptance.

The leader begins by asking each person around the table to mention one thing they are grateful for. I say I'm grateful that my friend asked me along, since I probably wouldn't have had the courage to come on my own. We then go around the table again, offering an update on our struggles or, in my case, an explanation of why I'm here.

Even at this first meeting, I receive so much information that it's all I can do to write it down in my spiral notebook. Best of all, I find that I'm not alone. In many ways, our stories are all the same. It is powerfully consoling to be among men and women who understand my journey and my sorrows. We close by going around the table one last time, sharing one thing we are looking forward to. It takes me a long time to think of something.

March 2007

Sober House III works for a few weeks. Danny keeps his appointments at a day program at the Bournewood Hospital, mainly because a van takes the residents there and back each day. This house has a cook who prepares dinner each night, so Danny finally has a healthier diet. There's a pool table and a basketball hoop, so I buy Danny a new basketball, hoping it will be a positive outlet for some of his anxiety and restlessness.

Every evening at 7:00 there is a twelve-step meeting. Danny attends fairly regularly, and gets to know some of the staff members who lead the groups. One night it's close to seven as I'm dropping Danny off, and the leader of the NA (Narcotics Anonymous) meeting asks if I'd like to join them. I've never been to a twelve-step meeting and I'm honored to be invited.

FIGHTING MAD

I sit on a metal chair near the porch and listen to Sam, a fortyish man in a wheelchair, talk about his past—the mistakes he made as a young man and the pain he brought to his mother. He has no illusions about himself and makes no effort to hide his tears or his shortcomings. I expect that kind of honesty to be accompanied either by self-importance or self-deprecation, but Sam's face is a picture of calm.

When he finishes, some of the others around the circle offer their stories. One resident has just arrived, and he says how determined he is to do whatever it takes to overcome his addiction. He wants to return to his wife and children, and try to be the husband and father they deserve.

Danny speaks too, saying how much he loves me and wants to do the right things so I can be proud of him. I spend almost the entire hour weeping. By the time we finish, I am acutely aware that I am the most spiritually stunted person at this meeting. The others no longer pretend that they are self-sufficient or in control, that they have no need of mercy and grace. They have been revealed as the walking wounded, and so are free to accept themselves and each other free of judgment. Many have an aura of peace about them that is almost saintly.

I'm afraid I'm not there yet, not willing to leave my mask behind as I get in my car, back out of the gravel driveway, and accelerate onto the highway. I know I live in the shadow world, but it's so much more comfortable there.

March 22, 2007

The staff at Bournewood Hospital day program are wonderful—capable, caring, concerned—and they keep Danny coming back, even though he is disciplined from time to time and has to leave the room. Today I have a meeting with the program director, Mrs. Percy. When I say I haven't been able to obtain any benefits for Danny except (sporadically) food stamps, she immediately sets to work on the applications for MassHealth and SSI benefits.

While we're talking, one of the doctors stops by to chat. Noticing my nervousness and exhaustion, he advises me to learn to relax. "Sit up. Put both your feet flat on the floor. Feel the floor. Feel your back against the chair. Feel yourself in your body." Mrs. Percy looks as puzzled as I am.

Later she finds Danny and asks him to join us for a few minutes. I produce a letter from my purse from MassHealth announcing that they will not provide insurance for my son. But Danny trumps me by producing a MassHealth card from his wallet: "Then why do I have this?" Mrs. Percy and I stare at the card in silence. Finally I ask, "Well, does this mean he has coverage?" Mrs. Percy recovers her composure and announces emphatically, "Oh, he has it all right. If he has a card, he has MassHealth." "Just like that?" "Yes. Just like that."

March 30, 2007

During his stay at Arbour Hospital, Danny was switched to an injectible form of his main anti-psychotic medication. Each injection lasts for two weeks, so it's easier to keep track of whether he's receiving it—he has to appear at a clinic to get the shot. Just as important, since the drug is long-acting, he doesn't completely crash if he gets the injection a day or two late. Danny's physician, Dr. Adams, was both pleased and relieved when he was able to switch to injections of this critical medication.

Today it's two weeks since Danny left the hospital, and so time for another injection. Dr. Feet-on-the-Floor writes a prescription and I bring it to CVS. Denied. MassHealth doesn't yet recognize that Danny is one of their beneficiaries, and our insurance company refuses to pay. I call the company and pitch the benefits of this form of the medication. Finally they agree to cover the cost, on one condition: the hospital must provide it directly to the patient and then submit a claim for reimbursement. They will not pay for it up front. A single dose costs over $500.

I call the hospital to ask if they can administer the medication and submit a claim for reimbursement. They reply that they don't stock the injectible form of this medication and never submit claims to insurance companies. I call the insurance company again and beg them to pay for the injection and allow me to take it to the hospital. After all, it doesn't include a syringe and will never be in the possession of the patient. The woman on the line (somewhere in Ohio) adamantly refuses. I ask to speak to the person who makes these decisions and get transferred to the company psychiatrist.

"I don't see why I can't carry my son's medication to the hospital," I begin, "since I'm allowed to have custody of the oral version of exactly the same medication." "Well, I'm afraid there's nothing I can do—that's our current policy." "OK, but it's a stupid policy." "Well, ma'am," a little huffier, "you're welcome to appeal the policy." "What's the process for appeal?" "You just write a letter stating your reasons for disputing the decision." "How long does it take to receive a reply?" "Oh, we always respond to appeals within [I wait with baited breath] six months." "Six months? But by then it will be pointless!"

Back and forth I go between the bureaucracies, trying to get someone to do the reasonable thing, the humane thing. At last it dawns on me that this is one of those tug-of-wars where my side ends up with hand burns and a mud bath, so I finally admit

170

defeat. But it feels like I've failed my son, even in this one small thing where I might have done something concrete to help him. Danny goes back to the oral form of his medication. It's more than two years before he receives the injections again.

April 2, 2007

Miraculously, Danny has finally been accepted as a client of DMH, so a case worker schedules an initial appointment with him at Sober House III. Sadly, just when she arrives, Danny is being grilled by the house director about drug use. He is extremely anxious and distressed, and finding it difficult to give the required urine sample. Everyone assumes he's been using. Concerned about potential reprisals, Danny calls me in a panic. I have a hard time making out what the problem is, but I drive to the sober house to see what I can do.

After calming him as best I can, I speak briefly with the staff. Eventually Danny is able to give a sample and it reveals no traces of street drugs. He's temporarily off the hook, if still a bit shaken. I meet Joan, the DMH case worker, and I like her immediately. She is in her late forties, with clipped salt-and-pepper hair and a no-nonsense attitude of concern coupled with unblinking realism. Over the next few months, she does a wonderful job of keeping Danny in a no-spin zone.

April 9, 2007 -- Monday of the Octave of Easter

Both our older sons, Joey and Alex, are behind in their respective rent payments and have no money for groceries. We give them each $200. Danny announces that he has lost $100 gambling and is also out of cash. Why are we getting buried the day after the Resurrection?

April 10, 2007—Tuesday of the Octave of Easter

Today, at the noon mass, we heard the gospel story of Mary Magdalene's visit to Jesus' tomb on the morning of the resurrection and her distress at finding it empty. Our Lord appears to her, asking, "Woman, why are you weeping?" Mary pours out her heart to this kind stranger in the garden. How good he is to ask, to reach out, to care. But she doesn't recognize him until he says her name, with that voice filled with love that she has come to know so well: "Mary."

So often we find this sensitive woman weeping in the Gospels, and not once does Jesus find fault with her tears. He is never ashamed of them, or impatient, or indifferent. Before he tells her who he is, before he shows her that her grief will be turned into joy, he asks, "Why are you weeping?" That's what Jesus does. He appears at the side of every grieving soul, asking why they are weeping. And he listens.

The clouds have lifted from my heart a little this week. Danny spent all of Lent in hospitals—first at the Arbour, where they bound up his wounds and cared for him for three weeks, then at the day program. I pray for him daily, especially to John Paul II, asking for comfort and strength and healing and hope. Danny finally has some treatment in place, and the medications are helping to clear his mind. His path has been full of detours and dead ends, but he is getting a little bit better as time goes on. Perhaps there is a resurrection even for this one; someone who hears his cries and comes to find him.

April 15, 2007

It's Sunday. Damian is away for the weekend at a conference, but Danny comes to mass with me and then to the grocery store to pick up a few things for brunch. Lily walks the two blocks back home from the store to take a nap. The parking lot is always crowded, especially on Sundays. I snake slowly up and down the rows of cars, hoping for a space to open up. At last I see a car backing out, so I stop to wait for the space. The driver hesitates, clearly worried about whether she has enough room to back up. I try to back up a little myself, but there's another car quite close behind me.

As I inch backward, the car behind me lurches forward, intent on forcing me to give up and drive on ahead. I ease back another inch, and the guy behind me lays on his horn. When the woman finally makes her way out of the space, we're still locked in place by the prevailing bumper car mentality. Finally, my tailgater finds enough of a gap between us to pull around me on the right, rolling down his window and offering a negative opinion of my driving as he does so.

I ignore him, but Danny is increasingly agitated by the honking and gesturing, and the unflattering remarks about his mother are the last straw. Incensed, he reaches for the door handle. I grab his arm and try to hold him back: "It's not worth it, Danny. Who cares what he thinks?" But words are useless at this point. Danny walks up to Road Rage's open window and shouts that he (f***in) better not talk about his mother like that. RR jumps out of his car too, cursing and stomping up to Danny's chest, offering a piece of his mind that he probably can't spare.

When RR shoves him backwards, Danny responds with a punch that knocks the man to the ground. Danny is on him in a flash, trying to get in a few more licks. RR lands a few punches of his own, but Danny is so enraged he barely feels them. Finally, some of the bystanders intervene and manage to separate the two. I plead with Danny to get back in the car, and we drive away in search of a different grocery store.

Just as I'm walking in the door of Grocery B, my cell phone rings. It's Lily. Apparently some of the concerned citizens at the scene of the parking lot slug-out recorded our license number as we drove away and called the police. Since the two officers who respond to the call don't find us at the scene, they appear at our door, waking Lily from a sound sleep and demanding to know where her mother is. She is frantic and terrified; I can hear the panic in her voice. I try to be reassuring, "Oh honey, I'm so sorry you were there by yourself. But everything's going to be fine, OK? Just let me talk to the officers. Danny and I will be home in just a few minutes."

The police assume we took off to avoid criminal charges, but it hadn't even occurred to me that this was a police matter. Maybe it's my rural background, or growing up in the Pacific Northwest where we still think we're on the frontier, but my experience was that a fistfight pretty much settled a dispute between two men. Well, we're obviously not in the Wild West any more. I don't mention the duke-it-out assumption to the police, however, as they are in a very bad mood. They order me to get back to Grocery A **immediately!** I do.

When we arrive, Road Rage is gone. The officers inform us that there is always a security guard on duty at the store. For some reason, however, no security was present when the fight broke out. Thus, the police won't file charges against Danny. They tell us that RR was injured though, with a broken nose and elbow. "Oh, I'm so sorry," I manage. And I am—I had no idea Danny had hurt the man so seriously. His own cuts and bruises are nowhere near that level.

RR has the right to file charges, of course, and he does so. Since Danny is on probation, this does not bode well for him. A hearing is scheduled for May 8th.

May 8, 2007

Danny and I appear at the district court today for a hearing on the assault charges. Mason, the lawyer who is always at Danny's side, sits with us on the bench outside the courtroom. Amazingly, RR doesn't show up, so the charges are simply dismissed. It's hard to know how I *should* feel about this, but what I *do* feel is enormous relief.

May 21, 2007

It's a day of celebration, since Joey is graduating from the University of Boston. My parents are here for the occasion, and Damian and I are dressed in our academic robes for the procession. Danny doesn't attend, but comes to the reception afterwards and seems genuinely proud of his brother.

I wonder what this day means for him. If his life had gone according to plan, he would be finishing his sophomore year at U of B. Instead, he has yet to receive a high school diploma, and has spent more than two years in and out of hospitals, courtrooms, shelters, and sober houses. I try to put this out of my mind and focus on Joey's achievement, making the day as celebratory as I can. Still, I wouldn't be surprised to find that Danny's mixed feelings on this occasion have something to do with the meltdown of the next few days.

May 23, 2007

Danny calls from the sober house to tell me that he and one of his roommates, Carlos, just 17 years old, have consumed entire bottles of cold capsules, hoping to get high without failing the random tox screenings. He feels terrible—nauseated, dizzy, and extremely lethargic. He's afraid to fall asleep in case he doesn't wake up again. He and Carlos have told the staff what they've done, so I ask to speak with the house director.

The director, James, tells me not to worry, "The cough medicine you can get over the counter doesn't have the 'good stuff' in it, so there shouldn't be any long-lasting damage even from drinking a whole bottle." I drive out to see Danny anyway, since he's not buying this benign version of the facts. We walk around the grounds for a while and talk about what a bad idea this was. Eventually, he is calm enough to go inside and fall asleep.

May 24, 2007

The next day, James calls me around 6:00 pm to report that Danny is dizzy and vomiting, completely garbled in his speech, and unable to think or speak coherently. He can't even walk on his own. They want me to take him to a hospital emergency room. I drop everything and drive to the sober house for the second time in two days. Danny has to be carried and dragged out to the car, then leans against the window without opening his eyes. He looks very sick.

James offers to show me the way to the nearest hospital, since it's getting dark and I have no idea how to get there. He takes a tortuous route, however, so it's forty-five minutes before we arrive. James helps lift Danny out of the car and into a wheelchair, then jumps in his car and drives off, leaving us both on the sidewalk.

I bring Danny inside and sign the list, then park my car and return to the ER to sit beside him, waiting to find out what could be wrong with my son. Grave possibilities cross my mind—drug overdose, brain damage, internal injuries. Danny slumps over

176

in the wheelchair, looking more dead than alive. Still, it's three hours before we're brought into a room.

Whenever Danny stirs, I try to get out of him what happened. It eventually comes out that he and Carlos tried the same stunt two days in a row, this time downing entire bottles of a different brand of cold medicine. Inside the ER proper, the doctor tells me Danny will be OK, and that he should suffer no permanent damage. They let him sleep it off in the ER and I go back home, wishing I could sleep it off too.

The next morning, Danny takes a cab back to the sober house, where the director tells him that he is now *persona non grata.* Since we have no other housing in place for him, Danny is homeless once again. He leaves the sober house without taking any of his belongings. No one informs us that he's gone.

That evening I'm attending a meeting of our condominium association at the unit downstairs from ours. Since there are only six units in our building, the conversation is generally informative and worthwhile, but I'm struggling to stay awake after the crises of the day. My parents are still staying with us, and around 8:30 pm my mother appears at the door. There's a call for me from the South Boston Police Department. Some Good Samaritan came across Danny wandering the city streets in intoxicated confusion and called the police. They picked him up, brought him to the station, and called our house.

I try to gear up for a drive to South Boston, but find that I can barely move. I have a splitting headache and, even though my son is in trouble, this time I lose the battle against fatigue. My father offers to drive downtown, but I know he's terrified at the prospect—he's used to a town of 800 with only one stop sign.

In the end, Damian (who does not drive), offers to take public transportation downtown to retrieve Danny. I'm so relieved and grateful, I want to cry. When Damian arrives at the precinct around 10:30 pm, however, he discovers that Danny isn't there. The officer on duty explains: "We're not a medical facility, and he hasn't committed a crime, so we had no grounds to keep him here against his will."

Searching the nearby streets, my husband finally finds Danny, who is seriously disoriented and under the influence of who-knows-what. He takes his troubled son to the nearest hospital, Boston Medical Center, but they refuse to treat him. In fact, they won't even allow him to come into the Emergency Room. Damian then steers Danny several blocks down to the MGH emergency room. They also refuse to treat Danny, but allow him to sleep for a couple of hours on one of the gurneys.

Damian calls to give me an update, and we scratch our heads trying to figure out why a hospital would refuse to treat someone. How do they know Danny isn't in danger from an overdose or a toxic combination of substances? Couldn't they at least give him a blood test? Desperate to find someone to care for our son, my husband calls the Arbour Hospital where Danny was last treated. At first they refuse to take him in, then decide they can admit him on the ground of non-compliance with his medications.

May 24 -31, 2007

E. Fuller Torrey, a leading expert on mental illness, states: "The greatest cost of schizophrenia . . . is the noneconomic cost to those who have the disease and their families. These costs are incalculable. They include the effects of growing up normally until early adulthood, then being diagnosed with a brain disease that may last for the rest of your life. Hopes, plans, expectations, and dreams are abruptly put on hold. Cerebral palsy and Down's syndrome are tragedies for families of newborns; cancer and Alzheimer's disease are tragedies for families of the elderly. There is no known disease, however, with noneconomic costs so great as for schizophrenia. It is the costliest disease of all."[32]

Damian and I visit Danny a few times at the Arbour hospital. He signs the relevant paperwork to apply for Social Security Income for the disabled (SSI). He still doesn't feel at all well. The doctor gives him a high dose of Haldol that renders him nearly comatose, so even when he's relaxing on the couch, his mouth sags open and his eyelids droop. Sometimes we have to wait several seconds for him to respond to our questions. It's hard to see our son this way. Probably the doctors are afraid he'll become violent, and their solution is to keep him heavily medicated, to keep everybody "safe."

I remember seeing this same expression on my brother's face during the early part of his stay at a mental hospital in Fort Lewis, Washington. He experienced a psychotic break just months after joining the army. He was 18 years old and stationed in Nuremburg, Germany when his mind unraveled. The long flight back to the States must have been a living nightmare for him.

I was 15 then, and little prepared to see my brother, my constant childhood companion, heavily sedated with Thorazine and shuffling around the hospital common room with a bunch of other young men with glazed eyes that looked without really seeing. Now I've had more experience with mental hospitals, but I find that I'm still no more prepared for this heartbreaking sight than I was four decades ago.

---

[32] Torrey, *Surviving Schizophrenia*, p. 428.

While Danny is in the hospital, Damian and I decide to contact an organization we've been told provides supervised housing for clients of DMH. Amazingly, they have an opening in a shared apartment just a few blocks from the hospital. Danny can live in a three-bedroom apartment with two other young men who are also "dual-diagnosis," suffering both from a mental illness and a substance abuse disorder, SAD for short (as if we needed the reminder).

A case worker will check on them each week and help Danny finish his high school diploma, find a job, get to AA or NA meetings, and so on. It sounds quite promising. The apartment is fully furnished and each resident has a bedroom to himself. There is a shared computer in the living room, a house phone, and a television, and Danny can come and go on his own schedule.

On the day Danny is slated to move into the apartment, he hasn't yet been discharged from the hospital, so my mother offers to come with me to the sober house to help pack up his things. I'm glad to have her company and moral support. She understands my situation better than most, having been through so many hardships and heartaches with her own son. When Mom and I arrive at the house, one of the residents bounds out to greet us. He's pleased to report that he has already started "packing" Danny's clothes for us. Great.

The upstairs room where Danny sleeps is in chaos, with four or five cots, various pieces of half-destroyed furniture, clothes, shoes, and garbage strewn randomly about, collecting dirt and the miscellaneous unidentified substances that cover the floor. The smell is difficult to ignore—a combination of mildew, body odor, unwashed clothes, and rotting food.

Danny's things have been crammed into the standard-issue black trash bags. There is some confusion over what does and doesn't belong to him. Mom and I try to pack his few remaining possessions into the boxes we brought, pulling them from under his bed or what seems to be the likeliest dresser drawer. We miss some things that are hanging in one of the closets. Not many are left when I return to fetch them two days later.

Some of the men help carry the bags and boxes down to the car, and my mother sits in the front seat while I supervise the loading of the trunk. When the job is finally finished, I say some good-byes and get into the driver's seat next to my mom, who is sitting very still. Glancing over, I see that tears are streaming down her face. She chokes back sobs long enough to say, "I don't how you do it. It's just so sad! It is too, too hard. I'm so sorry you've had to live with this situation for so long."

Too late I realize I should not have brought her along on this errand. I've had months to acclimate to the conditions in these houses, and of the three I've known this is hardly the worst. But my mother is new to it all, still able to be shocked by the truly marginal lives of men on the brink of death by addiction. Some are in their 50's and 60's and this is the only life they've known since their teens. Failure, and fear of failure, is etched into their faces. It stoops their shoulders and flits across eyes that rarely meet yours. My son is one of them. And, as Mom often reminded me, each one of these men is the son of a mother who loved and hoped and probably prayed for him.

All of this floods into my mother's heart, a heart that aches for her own son, for mine, and for all the broken souls in this world. Mary, Mother of Sorrows, pray for us.

12 Can You Relate?

June 1, 2007

Danny is discharged from Arbour Hospital and moves into the DMH-supervised apartment in Jamaica Plain. I help unpack boxes and talk up his new living situation. It's a real apartment, recently renovated, with all new furniture and kitchen appliances. New cookware, tableware, and small kitchen appliances are all provided—even sponges and dishtowels. Compared to the places where Danny has lived for the past fourteen months, it's a palace.

The neighborhood is a middle-class community in transition from slightly scary to cool and edgy. Next door to Danny's apartment is a large group home, and across the street another one for men with substance abuse and mental health problems who require more constant supervision. Next to them is a shelter for battered women. It's sobering to imagine the magnitude of human misery hidden behind the walls of these large, gracious homes, sharing the same tree-lined street with Boston's young lawyers and bankers.

June 11, 2007

Danny has an appointment at the DTA (Department of Transitional Assistance—formerly known as the Welfare Office). There he finally receives some housing assistance funds and a monthly supply of food stamps. Apparently, food stamps aren't stamps any more. Danny gets a blue card that accesses his food account. Money is wired into it on the 5th of every month, and he can use it like a debit card until the money is gone. It won't work for non-food items—not even toothpaste or toilet paper—but it will certainly help pay for his groceries in his new apartment setting. At least the refrigerator here is shared by three instead of thirty-three.

June 14, 2007

Danny has two housemates, both in their early 20's, Nate and Doug. Nate is a bear of a man, covered with tattoos from head to foot and piercings from ear to ear. Doug is the only one of the three who has a job. He's a mild-mannered, quiet young man, with the expression of someone who is either very vulnerable or very dangerous. Maybe both.

Yesterday, Doug complained to the DMH supervisors that Danny sometimes smokes in the house, earning Danny a housing violation. Danny later confronted him, calling him a rat and socking him in the jaw. Danny was nearly ejected from the apartment for this incident, but after a group meeting with Doug, some DMH staff members, and me, they decided to give him another chance. I'm not sure why. Maybe it's partly that Danny has only been in the apartment for two weeks, and they have no other place for him to go.

July 6, 2007

Danny and Nate discover a file on the shared computer in the living room in which Doug fantasizes in detail about raping and murdering the female social worker assigned to his case. The contents are stomach-churning, and Nate and Danny decide they should let the staff know about it.

When Doug finds out, he is furious. The DMH supervisor decides against removing Doug from the apartment, and Danny says that the same woman even continues as Doug's case worker. This seems like a very bad idea, but it's not my call. The only official reaction to this situation is to reprimand Nate and Danny for looking at Doug's personal files, though he had done nothing to hide them. Unsurprisingly, Doug remains hostile, in his quiet, passive-aggressive way, and waits for an opportunity to even the score.

July 8, 2007

We begin this day with plans to celebrate Danny's 20th birthday (officially July 10th) by making a family trip to the beach. When we arrive to pick Danny up at his apartment, however, he is high on marijuana. As soon as he gets in the car, he sinks into an antisocial funk. Not wanting to give up on the day, we soldier on toward the beach and spend a couple of hours playing in the waves and walking along the shore. Danny spends the entire time sleeping on a beach towel. When we start packing up to leave, we have to wake him up, which makes him increasingly irritable.

On the ride to our house for cake and gifts, Danny gets into an argument with Liliana, adding a few annoying shoves for good measure. When Lily complains that he won't leave her alone, he ratchets up the hostility and actually curses at her.

As far as Damian and I are concerned, this is the last straw. We decide to cancel the rest of the party for now and take Danny back to his apartment. He is clearly hurt by this, but too angry to apologize to anyone. As we pull up to his place, he jumps out of the car before it stops moving, slams the door, and never looks back. Happy Birthday, Son. Lily is in tears, and Joey and Alex sit in stunned silence. Damian's silent anger is almost a match for Danny's.

I don't know how to feel. Angry? Ashamed? Hurt? Depressed? It's so hard to judge another person fairly, and virtually impossible when that person is both your child and struggling with a mental illness. How much control does Danny have over his drug habit? His anger? His violent outbursts? If only we knew, we would have some idea of how to react to his troubling behaviors. As it is, we live with the sad reality that, most of the time, we are treating him either too harshly or too leniently. Not knowing which is one of the most distressing and frustrating aspects of his illness.

July 12, 2007

Today, Danny gets into a heated confrontation with his other roommate Nate, who responds with a punch in Danny's face that breaks his nose and opens a cut requiring some stitches (Nate was wearing a ring). Danny calls from the ER of a hospital I'm unfamiliar with. I'm embarrassed to find that I'm actually pleased about the change of venue.

Danny decides not to report the incident. In fact, his main reaction seems to be one of pride in that fact that he took the punch without falling down. When the staff hear what happened, they blame Danny rather than Nate, on the grounds that Danny had started the argument. It's hard for him to win these days.

185

FIGHTING MAD

When the ER doctor finishes the stitches, I bring Danny back to the apartment. Nate is still hanging around, and he greets us nervously, expecting the worst. Instead, Danny apologizes for antagonizing him. (Okay, so maybe the staff was right.)

While I attempt to clean up after the tornado that appears to have hit their kitchen, Nate tells me his life's story. He's been in trouble with both the law and the anti-law contingents in LA, often putting the rest of his family in serious danger. Fearing reprisal from some of Nate's enemies, his exasperated mother kicked him out of the house and LA social services sent him to Boston—as far away from his previous gangster environment as possible.

He confides that he has little hope of finding a job here in Boston; employers take one look at him, an enormous black man covered with piercings and tattoos, and run the other way. This is a quintessential New England city, and Nate has arrived with the wrong color of skin, tattooed with gangster signatures, and reeling from the double stigma of mental illness and substance abuse.

I try to say encouraging things, describing jobs where appearance doesn't matter or where toughness is a plus. But Nate has back injuries from life on the streets, and his weight makes them worse. He is clearly homesick, and trying to cope with that sadness on top of the others in his life. As he talks, I begin to see the frightened little boy inside the intimidating exterior. He needs a mother. Everybody does. I tell him I'll pray for him.

When I leave, I hug them both. Life really is a strange journey at times.

July 15, 2007

My husband is in New Jersey this week. I try not to think about the events of last year at this time—the arrest, the court proceedings, the humiliations. Never look back.

Since Danny hopes to start classes at U of B in January, he is required to attend a summer orientation seminar for incoming freshmen. He's signed up for the one that starts today, and has filled his backpack with the mandatory items. He's not ready to go when I get to his apartment though, so we arrive at the eleventh hour for registration and room assignments. On the way out, we miss the table with room keys and have to make an extra trip between the registration area and the dorm.

Danny is nervous and ill-at-ease in the crowd of self-consciously stylish U of B students. He feels conspicuous with stitches on the bridge of his nose and a dark bruise under one eye. When he is finally settled in his room, I ask if he plans to attend the opening orientation talk. But he is already sprawled across the standard-issue extra-long twin bed, with no plans to move from it for the next two hours. I encourage him to try to wake up in time for dinner at six and leave him in his room, falling asleep from exhaustion, while other students rush around excitedly, exchanging names and hometowns and tentative majors.

On my way back to the parking lot, I notice other parents who, like me, have just dropped off their sons or daughters for this first *bona fide* college activity. They smile conspiratorially, assuming I share their feelings of pride and excitement, and I try my best to smile back. But my heart isn't in it. I have to admit that I envy them, with their "normal" kids and obvious confidence in the bright future that awaits them. My son isn't

187

showing his younger siblings around the campus or joking with friends by the cafeteria.

Most of the time, I try to live in Danny's reality with as little self-pity as I can muster. But this time the contrast is simply too much to bear. Once inside the car, it's a long time before I can collect myself enough to start the engine and head toward home. From my memory's far recesses, I recall a warning from our driver's ed book: "Never drive when you're emotionally upset." Obviously, they didn't have a child with a mental illness.

July 17, 2007

Today I pick Danny up from U of B at the end of orientation and drive immediately to the doctor's office to get his stitches removed. I ask how the weekend went. He doesn't want to talk about it.

August, 2007

With fall approaching, I'm aware that the time is short for Danny to acquire his high school diploma before starting at U of B in January. It's been over two years since the graduation fiasco, and the charter school is a wall of silence.

When Danny moved into the DMH apartment at the beginning of June, I asked about tutoring to help him finish his high school diploma. It was weeks before any meetings with a tutor were scheduled, though, and then we found that the level of tutoring DMH has to offer can't help Danny with his high school requirements. Their primary focus is English as a Second Language and preparation for the GED.

I'm also growing increasingly frustrated over Danny's decreasing activity. I contact his case worker to explain that he has no structure in his day, and so spends much of his time looking for ways to get alcohol and drugs. He's also begun to take up gambling again. The case worker assures me that they are working on putting some programs in place for Danny. But as the weeks pass with no perceptible movement in that direction, the apartment begins to resemble an upscale sober house.

In late August, I contact the Massachusetts Board of Education to ask about possible options for Danny to get a diploma. I explain the reason he was denied one and mention that I had asked the charter school about possible testing for him, only to be told that it wasn't available through the school. "By now," I lament, "my son has tried three times to complete his senior year requirements, taking summer courses at the charter school and then at a nearby public school, but he was expelled from both programs. His backup plan to take two of the three required courses at Harvard Extension School fell apart when he was hospitalized. I'm sure some of this (maybe all of it) is his own fault, but I'm at a loss as to how he can ever earn a diploma."

The Board of Ed Liaison explains that since Danny was never expelled from the charter school, they are still responsible for helping him finish his diploma. Further, schools are required to offer and pay for educational testing if a parent requests it. I am shocked and angry. Letters, emails, and phone calls fly back and forth, but the charter school continues to drag its feet about paying for any testing. They then insist that since Danny is 20 now, he must ask for testing himself.

A school staff member calls Danny and lobbies him into accepting tutoring instead of testing, arguing that this will be a faster track toward his diploma. Danny accepts the deal, but the school year begins with only a list of assignments for the three courses he needs to pass. Not a single tutoring appointment has been made. Instead, in his only meeting with Mr. Cole, the math teacher who used to be his best advocate, he is told that he can do the work on his own—he doesn't need any tutoring. If I had been present at that meeting, I'd be serving a sentence for attempted murder.

At a loss to get any concrete help from the school, I finally turn to craigslist and hire a calculus tutor for Danny. Six sessions and $180 later, he finishes the required problem set. He and I then work together on the term paper for his English course, a lengthy assignment requiring footnotes and an annotated bibliography. I try to help Danny without writing the paper for him, but it's slow going. He frequently gets frustrated and goes outside for a couple of cigarettes, returning to tell me he can't focus on it any more today.

Eventually the paper is completed and turned in, so only the Spanish course is left. Danny is supposed to translate a three-page passage into English, which ought to be simple enough. But the text is filled with metaphors and is extremely difficult to translate. Danny gets nowhere with it. When he lets the Spanish teacher know that this assignment is beyond him, she drops it and arranges instead for him to take a written exam, which he passes. I'm not sure which of us is more amazed and excited.

Danny receives his high school diploma in the mail in October 2007, $2^1/_2$ years after his graduation ceremony. I haven't seen him smile like this in years. The whole family celebrates over dinner at Uno's and cake and ice cream back at the house.

August 31, 2007

I'm spending the day with Alex, bringing the car over to his apartment to transport the boxes of his belongings to his new place. Most of the buildings around U of B are filled with students, who pack as many live bodies as possible into each one. The local landlords rake in thousands of dollars a month from students who need to live within walking distance of the school and so are forced to succumb to exorbitant rents while putting up with everything from broken glass to bedbugs.

Alex quit attending classes this past semester, feeling intense pressure in his academic work and an ongoing disconnect from the preppy scene at U of B. Unfortunately, Damian and I were the last to know. I have noticed that children of academics often fail to flourish at the colleges where their parents teach. Over the years I've developed, then discarded, many explanations for this. Class differences? Intellectual interests? Cynicism about university culture? I'm pretty sure my children know, but I'm afraid to ask them.

In Alex's case, dropping out of school did not coincide with seeking additional employment, so his resources are pretty thin. He's been working at part-time jobs and is several hundred dollars behind on the rent at his present apartment. But he's assured me that everything is set for the new place. The other residents are international students, and the apartment was arranged by University of Boston's off-campus housing office. I should have known that this was way too easy. When I arrive at his apartment, Alex informs me that, since he never placed a deposit or signed a contract, the room has been rented to someone else.

In a panic, I track down the relevant office at U of B, only to find that there's nothing available at this late date. Our next stop is a local realtor, who shows us a place far beyond our means. As the afternoon wears on, Alex suddenly remembers that he has to be at work at 4:00 pm. With no place to move his furnishings, we prevail on Joey to let us use part of the basement in the house he is renting with three other U of B students.

Alex is the last of four housemates to move out of the apartment, so there are several pieces of furniture lying around that don't belong to him. We leave them stacked along a wall of the garage, as Alex assures me that this was OK'd by the landlord. It wasn't. Alex is charged $200 for the cost of removing these items from the garage and another $300 for unpaid rent. From the deposit of $525 Damian and I put up for him in September, we recover $25.

Alex will have to live at home until he finds another room to rent and a job that will pay for it. No one is pleased at this prospect. As he and I stand in the middle of his bedroom, surrounded by half-packed boxes and half-baked plans, my cell phone rings. It's Danny. He and Doug (of the computer caper) got into yet another argument, this time about Doug's refusal to take his clothes out of the dryer. In frustration, Danny gave him a hard shove, knocking him down. This, alas, is the tipping point.

The staff advise Doug to take out a restraining order against Danny, which means he must leave the apartment immediately. When he calls, Danny is distraught. He's not even allowed to go back inside to get his things without a police escort. I tell him I can't come over there for at least two hours, since I'm still helping Alex move out of his place, but that I'll call when I'm on my way.

I try to encourage him, "Danny, I know this is a real blow for you. And it's scary to think about contacting the police. But I'm going to help you with those things, OK?" "But Mom, what are we even going to pack my things in? I have a lot of stuff there." "That's true. But we'll pick up some boxes when I get there. We can do this, Son. Just hang in there." Feeling a little better, Danny hangs up the phone.

Now the moving project kicks into high gear. Since Alex has to leave for work, Joey and I end up with the job of unloading the boxes and furniture into the garage at Joey's apartment. (His landlord is unimpressed with that solution, so in a few days we have to move them again from the garage to the basement.)

Tired, but relieved to have one move out of the way, I drive toward the southern suburbs of Boston to find my youngest son. He is angry and frustrated. I can barely hold it together myself, having worked all day at Alex's apartment and come up against countless dead ends. This morning both boys had a place to live; now neither does.

Danny asks where Alex moved to, and I have to admit that Alex doesn't have a place after all and will have to stay with us for a few days until he finds something else. Danny tells me he has to stay away from Doug and the apartment for two weeks. Then a hearing will be scheduled to determine whether the restraining order will be dismissed or continued for a year. He asks if, like Alex, he can live at home for the next two weeks. Again, I have to tell him that it's not possible for us to have him there.

Since Alex is allowed to come home, and on this very day, Danny is understandably hurt and angry. Explanations are pointless. He already knows why he can't live at home. Or he doesn't know, but the fact of the matter remains. I find that I've had to say to own son, my most vulnerable child, many times over, "I'm sorry, but no—you can't come home." It never gets easier. It's gut-wrenching, and fills your whole soul with guilt and grief. But I know that with Danny at home I would fall apart in a matter of days, and *I must not fall apart*. At times like this, I'm all he has.

Danny and I meet at a coffee shop, where I order a double shot of espresso to gear up for this next task. We stop at a liquor store for cigarettes and a few boxes to use for the move. Next, it's a trip to the police station to arrange an escort. They are surprisingly kind to us, but I still feel like a criminal. Back at the apartment, it doesn't take long to pack Danny's things. He has no furniture and very few books. Just clothes, shoes, his signature baseball caps, a small rug, and some office supplies. For the next two weeks, Danny lives with Joey, sleeping on the couch and waiting for his court date.

September 14, 2007

Today, the relevant parties convene at the courthouse. Danny and I appear at 9:00 to await the judge's verdict. The judge is a woman, which gives me a small spark of hope. Maybe she'll have some sympathy for Danny's predicament, and for mine as his mother. Doug is not in the courtroom yet, but appears just before 9:30. He's not an especially combative person, so we're surprised that he came to press for a continuation of the restraining order. But Mr. Pomposa, the director of the housing program, has brought Doug to court to make sure he doesn't back down.

The judge calls everyone up to the bench. She hears from Doug, then from Danny (who says nothing), and finally from me. Without further ado, she declares that the restraining order will remain in place for one year. I am shocked. I beg her to reconsider. "Danny has no place else to live. What's he supposed to do now?" She looks unimpressed. "I'm sure DMH will find another placement for him." "But Your Honor, that's not going to happen. He's already lived in five different places in eighteen months—he's been in shelters and sober houses and on the streets. This is the first normal living situation he's had."

No response. The decision is made. What is it to her if this difficult and disheveled black teenager has no home? We're told to wait for the bailiff to prepare some papers, but I'm already in tears and ask to be excused. Exiting the courtroom requires walking in front of the whole assembly—lawyers, clients, defendants, and their dispirited relatives—until I reach the door at the back of the room. A walk of shame if there ever was one.

Danny and I have to arrange yet another police escort in order to move the rest of his things from the apartment. He spends the next three nights at Joey's place, but Joey's landlord and roommates complain that they hadn't planned on a fifth person in the apartment, and Danny has to leave.

September 17-20, 2007

Danny's DMH case worker, Joan, hopes to place him in a different supervised group home—this time in Boston—and so begins the application process. Meanwhile, Danny has no place to go. He uses some funds he received from retroactive Social Security payments to stay three nights at a Motel 6 in the far pavilions of the Boston area. But he's lonely there—there's nothing to do, and he can't afford it for very long anyway. It's colder now, so sleeping on the streets is a more forbidding option. Time is running out.

Timeout: Greyhound Therapy

Fighting homelessness is both costly and frustrating, and large US cities increasingly find their resources and expertise inadequate for the task, especially in the case of homeless individuals with mental illnesses. A 2006 report from the National Coalition for the Homeless noted that "Approximately 20-25% of the single adult homeless population suffers from some form of severe and persistent mental illness."[33] Many would put the percentage much higher.

One strategy for coping with this problem, informally known as Greyhound Therapy, is to buy a person a one-way bus ticket to a city some distance away. Problem solved. One such program, Homeward Bound, purports to relocate homeless people in the places they're originally from. This is made difficult by the fact that many homeless persons, especially those with mental illnesses, are no longer "from" anywhere; their families may have moved or disowned them, and they have no connections to social services in places they left long ago.

---

[33] "Mental Illness and Homelessness: NCH Fact Sheet #5," *National Coalition for the Homeless*, June 2006. Available at *www.nationalhomeless.org/publications/facts/Mental_Illness.pdf.*

In 2006, a *New York Times* article reported: "In the past, the city [of New York] contracted with the Salvation Army for a now-defunct program called Homeward Bound, but only for single adults and couples, not families with children. Both versions followed the example of Travelers Aid, a 150-year-old nonprofit organization that provides stranded and homeless people emergency aid so they could [sic] return to their homes, and which still exists today. Other cities have experimented with similar programs."[34]

Unfortunately, Homeward Bound is not defunct after all, though there is no mention of the one-way ticket program on their current web page (*www.hbphx.org*). A 2006 article in the *Sacramento Bee*, however, describes San Francisco's policy of sending homeless persons to a distant county:

"[San Francisco] city officials created a program last year to give homeless people one-way bus tickets out of town. Thus far, more than 960 homeless have left San Francisco under the program, Homeward Bound. . . . City welfare officials have agreed to stop sending homeless people to Humboldt County without notifying their counterparts in the far northern county. The agreement reached Friday resolves a dispute that began after Humboldt County officials learned that San Francisco had sent at least 13 homeless people north on one-way bus tickets over the past year. San Francisco officials said they will start informing Humboldt officials whenever homeless people are sent over its borders through the city's Homeward Bound program. They will also verify beforehand that the person is

---

[34] Julie Bosnan, "City Aids Homeless with One-way Tickets Home," *New York Times*, July 29, 2009, A1.

actually from Humboldt, located about 200 miles north along the coast."[35]

Over the past fifty years, many individuals and organizations have complained about the barbaric practice of forced relocation, but the general public is still largely unaware of it. No doubt many would find it hard to believe. Public ignorance, combined with skewed perceptions of the homeless, are major motivations behind a forthcoming independent film, directed by Steven Oakey and titled *Greyhound Therapy*.

A journalist who interviewed Oakey about the movie explains: "No one wanted to know the stories of the homeless. They only want them to disappear. This antipathy is what originally awakened something deep within Oakey, and he poured the simmering contents of his soul onto paper and onto the big screen."[36]

This movie will surely help to raise public awareness of the plight of the homeless. But what we need even more than knowledge is a workable plan for caring for those who wander our streets night and day, often without help, and sometimes without hope.

---

[35] Leonidas, "Suspected Greyhound Therapy Confirmed," *Fighting in the Shade* (an online blog), January 29, 2006, available at *http://fightingintheshade.blogspot.com/2006/01/suspected-greyhound-therapy-confirmed.html*.

[36] Terry Shropshire, ""Greyhound Therapy' Makes Issue of Homelessness Matter to America Again," *Rollingout.com*, May 7, 2011. Available at *rollingout.com/cities-events/greyhound-therapy-makes-issue-of-homelessness-matter-to-america-again/*.

13 Sorrow upon Sorrow

September 20 – October 8, 2007

Joan found a bed for Danny in a shelter in Cambridge run by the Salvation Army. It's located about a mile from Harvard Square. This shelter allows residents to keep the same bed for the length of their stay, even providing a locker for clothes and toiletries so the men don't have to carry them around all day. Danny is pleased to be able to move from Motel 6 to a place better than the streets. He stays at the shelter that night, but he's been invited to spend Friday night at Joey's house and doesn't want to miss out.

The only problem with his plan is that, according to shelter policy, if you miss a night, you have to stay out for a total of four nights before you can return. So Danny has three more nights to cover. He stays an additional night at Joey's, but on Sunday he has no place to sleep. His call comes at 5:00 pm, so the other shelters I know about are closed for the night—some shut their doors as early as 4:00.

I contact Joan for an alternative and she tells me about a place that accepts the homeless until 9:00 pm—the Boston Night Center, located in the heart of downtown Boston near the commuter rail station. I drop Danny off around 8:30. Catching sight of the ragged others lined up by the door, he's reluctant to get out of the car. But it's been a long day, and I have neither the strength nor the patience to wait another half hour until the doors open.

So Danny gets in line with the rest of the city's desperados, the most homeless of the homeless. The Center is actually the lobby of an office building. There are no beds, no food, no TV, and no real security. The only thing to be said for it is that it isn't the street. At 5:00 am, everyone has to clear out. Danny has barely slept, worrying all night about being assaulted or robbed. At five, he crosses the street to the train station and immediately falls asleep on one of the benches. When he wakes up, his wallet is missing, having been safer at the Center than at the train station it seems.

For three weeks, Danny stays at the Salvation Army, though not continuously. In order to get a bed every night, residents are required to attend the religious services and day program offered there. Since Danny is Catholic, he has little interest in the Protestant services, and his record with day programs is, well, appalling. Those who don't attend the day program are allowed only six consecutive nights at the shelter and must find another arrangement for the next four nights. But their beds are held for them, so they can return when the four nights are up.

It's the weirdest system I've encountered so far, and it has the effect of making Danny's life increasingly dysfunctional. During his exile from the Salvation Army, the closest alternative is the Albany Street shelter in the neighborhood of the Massachusetts Institute of Technology, also located in Cambridge.

Albany Street is a "wet shelter," accepting those who are clearly under the influence of alcohol or drugs. Since wet shelters are rare, the sober homeless are turned away, presumably on the assumption that they can find a bed elsewhere—say, at the Salvation Army, which is a "dry shelter," admitting only those who are (or at least appear to be) clean and sober.

The bizarre result is that Danny spends six days in a row trying to "keep it together" so he can qualify for the Salvation Army, then four days in a row trying to drink enough beer so he at least smells of it and can gain admission to Albany Street. Six sober, four drunk, six sober, four drunk. This is what we offer the homeless mentally ill in the shadow of Harvard University and MIT.

September 25, 2007

Alex has been living at home for a month now, and we continue to press him to find another apartment to rent. At last he finds a room in a Boston apartment with an easy commute to his workplace and to the state college where he hopes to take a few courses, having given up on U of B for the time being. The neighborhood doesn't have the best reputation, but I notice that there are several families living on the block. I help Alex retrieve his furniture from Joey's basement and move it into his new, second-floor apartment. His is a tiny room at the back, just off the kitchen.

His roommates are an international student newly arrived from China, and a married couple in the bedroom next to his. He has a part-time job at Starbucks and is able to pick up a few hours of extra work at area bookstores during the book stampede at the beginning of each semester. There are fifty-four colleges located inside Boston's interstate highway loop, so every September and January is a textbook lollapalooza.

October 8-22, 2007

On Oct. 8th, Danny breaks the rules at the Salvation Army and is banned for two weeks. DMH still has no housing for him. He sleeps on the couch at Alex's apartment for one night, then Joey offers to take him in for a couple of weeks. When Joey's landlord boots him out, Danny again dips into his SSI money, this time to rent a room by the month in a three-story house in a yuppie neighborhood south of downtown. By the time we find out about this, it's a done deal.

A Chinese family occupies the rest of the house and Danny seems to be their only renter. He shares the bathroom with the rest of the family but is banned from their kitchen. There's a mini-fridge and a small microwave in his room, though, so he's able to prepare some of his own meals. I bring his clothes and a few other things to his room, planning to help him fix it up and make it feel more like his own space. The room is dark and gloomy even with the lights on, so I do some cleaning and then head to the store for a new window shade, a mirror, a coffee maker, and a few other things to brighten the room.

Danny is proud to have a place he found and paid for himself. There is no rental contract, just a verbal agreement with the young woman who seems to be the only member of the family who speaks English. As the days pass, Danny starts to understand why the room is so affordable. The family dog has free reign of the house, and no one seems bothered by the fact that he defecates in the hallway on a regular basis. If Danny steps out for even a minute without locking his door, the ever-vigilant dog zooms in and helps himself to whatever he can find. Bagels are a special favorite, cream cheese and all—he will chew through a plastic container of cream cheese in order to get to the good stuff. Still, the room is a place to sleep, and it beats the hell out of the street and the shelters.

October 17, 2007

Meanwhile, three weeks after moving to his new apartment, Alex is miserable. The house is empty most of the time, but his sleep is disrupted every night at midnight when the husband in the neighboring room returns from work. He and his wife get into loud and violent arguments every night until 2:00 am, separated from Alex by a very thin wall. In spite of the presence of families living close by, Alex is afraid to go outside alone after dark. Since the walk to and from the train station is utterly deserted, twice a day his heart revs up to a high pitch until he gets to a well-lit, populated area again.

To make matters worse, things are going badly at work, so Alex fears he's on the verge of losing both his job and his apartment, with no idea what to do next. Maybe it's more than that. Maybe it's that he doesn't even know what he *wants* to do next. Ever since U of B fell through, Alex views his life as stamped with failure. I invite him to spend a couple of nights with us so he can think about the direction he wants to take. Then he returns to his lonely apartment to try to make life work again, at least for now.

Since Alex left some of his things at our house, he returned this evening to retrieve them, but was met, practically at the door, by my frustrated complaints about the condition in which he left the bedroom and bathroom. I'd spent hours cleaning and putting things away that day. I could see that Alex was deeply hurt by this attack, and instantly I regretted jumping on him like that. I hadn't even asked how he was doing.

But there's no opportunity to take it back. Agitated and upset, Alex grabs his coat and bag and practically runs out the door, fighting back anger and tears and despair. I know he is deeply wounded. I want to run down the street after him, but the day has stolen my energy; I have nothing left. I ask Damian to go after Alex and catch up with him. But when he asks, "Why? What am I supposed to say?" I don't have an answer. I just want someone to console Alex, to encourage him, to tell him how much we love him—because anything else would only deepen his distress. I call his cell phone several times, but he doesn't pick up. So I wait. And hope. And pray.

Damian and I finally turn in, but I can't get to sleep. I get up and try to keep myself occupied, picking up the living room, folding clothes, filing a few papers. At 1:30 am, Alex calls. He sounds very sad, and very far away. I ask what's wrong, and eventually he admits that he's tried to cut his wrists with a broken bottle, under cover of the dark corridor between the train and his apartment. I never get the whole story, but it seems that a police officer came along and was very concerned about Alex. He advised him to go back to his apartment and call a suicide hotline. Thankfully, Alex decided to follow the advice.

After an hour or so of conversation, the hotline volunteer suggests that Alex call someone who cares about him—someone he can confide in. May God bless that person, wherever they are. And I can never be grateful enough that Alex felt he could call me, that in spite of my earlier harsh words and seeming indifference to his pain, he still knew that I loved him.

When he calls, I ask Alex to wait at his apartment—I'll be there in just a few minutes. My heart aches for my son. I'm angry at myself that I didn't follow my instincts and run after him when he left our house in such distress. How could I have missed the depth of his despair? Alex is so quiet in comparison to our other children—it's been easy to lose track of him in the general chaos.

I'm afraid I've been so absorbed in Danny's problems, and the constant crises they provoke, that I've barely noticed how Alex (or anyone else in the family) was doing. He must have felt so alone and forsaken. I feel tried and convicted of failing my son. In his moment of deepest agony, balanced on the razor edge between hope and despair, it was a stranger on the phone who listened and cared. Not his family. Not I.

The drive to Alex's neighborhood takes an eternity, but I'm able to persuade him to speak to the doctors at the psychiatric ER at MGH, just to see what they think he needs. By now it's a familiar setting for me. But on this visit, at 2:30 am, we meet with a strange resistance from the staff. "Why are you here?" "So what's the problem, really?" A young intern interviews both of us at length, and presses Alex for details about his suicide attempt. He has deep scratches and cuts his wrists, but they're not bleeding right now. Maybe she's looking for something more dramatic.

Finally, reluctantly, the doctor tells Alex that he can choose between two options—admission to a hospital or going back home (!) and returning the next day to attend an out-patient program. Alex asks to be admitted, and the intern departs to tend to the preliminaries.

As we wait in the small conference room for the system to rouse itself at this hour of the night, another physician walks in. He's significantly older than Dr. #1, and an air of authority and entitlement breezes in with him. I have only a vague understanding of the relationship between this man and the young woman who preceded him. After all this time, hospital pecking order remains a mystery to me.

Doctor Superior expresses doubts about the severity of Alex's depression, and badgers him with questions about just how suicidal he really is. After all, he can come back as soon as the next morning to begin the partial program. I interrupt to explain that Alex's living situation is a contributor his current despair and the scene of his recent suicide attempt, so it doesn't seem wise for him to return there just now. "Can't he just stay with you?" he asks, casting his accusing eyes toward me. "Not really. Our family is a stressful place for Alex right now, not exactly a safe haven."

Dr. S grows increasingly exasperated. Finally he leans forward, inches from Alex's face, and barks, "Do you mean to tell me that you can't keep yourself safe for the next seven hours until the day program starts?" I cringe at his tone. This is an interrogation, not an interview. My son is the accused. Did I miss something? Has despair become a crime? I expect Alex to wilt under this intense pressure, but instead he replies calmly and evenly, "No. I don't think I can." I cheer inwardly, amazed at his ability to stand up to this arrogant jerk.

Given this unequivocal answer, Dr. S finally relents and leaves the room in disgust, throwing back over his shoulder that it's going to take *hours* to find a hospital bed for Alex. He'll just have to sit here until they do. As if he'll change his mind because we don't have the time to wait for the paperwork. It's now 4:00 in the morning for Pete's sake; what else is there to do?

When Good Cop returns, she offers to let Alex change into hospital garb and lie down in one of the rooms until arrangements can be made to transfer him to a hospital. She explains to me that there's nothing more I can do right now. So I drive back home at 5:00 and fall asleep in my clothes, feeling close to suicidal myself. Alex is transported to McLean Hospital before 8:00 am.

October 18-24, 2007

Alex spends a week in the hospital and seems to find it enormously helpful. He takes advantage of the groups and the therapy, and gets onto a medication that mitigates his anxiety and depression. The rest of us visit him frequently, going for long walks on the beautiful grounds surrounding the hospital.

Once Danny remarks, "It feels weird being here as a visitor instead of a patient." "I'm sure it does, Son. It feels a lot better though, right?" I don't add that it feels weird to me too, visiting yet another of my children who knows so much sorrow. I can't take it in right now; it's too much to bear. Only the Psalmist has words for my grief: "Save me, O God. . . . I sink in deep mire, where there is no foothold; I have come into deep waters and the flood sweeps over me."[37]

Poor Lily is shell-shocked by Alex's suicide attempt, coming only two-and-a-half years after Danny's psychotic break. She's just turned 15, and these events have hit her like a train. But I'm ashamed to say that I don't pick up on her agony of heart. Maybe I'm having too much trouble assimilating it all myself.

Turning away from this mountain of grief, I try to focus on the practical things I can do something about. Will Alex be able to return to his apartment? Probably not. Can he break his lease?

[37]Psalm 69:1-2.

Even if he can, will he be able to find another place to rent in the middle of October? As daunting as these problems seem, they are infinitely easier than the questions that surface whenever I let down my guard: What makes Alex afraid to go on living? Will he get better? Did I contribute to his sense of abandonment? If I did, will he ever be able to forgive me? And the hardest one of all—will I ever be able to forgive myself?

October 24, 2007

Alex is discharged from McLean Hospital today and referred to a day program at a clinic near Fenway Park. Danny is staying at Joey's apartment tonight, and they invite Alex to come over too. The three celebrate Alex's release by having way too much to drink. Danny ends up saying some very cruel things to Alex, which results in a shouting match that quickly threatens to turn into a boxing match. Joey takes Danny outside for a smoke, hoping to get him to cool off.

They're walking down the middle of the street, for some reason, leaving little room for cars to pass, so it's not surprising that one comes close to grazing them. The driver screeches to a halt, cursing them up and down and leaning on his horn for emphasis. As he starts to drive away, Danny kicks his fender. Immediately, the guy stops his car again and rolls down the window. Not a wise move. Danny walks up and punches him in the head so hard that he falls unconscious onto the steering wheel.

What is it with my son, I wonder? Why not meet words with words? I'm sure he knows how to curse with the best of them. I marvel that Danny's not in prison. The mental health providers press him to attend anger management groups and occasionally he does; he says they have some good

208

suggestions, but he never remembers them when he's really angry or upset.

I've sometimes tried phrasing it in terms of a cost/benefit ratio, pointing out the few pros and many cons of expressing his anger with his fists. But the professionals would say I'm wasting my time; schizophrenia impairs a person's ability to recognize cause and effect connections from one context to another. Further, several factors interfere with their awareness of their current set of motives for action, and hence with the ability to sort out the good from the bad.

Schizophrenia specialist Dr. Torrey explains, "Paranoid delusions may on occasion be dangerous. . . . The paranoid person my strike first when the threat is perceived as too close. Facilities for the criminally insane in every state include among their inmates a large number of persons with schizophrenia who have committed a crime in what they believed to be self-defense."[38]

Awakened by the honking and cursing surrounding the whole affair, Joey's neighbors call the police. My sons are examining the driver of the car to see if he's seriously injured. Just as he starts to regain consciousness, they hear sirens coming in their direction, so take off running for the cover of the nearest woods. Following a circuitous route to a T stop, Joey puts Danny on the train back to his apartment. It's a long time before Alex will speak to Danny.

On the day Alex is released from the hospital, things have to go like this? Sometimes I despair of all three of them.

---

[38] Torrey, *Surviving Schizophrenia*, p. 29.

14 Catch-22

October 28, 2007

Danny has strep throat, so I spend several hours with him at the emergency room. I'm embarrassed to find that I'm practically giddy over the occasion. It's so rare to be in a hospital with only a medical problem to deal with.

October 29, 2007

Alex and I make a trip to the apartment he lived in for only five weeks. We leave the dining room table and TV for the other residents to use. The Chinese-speaking landlord is displeased about the TV, and refuses to return the rent deposit until we come and remove it. Whenever I call, it takes a miracle of communication to understand his accent, and it's almost Christmas before I can finally arrange to meet at the apartment.

I head up to the second floor with the landlord and carry the television downstairs with ease, which makes it all the more puzzling that he would wait two months for someone else to remove it. In any event, he finally returns the deposit, minus two weeks of rent, since Alex failed to provide two weeks' notice that he was vacating his room. OK, sure. It's true that he didn't give notice. But isn't part of the definition of a crisis that you don't know it's coming two weeks in advance? Under the circumstances, I hoped the man might make an exception. But, looking into his expressionless eyes, I sensed that it just wasn't in him. It's odd, though, the way money seems to trump everything else. Even at Christmas.

November 7, 2007

Alex arranges to stay with two of his U of B friends in their two-bedroom apartment. They charge him $300 a month to sleep on the living room sofa. He also has access to a closet. Period. Most of his furniture returns to Joey's basement. He does attend the day program recommended to him in the hospital and finds it both informative and encouraging. Ultimately, he moves all his medical care and records to that clinic, and continues in counseling even after the day program ends. He has no problem taking the prescribed medication and seems glad for the support he's receiving. Slowly things become a little easier, and Alex is able to think about the future with a small reservoir of hope.

November 30, 2007

"All your base are belong to us."[39]

Getting Danny into Boston-based supported housing has turned into a bureaucratic nightmare, a fiasco worthy of the theater of the absurd. To get into a DMH-supervised house in the city of Boston (aka The Promised Land), you must first pass through the Slough of Despond. If you succeed, you will

---

[39]1991 European Sega Mega Drive version of the video game *Zero Wing* by Toaplan.

arrive at the door of the Boston Housing Authority (aka Evil Empire), where you must prove that you are (a) truly homeless and (b) genuinely disabled. This is hard to manage when you've just been up to your neck in the Slough, but never mind.

Danny's application to BHS went in on Sept. 1, 2007. By mid-October, with no word from anyone, he had arranged to rent the room he's in now on a month-to-month basis. He's paid through today, November 30th, but doesn't have enough funds to pay for December, so he's moving out this evening.

As fate would have it, BHA calls on this very day to say that Danny's application for public housing has been approved (cue the angelic hosannas)! He just needs to come in and sign the final papers. When they ask the million-dollar question: "So where are you living now?" Danny says he's living in a room that he's rented by the month for about six weeks. When BHA learns that he has a place to live, if only until the end of the day, they declare that he's not officially homeless after all, and revoke his housing voucher then and there. It's not called the Slough of Despond for nothing.

Danny's case worker urges us not to despair. A letter from BHA announcing their negative decision will arrive in the mail in a few days. As soon as we have the letter, we can file an appeal. There's no reason for the appeal to be denied, since Danny is no longer renting a private apartment. Mercifully, DMH offers him a bed in a respite house while he waits for the appeal. This worries me. "If he has a place to live, won't they just deny his application again?" "Not at all! Living in a respite house qualifies as being homeless."

In other words, on Nov. 30th Danny is homeless, having no place to live the following day, but he's not *officially* homeless. On December 1st, when he's living in a lovely Victorian house with free food in the refrigerator, he *is* officially homeless. I keep looking around for the Mad Hatter.

We wait through the month of December with baited breath for the letter from BHA, though nobody knows when or even where it will be sent. It feels like waiting for Godot. Perhaps BHA sent the letter to Danny's former apartment address. No one there tells him he has mail, but I suspect it might be there anyway. However, our many calls to the young woman who arranged the rental are unreturned.

After several fruitless trips to that apartment and numerous phone calls, we discover that the woman in question has left for a two-month visit to Peru and has locked all her things in her room. Those things include all of Danny's mail. There is no getting into her room until she returns and no phone number where we can reach her. Without the letter, we can't mount the appeal (or so we are told). Checkmate.

Danny asks for another copy of the letter to be sent, this time to our home address. A troll at the Evil Empire insists that this constitutes an official change of address on his application, and changes of address must be made *in person* at Empire headquarters in downtown Boston. So, on a January day when the temperature bottoms out at two degrees and the wind chill is minus fifteen, Danny wanders the streets near the Boston Common searching for the headquarters of BHA. Frozen and forlorn, he finds it at last, fifteen minutes before closing.

But trolls are not easily appeased. Now he's told that the change of address is moot, as there *is* no appealing the decision made in November. (Apparently not everyone received that memo, since we've waited these past five weeks for our chance to file said appeal.) Rather we must begin again,

213

filing a *new* application and awaiting BHA's decision once more. Wailing and gnashing of teeth are heard in all the land.

December 2007

On December 1st, I go with Danny to the ill-fated apartment to clean his room and move his clothes and furnishings. Some I bring to our house and others we give away. Our next stop is the respite house. Danny shares a room on the third floor with another client of DMH, a fifty-year-old disabled alcoholic who is frequently off the wagon, but who also creates beautiful abstract drawings using only construction paper and crayons. I purchase one and have it framed as a Christmas gift for Danny.

The other room on floor three is occupied by a thirtyish, heavy-set woman with severe paranoia. She bickers regularly with staff members and often calls the police to complain about them, accusing them of threatening to harm her or one of the other residents. There are curfews and smoking restrictions, and Danny is not allowed to administer his own medications. On the other hand, he's not allowed to *miss* any doses of his medications, which makes for a rather demanding schedule of appearances at the appointed times of day. Still, I'm grateful that this introduces some stability into Danny's therapeutic plan.

The respite bed is supposed to be only temporary—a brief stopgap measure until the problem with BHA is straightened out. As it turns out, Danny lives there for three months, even though classes at U of B begin on January 14th. It is Dr. Ogunde's worst nightmare. But Danny insists on going ahead with his plan to start college. It's been 2 ½ years since he was supposed to receive his diploma, and those years have been a sojourn on the brink of hell. A new start is long overdue.

Would there be an apartment in the vicinity of U of B that Danny could afford on his SSI income? Not a chance. As for public housing, the Promised Land seems farther away than ever—perhaps Danny will never reach it. We decide to call a truce with the Empire for now, perhaps taking up arms again in the summer.

January 2008

But wait! On January 10th rumor reaches our ears that it may yet be possible to appeal BHA's earlier decision to deny Danny's application. Don't we need the letter? Oh no, we are told. (What?!!) Just call this number and offer your grounds for the appeal, letter or no letter. But (there's always a catch) do it *today* (Jan. 10th), because the appeal must be made within thirty days of the date on the letter, which (we just now learn) was December 12th. Yikes! Mobilize the troops! All hands on deck! Danny is marshaled to make the required phone call to the specified number, exactly these thirty days after Dec. 12th. And . . . nothing.

It's not the *phone call* silly! You have to send an appeal *in writing*! What about the thirty-day deadline though? Ohhhh . . . well, as a matter of fact, you've already missed it, since thirty days from Dec. 12th is January 9th, not the 10th. But let's see . . . yes, you can *still* file your appeal, including a further explanation of why you missed the deadline, and it's just possible your appeal will still be considered. No guarantees of course. How long will that take? Three weeks or so. Or, as the next person we called told us, thirty days. Or . . . well, just pick a number. Oh, and Danny needs an official document certifying that he is indeed homeless. (Where are homeless people supposed to get such a document? We seem to be playing roles in a very dark comedy.)

We decide to continue on both fronts, mounting an appeal of BHA's earlier decision and sending in a new application as well. The DMH case worker will complete the certification of homelessness status for Danny. However, *that* form requires a detailed accounting of every place Danny has lived for more than a month over the past three years, complete with dates, addresses, contact phone numbers, and reasons for leaving.

Hours later, with a few gaps, I am able to create a list that goes back to January of 2005 when Danny was still a senior at the charter school and living at home. There are thirteen entries. Reasons for leaving range from parents' decision (too painful to discuss) through loss of jobs, vandalism, and assault, to drug violations and involuntary hospitalizations. Will the story end with supervised housing in the Promised Land? Somehow it doesn't seem so likely any more. But we soldier on with the application process.

BHA claims they can "fast-track" the application this time, since the background check has already been done. How to get on the elusive fast track? Yes, you guessed it! There's another form—the fast-track form! Do we fill it out? No. The manager at the Promised Land? No, not exactly. Then who? The people who *own* the Promised Land. The manager must get that form and send it to the property owners, who must then fill it out and send it to the headquarters of the Empire. *Then* you'll be on the fast track. (Get it? There *is* no fast track! Laughter all around.)

January 11, 2008

Danny's therapist Dr. Ogunde calls to berate me for even thinking Danny can start classes at U of B without a permanent place to live. He backs off only when I inform him that Danny can put off starting at U of B until the summer or even the fall if he wants to. It's his decision to start in January, not ours. A few days later, Danny decides he should probably postpone U of B, waiting for his housing to be resolved before taking on the stress of college classes and a long commute. Two days later he changes his mind again and enrolls in four classes.

According to Dr. Ogunde, we're setting Danny up for a major disappointment, and should at least be paying for room and board on campus or an apartment near the school. (It's unclear how we are supposed to finance this. Maybe Danny misled him about the extent of our resources.)

Dr. Ogunde is clearly a man with little experience of the "social services" available to the mentally ill. Even if we could find the money to pay for Danny's housing during the school year, it would make him ineligible to live in the Promised Land if and when his application succeeds. Catch-22. It's becoming a very familiar game for us.

.January 14, 2008

With Danny voicing concerns but still insisting on working for his goals, I decide to go against the advice of Damian, Dr. Ogunde, Joan, and Dr. Christianson, and help Danny register for four classes at U of B. Again, there's the major expenditure for books and supplies—$500 this time—knowing it may all be for naught.

But seeing Danny's face on the first day of school as he heads toward class, sporting new clothes and new shoes, and carrying his laptop computer (a graduation gift) in its matching briefcase, makes all the effort and sacrifice of the last three years melt into the snow. There goes my son, a freshman at the University of Boston. Just a normal kid, doing what other twenty-year-olds are doing, with pride and hope in his eyes for the first time in years.

Timeout: Waters of Peace

January 31, 2008

Last night I took the medication my primary-care doctor prescribed for the pain caused by shingles, an affliction that set in two weeks ago and is departing with a final spasm of agonizing pain at the site of the infection. As the pain medicine began to take effect, I felt myself relaxing and growing calmer, tensions and anxieties gradually disappearing along with the pain. I realized that it's been years since I felt this way—totally relaxed and at peace.

These moments of calm and clarity gave me opportunity to reflect on the many ways God has blessed my life and the lives of my family. Damian and I spent yesterday together, going first to the clinic, then to the post office and pharmacy, dividing our errand list so we could finish quickly and get in on the lunch special at Uno's. Then home to rest, work a little, dine on soup and crackers with brie, and spend some time with our daughter.

Suddenly I was overwhelmed with a deep sense of gratitude for these things—for the comfortable relationship between Damian and me these days; for Danny having a place to move into soon, and doing well at school and making some new friends; for Joey's success at work and his desire to deepen his education by reading great books and exploring classical music; for Alex finding the courage to read his poems at the local coffee shop on open mike nights; for Lily's confidence and compassion and wonderful smile.

God has truly showered me with so many amazing graces. It's been a long time (years?) since all I wanted to say to God was "Thank-you." But last night, I was given a brief glimpse of his faithfulness—his presence with me, even at the edge of the abyss.

The Psalms are my constant companion on this journey— putting my grief into words, and reminding me that God is my strength and shield. These one hundred and fifty prayers and songs, written so many centuries ago, speak to me and for me in countless ways, as though the author was reading not only my mind, but also the depths of my heart.

In the small copy I carry, the Psalms are divided into five books. The first four are filled with the turbulence of life—fears, sorrows, sins, and enemies. The Lord comes to the rescue in these Psalms, at least in the long run—healing, consoling, defending, and forgiving. Still, it's clear that we're in the heat of a fierce battle, and our enemies often seem to have the upper hand.

But the fifth book of Psalms begins with these words: "O give thanks to the Lord, for he is good; for his steadfast love endures forever,"[40] and ends as it began: "Let everything that

---

[40] Psalm 107:1.

has breath praise the Lord! Alleluia."[41] These last psalms are full of gratitude, recalling God's mighty deeds in times past and his providential care for his people. It's as if the turmoil of the earlier books has been caught up into the Lord's peace; not dissolved, but transformed. A divine alchemy has turned the suffering and sorrow into gold. May it be true for each of us that, in the last chapter of our lives, all our prayers are praise.

---

[41] Psalm 150:6.

15 Pinball Wizard

March 1, 2008

At last DMH finds a permanent housing arrangement for Danny, a two-bedroom duplex that's close to public transit and only a ten-minute walk from our house. He has just one roommate who spends virtually all his time with his girlfriend in another town, so Danny usually has the place to himself. The house sits well back from the street in a quiet neighborhood, flanked closely by other duplexes that are either attached to one another or separated by just a few yards.

There's a covered porch across the front of the building and Danny is allowed to smoke there. His bedroom is quite large, with windows on three sides that let in plenty of natural light. Most of the apartment is recently painted, there are several new pieces of furniture, and the kitchen is fully furnished. Given the amount of space, I offer to help Danny set up his drum set in his room. It faces the back of the apartment and is separated by a high fence from a parking lot. Also, that side of the house is several yards away from the closest neighbors.

221

I reason that if Danny limits his playing to daytime hours, most of the neighbors will be at work and it won't be a problem for them. Stupid? Yes it was. Looking back, I'm sure I ignored the obvious problems with this plan because I wanted so much for Danny to be able to play. The drums were a graduation gift, but he hasn't been able to use them in almost three years. I hoped playing again would be good therapy for him, something positive that would fill some of the lonely hours in his day and make him feel better about himself.

Danny's food stamps cover his groceries, and the apartment costs only 35% of his income, so he has enough money to take care of himself now. His medical care and prescriptions are free of charge. All that remains is the daily struggle—to stay clean and sober, keep his scheduled appointments with the psychiatrist and probation officer, take his medications on time, cope with their unpleasant side effects and the symptoms they never fully suppress, fight against loneliness and despair, overlook people's negative comments and faces filled with fear or disgust, believe that it's possible to make real friends, and dare to hope that, someday, he will find someone to love who will love him back.

Danny asks me sometimes, less often now, but still with the same concern in his voice, "Will I be OK, Mom? Will I ever be able to have a normal life?" "Of course you will," I assure him. "You will always have some challenges to deal with, but I think you can learn to manage them so that you'll have a good life." It's what I believe. But I suppose it's also what I have to believe. And, please God, let it be true.

March 1 – May 31, 2008

Danny lives contentedly in his apartment for three months, commuting to the University of Boston for classes and entertaining friends in his new place. On one of the case worker's routine visits to the apartment, Danny's friend Charlie answers the door with a beer in his hand, so Danny receives a housing violation for having alcohol in the house, but this isn't treated as a major infraction. Sometimes he plays his drums, pleased that he hasn't lost a feel for the rhythms and happy to have an acceptable way to blow off steam or ease his anxiety.

However, Danny's happiness is inversely related to the happiness of his neighbors—one of those paradoxes of utilitarianism. The woman who shares the long porch with Danny is afraid of him. It's not clear whether this is based on something he did or general nervousness about living next door to a young black man with a mental illness. Danny is not allowed to smoke in the apartment, so he smokes outside on the porch instead, sitting on an overstuffed chair and using a sand-filled bucket for an ashtray. He makes calls to friends and family from the porch, since he gets a better signal outside, and in these winter months he often feels lonely sitting by himself in the cold and dark.

But one neighbor complains that, when Danny is out on the porch at night, smoke drifts into his open bedroom window—which happens to be located only about twenty feet from the porch. Also, Danny's phone conversations in the middle of the night are too loud, disturbing his sleep. As for the drums, they simply have to go. The landlord owns this entire configuration of apartments, and is trying manfully to make everybody happy. He and Danny meet several times to discuss the neighbors' complaints and what adjustments he can make to keep them satisfied.

But Danny grows increasingly frustrated with the many restrictions this involves. There is no space at the back of the apartment, so if he's going to smoke outside, it has to be in the front. And unless he goes to bed as early as everyone else, he'll sometimes be smoking when the neighbors are sleeping. He tries to speak more quietly on the phone, but often forgets.

During one late-night phone conversation with Danny, in an effort to help, I ask, "Do you think you can speak more quietly, Danny? You're almost shouting right now." "Oh, yeah. Sorry, Mom. It's just hard sometimes." "You mean it's hard to talk quietly?" "Well, yeah." "What makes it hard?" "Um, it's just that a lot of times I hear other voices in my head and I get confused about what I'm trying to say. So sometimes I have to talk louder so I know which voice is mine." "Oh. . . . I'm sorry, Son. That must be really hard." "Yeah. But it's ok. I'm used to it, you know?"

Actually, no. I didn't know. Over the years of Danny's illness, I experience numerous moments like this. They bring me up short and make me realize how little I understand what his life is like. I only see the outside; what is it like to live on the inside? I'm reminded of a line from one of my favorite poets: "O the mind, mind has mountains, cliffs of fall frightful, sheer, no-man-fathomed. Hold them cheap may who ne'er hung there."[42]

May 12, 2008

Yesterday was Mother's Day. Lily and I drove out to a beautiful reservoir west of the city to explore the trail along its edge. We even climbed over the fence to take a forbidden dip in the cool, crystal clear water, our underclothes substituting for swimsuits. Later that evening my husband surprised me by taking the family out to dinner at a very elegant restaurant. It was a lovely

---

[42] Gerard Manley Hopkins, "No Worst, There is None," in W. H. Gardner, Poems of Gerard Manley Hopkins, 3rd ed. (New York: Oxford, 1948), pp. 106-7.

setting and a delicious gourmet meal. Only Danny was missing. Sometimes he has a hard time knowing who is on his side.

It's been a trying month, but also one of new lights and new hope. In spite of everything, Danny will pass two classes at U of B and is already registered for two summer courses and four more in the fall. So he has begun, and is on his way to his future at last. Admittedly, it's still a little uncertain what that future holds.

June 1 – July 16, 2008

At the end of May, Danny is forced to leave his apartment. The neighbors have complained so often and loudly to the landlord that he tells DMH to remove Danny or lose the lease. There is space for now in a group home located near a shopping mall and train station, so Danny is told he will have to move there for the next few days, pending a transfer to something more permanent. It's a short-term solution at best, since DMH is vacating that property by the end of the month.

Half of Danny's belongings are still in his apartment, and we have to arrange for the case worker to let us in if we want to retrieve them. The staff at the swiftly-shrinking group home seem to have vacated already. I never see them engaged in an actual activity. Danny is given a room in the attic that is suffocatingly hot and ankle-deep in used coffee cups, old newspapers, discarded clothes, broken furniture, and dust.

I do what I can to sweep up the dirt and get rid of the trash, but the condition of the kitchen and bathrooms is abominable, and there's nothing I can do about those. The staff seem oddly indifferent to these conditions, as well as to the residents, who wander in and out like sheep without a shepherd. Disputes among them go unresolved. I try not to see this pitiful, dilapidated house as a forecast of Danny's future.

July 16 – August 20, 2008

When the little house of horrors finally closes, Danny moves back to the respite house where he had lived earlier in the year. On August 20th, a fire on the first floor forces the evacuation of all the residents. No one is allowed to go back inside to retrieve his belongings. In fact, it is six weeks before Danny can recover his clothes and shoes. Meanwhile, the residents are housed at a nearby hotel for two nights, then moved to a different hotel that is closer to public transportation.

August 20 – September 15, 2008

Danny shares the hotel room with his new roommate from the respite house, a young man close to his age who suffers from hearing and speech difficulties. DMH purchases a different house in the same neighborhood and begins renovating it to prepare for the return of the residents of Hotel Respite, who are living large on catered food and cable TV. Their only burden is that they have to wear the same clothes every day.

One day, Danny and his friend take the bus to the station where they will catch a train to downtown Boston. When they reach the station, Danny jumps off the bus without taking his backpack, which is carrying his notebook computer. He realizes it almost immediately, and contacts the dispatcher at the T station, who tells him that they don't try to recover lost items. "Don't you have security cameras in all the buses?" "Yes, but the police use those to arrest anyone who attacks the driver or the other passengers." "Can't they use them to see who walked off with my backpack?" "No, sorry. We don't do that. It violates passenger privacy."

Later I phone the transit authority and police department to question this policy. The dispatcher at Sullivan Station finally agrees to ask the bus driver from that day and time if he found a backpack with a computer in it. Of course the answer is no.

September 15 – November 2, 2008

When the new respite house is ready, most of the hotel crowd relocate there or to another DMH group home. But Danny seems to be out of chances. His only option is a room at an SRO (Single-Room Occupancy building) operating on one side of the Cambridge YMCA. The Y offers no on-site social services and support of any kind is available only from 8 to 5 on weekdays. At the respite house, a staff member dispensed Danny's medications twice a day. Now he is expected to handle the meds on his own.

Fifty men share the bathroom facility at the end of the hall. There is no common room and no kitchen, but Danny is expected to prepare his own meals. He uses some of his SSI money and we throw in a few dollars to purchase a mini-fridge and microwave for his room. I pick up another coffee pot and toaster, hoping to make life at the Y feel more normal. With a few milk crates to hold the groceries and household supplies, Danny's small space begins to look more like a dorm room and less like a prison cell.

Timeout: Corrective Lenses

One of the most positive developments in the nearly five years since Danny became ill is that the media are paying much more attention to the problem of mental illness, trying to create greater knowledge and greater compassion for those who live with these difficult diseases. Mainstream media outlets are giving more attention to this issue than ever before, working to help overcome the stigma that sticks to Danny and millions of others like a second skin.

In the opening chapter of his book on schizophrenia, Dr. E. Fuller Torrey explains that in order to sympathize with other people, we must understand them, at least to some extent—we must be able to put ourselves in their place. Sadly, Torrey continues, "Because there is little understanding of schizophrenia, so there is little sympathy," and "the paucity of sympathy for those with schizophrenia makes it that much more of a disaster."

The good news is that it's possible to arrive at a deeper understanding of this disease, which in turn makes it possible to sympathize with friends and loved ones affected by it. Torrey contends, "The best way to learn what a person with schizophrenia experiences is to listen to someone with the disease."[43]

This is the goal of a series that appears in the online *New York Times* health and wellness section. The series focuses on a different mental illness each week—Alzheimer's, Bipolar Disorder, Autism, etc. Each column includes a link to short videos in which the people interviewed for the article describe their experiences in their own words.

News programs like this one are among the best things going for people who struggle with mental illness. As you watch these men and women speak about their lives, you recognize them as ordinary people who were struck with an illness that is extremely difficult to treat and often hell to endure. They are not the stereotypical "crazies" with electric-shock-hair that appear distressingly often in movies, on television, and even in Saturday morning cartoons.

It can be tempting, in some cases, to reduce a person to his or her illness, especially if it's what is most obvious or visible about them. Once labeled, we can lump them into a category with others who are similarly afflicted, and it's a short step from there to broad generalizations about the group as a whole. Since many people suffering from mental illnesses are not adequately cared for, they can easily become poster children for virtually every socially stigmatized group. They are the unkempt homeless, chronically unemployed, weirdos, and beggars that litter our sidewalks and interrupt our trips in and out of the drug store.

---

[43] Torrey, *Surviving Schizophrenia*, 2-3.

But no one is an illness, and surely a person's illness is the least interesting or important thing about him. The challenge is to see beyond appearances and get to know the individual who is trying to make sense of a fractured life. When we do, we find ourselves thinking of that person as Sophie or Mark rather than as a mental patient. In the same way, to listen to the people Karen Barrow interviews is get to know them, at least a little, and to recognize them as our brothers and sisters who are on a very difficult journey.[44]

****

"Few mental illnesses are as complex and confusing as schizophrenia, a mental disorder in which people may experience hallucinations or delusions, hear voices or have confused thinking and behavior.

Although the word "schizophrenia" means "split mind," the disorder does not cause a split personality, as is commonly believed.

The latest Patient Voices segment by Karen Barrow, a Web producer, offers rare insights into schizophrenia and schizoaffective disorder, a related condition that combines thinking and mood problems, as seven men and women share their experiences.

---

[44] Tara Parker-Pope, "The Voices of Schizophrenia," *The New York Times,* Health Section, September 15, 2010, available at *http://well.blogs.nytimes.com/2010/09/15/the-voices-of-schizophrenia/.*

'It disrupted my education, my relationships, it disrupted friendships,' explains Alita Van Hee, 32, of Santa Cruz, Calif. 'I was so bombarded by voices. They would tell me things like "Don't trust these people," "Don't talk to your friends," "They're not real friends," things like that. It's kind of like having a TV or radio on blasting inside your head just all the time that you can't turn off no matter what you do.'

You'll also meet Michael Runningwolf, 40, of Tempe, Ariz., who wants to change people's perceptions and fears about schizophrenia. 'I wish I could get a T-shirt that says, "We're more afraid of you than you are of us,"' he says. 'There are people with schizophrenia every day that are doing things to break down the stigma. They hold down jobs, and they're out there every day giving it everything they've got. Even though schizophrenia is a disabling illness, it's not the end. There is recovery.'

Susan Weinreich, 54, of Mount Kisco, N.Y., says that although her illness has made life difficult, it also has become part of her art. 'I believe my art was a vehicle for me to be able to express some things that were very deep, deep down inside and that were trapped and difficult to get out and communicate,' she says.

Another artist, John Cadigan, 40, who is Ms. Van Hee's partner, says the challenges of his illness have also played a role in his art. 'The difficulty is I'm not always cognizant of what reality is,' he says. 'I can't trust my own brain…. When you have a brain disorder, it unlocks parts of the brain I think normal people don't have any knowledge of. I think I translate that into my woodcuts.'

To hear these and other stories of schizophrenia, go to *www.nytimes.com/interactive/2010/09/16/health/healthguide/te_s chizophrenia.html*."

16 Meltdown

November 2, 2008, Sunday

After three weeks at the Y, Danny quits taking his medications altogether. Zyprexa makes him groggy, so it's difficult for him to get up in the morning, and he's put on a lot of weight as a side effect of Haldol. His new psychiatrist at the Arbour Counseling Center, Dr. Botkin, refuses to change either the medication or the dosage. Danny pleads with her every month to re-evaluate the meds, complaining that Zyprexa doesn't make a dent in his psychotic symptoms and only serves to "zombify" him so much that he barely has a life.

After three months, Dr. Botkin finally agrees to *consider* making a small reduction in the dose of Zyprexa. But (there's always a "but") she won't make any adjustments at all for the next six months. Danny is disgusted, frustrated, and furious. He can't believe that his doctor, the person entrusted with conforming his treatment to his symptoms, has ignored every iota of feedback from her "client," stubbornly refusing even to consider the possibility that her treatment plan *isn't working*.

Predictably, Danny gives up on the whole mental health establishment. He stops his medications as a form of protest against the implacable Botkin. Her betrayal (as he sees it), combined with the creeping paranoia that advances as his medication recedes, makes him deeply suspicious of everyone—doctors, social workers, therapists, even his family and friends. He tells me that he's sick and tired of being told what to do, of being pushed around from square to square on the DMH checkerboard, of being told on a daily basis what he's doing wrong. Most of all, he's tired of failing. He feels that his life has been ripped out of his hands and parceled out to a continuous parade of well-meaning "providers" who cycle through his life like horses on a carousel.

As I listen to Danny describe his deepening despair and helplessness, the fear that always gnaws in secret on the ragged edges of my heart threatens to burst from its heavily-defended fortress and utterly consume me. Danny and I have always understood each other effortlessly, knowing that we are kindred souls, attuned to the emotions and sensibilities of those around us and unable to treat them with indifference or steel our hearts against them.

When I visit Danny at the Y, bringing socks or candy or forms for him to sign, I read his face and see the fear and isolation and inconsolable sorrow that draw him ever closer to the abyss. Until now, he has held onto hope in the future, in a life free from the demons that taunt him and poison his thoughts. But hope is slipping away from him now, and mine recedes with it like the outgoing tide. Is there no one to pull my son back from the edge?

In the crises that have punctuated our lives over these past few years, I've usually been able to turn to a doctor or case worker who had been working with Danny and knew him fairly well. But when he moved to the Y, DMH transferred his case to a different contractor. I know nothing about them. In fact, I didn't know that DMH "subbed out" its clients to an array of independent contractors, and that decisions to move a client from here to there are made without consulting the client and even without notifying him or her. So far, no representative of "Under New Management" has appeared at the Y. "We're small," they explain, as if that means anything to me, and I still don't know what role they play in the lunatic stage production we call the mental health system. Like visitors to Oz, you keep wanting to look behind the curtain.

Around this same time, Joan, the DMH case manager who has worked with Danny for eighteen months, was promoted to a supervisory position. Her replacement is a kind, experienced, and capable woman, and Joan assures us that she will still be in touch with Danny in her supervisory role. We never hear from her again. Nor do we hear from her replacement. Apparently, someone from UNM is supposed to take up this role.

Dr. Ogunde, Danny's therapist, refuses to communicate with anyone—Danny, me, DMH—even the other doctors who are trying to continue his treatment. It's the one area in which he's been perfectly consistent, proving to be an equal-opportunity pompous ass. Even Danny's probation officer seems content to ignore him for the time being; her caseload is running over with so many others who require constant scrutiny.

When Danny's siblings find out that he has quit taking his medications, they steadfastly refuse to see him, and Damian feels the same way. But I can't bring myself to abandon him now. I have to know how he is faring, for better or worse. I have to try every way I can think of to reach him—to make him know that he is loved. I realize now that I would gladly give my life in exchange for his comfort and peace; not because of some special virtue in me, but just because I am his mother. Every mother I know would make the same choice without a moment's hesitation.

Danny remains adamantly opposed to receiving help from anyone, and grows increasingly anxious and irritable. Last Wednesday, he came by the house unannounced, looking for food and money. He said he would contact me the next day about picking up his weekly spending allowance a day early. But I didn't hear from him that day, or the next, or the next. Since he usually calls at least once a day, I'm beginning to worry that something serious might have happened to him. Surely he wants to get his money for the week. But all my calls go straight to his voicemail. It's Sunday, and no one has heard from Danny for four days. We attend mass in the morning as usual, but by the time it ends I am beside myself with anxiety and dread. Is my son in a hospital? a prison? the morgue?

Damian and I have plans to stroll along the Charles River after the service. The Head of the Charles rowing competition takes place this weekend and the crowds along the river's edge are treated to free food samples, live music, and hot apple cider. It's a beautiful day and I know Damian really looks forward to joining the festivities. But I am worried sick about my son, and can think of nothing else until I know where he is. So, at my insistence, Damian and I walk first to the Y to see if Danny is in.

We're told he's in his room—so at least he's still alive, thank God. When Danny comes downstairs to the lobby, he is so pale and gaunt that I barely recognize him. The anguish in his heart is written on his face, and I can barely maintain the casual manner I'm determined to project. I offer him the envelope with his weekly allowance, hoping it will open the door to his dungeon, if only just a crack.

235

His expression offers no encouragement on that front, but I soldier on with my plan to re-connect with him over something—anything. "Danny, I know you're really fed up with Dr. Botkin, and I can't blame you. I was wondering if you'd like me to help you find a different doctor, someone who actually listens. He might be able to find a medication that would work a lot better for you." No response. I should have quit while I was ahead, but my garrulous nature abhors a vacuum. "I just heard about a clinic near our house that is supposed to be really great—more like a house than a medical facility."

Meanwhile, Danny is growing increasingly agitated and angry, and suddenly he shouts over me with pure venom in his voice: "Look Mom, why don't you just stop talking? I'm the only one who knows what I need! You don't know *anything about me*! I mean, you wouldn't take my advice about *your* medications, so you should stop giving *me* advice!" By now he is inches from my face and virtually screaming: "**You never really cared about me anyway!**"

It's a body blow, and I fall back reeling. I want more than anything to be able to pick him up as I did when he was small, holding him on my lap until the fire subsides into coals. But today my very presence only adds fuel to the flames. Damian has been standing by silently until now, but at this unprovoked verbal attack, he steps toward Danny, giving him a look that could melt the paint off the walls, "You have no business talking to your mother like that. You're out of control . . ." He is cut off by a string of curses screamed into his face and shouted after him as he turns to go. "Listen, Dad, I don't f***ing care what you think! You're such a f***ing asshole! As if you ever gave a *shit* about me!"

Suddenly I'm aware of the silence. Everyone in the lobby, from the disheveled homeless men sunk into the ancient sofas to the young women waiting for the mommy-and-me swim class, is riveted to this astonishing barrage of hatred and contempt, hurled into the faces of two bewildered, middle-aged academics dressed in their Sunday clothes. We seem to have become the event du jour. Damian is already wheeling around to find the door and, helpless to withstand the hurricane, I walk away too, with Danny's accusations still ringing in my ears. Our exit feels weirdly anti-climactic.

I follow Damian out onto the sunlit autumn sidewalk, where the air smells wonderful—crisp and fresh, with the scent of fall leaves and fireplaces. So why can't I breathe?

Damian is deeply troubled by this experience, seeing the whole visit as unnecessary and predictably counterproductive. As happens so often, we are pulled apart by our conflicting reactions to Danny's illness. I know too that the rest of the day will be ruined for us because of this sad encounter with our son. But I simply had to know. Even if my worst fears were confirmed, that would be easier to bear than the gnawing dread and uncertainty.

November 3, 2009, Monday

The day after our visit, perhaps prompted by it, Danny's newly-assigned case worker from UNM comes to see him. She is a soft-spoken young woman, probably just out of college, filled with optimism and a desire to do good. Sadly, she is greeted by a client who is very ill and very angry, and bears the brunt of a belligerent, oath-laden barrage from Danny.

Overhearing this "exchange of views," the staff at the Y begin to realize that Danny is out of control. They hadn't witnessed his conversation with us on Sunday, but they'd probably been told about it. Not knowing what to do next, the young case

237

worker calls for backup from one of the senior staff members at
UNM, an older woman with more experience but no more
success with Danny. Refusing to answer any questions and
growing increasingly agitated, Danny finally stomps out of the
room, muttering some unpleasant opinions about the women
who have come to help him.

The case workers and YMCA staff opt to call the police and
have Danny taken to the nearest hospital for an evaluation.
Meanwhile, Danny has decided he needs something to eat. He
puts a hot pocket in the microwave and takes it out while it's
still too hot, burning his right hand rather seriously. Furious, he
flings the offending pastry against the wall, then begins
throwing other objects after it. When he heaves a metal coffee
can toward the wall, it shatters the window instead, sending
shards of glass around the room and onto the street three
stories below.

Inspired by the resulting crash, Danny begins to pitch
everything he can get his hands on through the window—cell
phone, coffee mug, desk lamp, even the flat-screen computer
monitor he had just acquired the week before. Some weeks
later I ask Danny if he was tempted to throw himself out too. He
admits that he had thought about it, and had even tried to climb
out the window. But between its small size and the broken
glass everywhere, he couldn't manage it. When the police and
ambulance arrive, the staff at the Y convince Danny to go with
them willingly to the Psych ER.

Oblivious to all of this, I sleep late today, exhausted from the
emotional strain of Sunday's events. Alex has spent the night
at our house, since yesterday was the one-year anniversary of
his suicide attempt and we don't want him to be alone. He
continues to struggle with depression and anxiety, but has a
good therapist and some helpful medication and significant

insight into his illness. He has held a full-time job for a month, a promising step for him. We talk for three hours about his financial situation and plans for the future.

Following that conversation, my hand is on the doorknob to leave for my daughter's soccer game when the phone rings. The UNM social worker informs me that Danny is at the hospital; the police have taken him there by ambulance. As has happened so many times, my daughter's needs are put on hold as I rush to the hospital instead.

Arriving around 3:00 pm, I find Danny speaking earnestly to a social worker, conning the guy into releasing him to the hospital's day program. Since the social worker leaves for the day at 4:30, he is in a rush to get the necessary paperwork done. He explains that he has no time to speak with me privately, and continues to come and go at random intervals. Whenever he enters, Danny sits up on the examination table and puts on an impressive show of normalcy, assuring this man that he will be happy to participate in the partial hospital program if only they will discharge him. Eventually the social worker comes to the end of his shift. He leaves and we stay, awaiting a signature from the psychiatrist.

When she arrives two hours later, Danny is already fixed on leaving the hospital. By now it is 7:00 and he is hungry and sorely in need of a cigarette. The psychiatrist leaves us alone for a while longer. While we wait, I notice Danny is exhibiting clear psychotic symptoms. His thinking is scattered and unfocused, and he mouths severe scoldings to someone I cannot see. The psychiatrist has picked up on this as well, so she is reluctant to release him. She and I make some unsuccessful attempts to convince him to spend a few days as an inpatient, perhaps at the Arbour Hospital since they allow smoking breaks. No go.

239

In the end, she simply decides to discharge him. I am stunned. She insists that she lacks sufficient grounds for keeping Danny in the hospital against his will, since he is not an immediate danger to himself or others. I counter that if someone is throwing large appliances out a third-floor window, he is at least a danger to others if not to himself. Besides, he cannot take proper care of himself in his current condition and there's no way he will show up for the day program at the hospital. But the doctor is adamant. She keeps repeating the "imminent danger" clause, and I have the impression she's inviting me to make something up—yes, Danny has threatened to kill himself; yes, he's threatened to harm me and I'm afraid of him.

I know the drill. Others in my NAMI group have explained that sometimes you have to lie in order to get help for your loved one. I wonder whether a false statement in these circumstances even counts as I lie. But I'm too tired and disgusted to play games right now. So at 8:00, Danny and I leave the hospital and begin our rounds—to Burger King for something to eat, to Target for a prescription and a new cell phone, to the Seven-Eleven for cigarettes. I know I'm just going through the motions, but I don't know what else to do. The cell phone disappears the next day and, as predicted, Danny never returns to the hospital. He continues to insist that he doesn't need any doctors or medication "The doctors don't pay attention to me, Mom, and they don't care about me either."

The fear that stays deep inside my heart grabs hold in earnest now. My son is on the verge of a psychotic break, and no one will help him. All the hospitals and doctors and social workers— the so-called "providers" of mental health services—what good are they? Why do they abandon the patients most in need of their services so often and so easily? It seems everyone who winds up in a psychiatric emergency room has to audition for a place on the in-patient team. Dr. Hart, my therapist and friend, keeps telling me I have to learn how to yell, to go postal sometimes, so I can get their attention. But I just can't do it. Years of past abuse taught me never to provoke a strong reaction in anyone—things might turn ugly.

Still, I hate it that I can't make doctors listen to me even after four and a half years of dealing with them. It feels like my failure as much as theirs. How do you keep from hating yourself when you can't get your child even what help the professionals have to offer? I try repeating the mantra others have offered to stave off the guilt: "There was nothing else you could do." But that's not the point. *Why* isn't there anything else I can do? Why isn't there something *somebody* can do? And buried underneath those questions, Why doesn't *God* take better care of my vulnerable son? "Isn't he your son too, Lord?"

November 5, 2008, Wednesday

Danny has missed several classes at the University of Boston, so he's decided to withdraw from school and look for a job instead. Today, since his phone isn't working, I decide to stop by the Y to see if he's in. He isn't, but a half-hour conversation with one of the staff reveals that his window has been patched with cardboard and his room is "kind of a mess." Apparently Danny has been instructed to clean it up himself—a ludicrous idea, but I seem to be the only one laughing. I offer to try to do something about the room, since Danny is growing increasingly unstable and I fear he'll soon find living there intolerable. In fact, I fear he'll find living itself intolerable.

The staff worker unlocks the room to let me in, suggesting I keep it locked from the inside while I'm there. Some of the men on the floor don't have the best track record. The hallway smells even worse than usual, and we pass a room with an open door and a mattress propped outside against the wall.

Apparently the occupant passed away. I wonder how long it took them to find him.

I try to prepare for the worst when I enter Danny's room, but the scene that greets me is beyond imagining. Shards of glass, garbage, empty food containers, liquor bottles, and energy drink cans are scattered everywhere—on the floor, the desk, the dresser, the bed. An amazing variety of food is splattered on all four walls, and there is vomit on the bed, the floor, and even the small refrigerator. Over the whole mess is a wall-to-wall layer of trash, cigarette butts, dirty clothes, ashes, coffee grounds, and syrupy goo sticking to the desk and floor. The window is covered with the end of a cardboard box held in place by duct tape, but jagged pieces of glass still stick out of the frame. The room is stifling hot, but there's no escaping either the heat or the horrible stench, since the window can't be opened.

I hadn't come prepared for this operation, so all I have to work with is a combination of the paper towels, wet ones, and Windex I had given Danny when he moved in. My friend from the front desk offers a large broom and some trash bags, and I begin to fill them with the things we've given Danny over the past two years. Most of his bedding has cigarette burns and can't be salvaged. Amid the sticky mess on the floor, I find the books and school supplies we had purchased when he started classes in the fall. I try not to think about the hopes I had then, just five weeks ago.

The broken glass is the hardest part. I cut my hand trying to pry loose some fragments still left in the window frame, and suddenly I can't contain my grief any longer. I sit on the edge of the stained mattress and let all the pain pour out of my heart, using up the few tissues that are left in the ash-covered box on Danny's desk.

After two hours of steady work, I've done all I can with the paper towels. I stuff what is left of Danny's bedding and clothes into a trash bag to take home for washing, leaving on his bed the only clean blanket I can find, a small flannel throw that has no chance of covering his tall frame. Danny still hasn't returned and I have no way of reaching him.

There is no doubt in my mind that it's only a matter of time before his illness drives him into another crisis. Leaving the barren room and the rancid stench of the third-floor hallway, I take the ancient elevator to the first floor and walk out into the freshness of a crisp fall evening. It's hard not to feel ashamed, knowing that I will return to a clean, well-furnished home and a warm bed, while my son will sleep among the remnants of his life in a dismal room with little light and even less comfort. I would gladly trade places with him—or so I tell myself. Maybe it's only possible to believe it because I know I won't have to.

November 7, 2008, Friday

I've been invited to speak at a conference in Princeton, and I decide to bring Lily along so she can look over the campus. She's a high school junior now and starting to think about colleges and majors. Besides, I'd like to have some time with her, just the two of us, when for once she is the center of attention. So this morning we board an Amtrak train for the trip to New Jersey.

The train has barely left South Station when I receive a call from the YMCA. Danny is taking yet another police-escorted trip to the hospital. "What happened?" I ask, not sure if I want to know the answer. Apparently, he was up most of the night trying to break into a small locked closet next to the bathroom, where "they" were hiding the body of Thomas Jefferson—or somebody's body anyway. The only way into the closet, other

243

than the heavy door, is through the wall of the bathroom, so Danny spent hours using only his hands and a sneaker to rip the tiles off the wall and tear through the plaster, eventually making a good-sized hole leading into the closet.

Perhaps because he found it empty, or because his paranoia was at a fever pitch, he developed the fear that someone wanted to kill him, and ran up and down the hallway countless times trying to escape his attacker. He thought about jumping from his window, but the cardboard and duct tape made it difficult. For some reason, neither the night staff nor the other residents tried to find out what was causing all the noise in the bathroom and hallway. Some thought there was construction going on, though I don't know many plumbers who will make a service call at 2:00 am.

When the day staff arrived at 8:00, they found a large section of the third-floor bathroom wall completely destroyed—the damaged area measured about ten feet by five feet. It didn't take long to find the culprit, since Danny left his sneaker behind. Hence the escorted trip to the hospital's psychiatric emergency department, just three-and-a-half days after they discharged him.

As I listen to this sad story unfold, I have no idea what to do. The train rolls relentlessly on, and the next stop is some distance from Boston. Damian doesn't pick up his phone, but I manage to reach Joey and ask him to go to the hospital right away. I hate to ask him to leave work in the middle of the morning, but I can't allow the hospital to discharge Danny again. "Don't let them send him out, OK? Just *insist* that he needs to be hospitalized. His life is at stake, Joey. He can't be left on his own right now."

Before Joey leaves from work, Damian calls. I explain the situation and he says he'll go to the hospital right away. I call Joey back to tell him he's off the hook. Once again, I emphasize to Damian how important it is for Danny to receive some treatment, but he doesn't take much convincing. We're both in shock over the severity of this psychotic break, wondering what it portends. Will Danny recover? And the question we don't acknowledge, except in some remote area of our consciousness: What if he doesn't?

Damian insists he can handle the current crisis on his own and that I should fulfill my obligation to speak at the conference. So Lily and I continue the trip to Princeton, trying to be brave for each other's sake. When we arrive at the hotel, I hear again from Damian. The hospital (belatedly) recognizes the seriousness of Danny's symptoms, so they are sending him to Arbour Hospital. They've given him some strong sedatives, so he is calmer but still confused. The director of the housing program at the Y takes out a one-year restraining order to prevent Danny from returning to the building, as she doesn't want to give the hospital an excuse to send him back there again (or so she says).

Lily and I attend the opening dinner for the conference that night and are seated with the other speakers, their spouses, and miscellaneous local dignitaries. I sit next to the donors who made the conference possible, so I say positive things about the importance of the project and the enthusiasm it's generated. But my heart isn't in it. Lily and I are both exhausted from the trip and the emotions of the day. She barely touches her food, and asks to be excused before dessert is served. When I return to the room an hour later, she is tossing in bed and groaning with severe flu symptoms. She is badly congested, her stomach is flip-flopping, and she has a splitting headache. After a trip to the drugstore for cold medicine and ibuprofen, I collapse beside her and try to get some sleep.

My presentation is scheduled for 11:00 am the next day, and Lily drags herself out of bed to come and support me. There is a lunch afterwards, but she just wants to go back to the room and sleep. Though we planned to stay until Sunday, the weekend is starting to feel like slow torture, so I manage to exchange our tickets and we return to Boston late Saturday evening instead.

In a few days, I gather enough fortitude to return to the Y to clean Danny's room and remove the rest of his things. The director generously offers to forgo charging us repairs to the window and the bathroom, for which I'm eternally grateful. Not much has changed in Danny's room since the last time I was there. The prescription we had filled when he was discharged is lying on the floor in the stapled bag it came in. Since his door was left unlocked when he was taken to the hospital, many of his things are missing. One of the staff members helps me carry Danny's remaining furniture and boxes down to the car. He gives me a big hug and tries to be reassuring.

I take a final look at the building where my son very well might have died. There's a strange irony in its two faces—one side devoted to children's swimming classes, Pilates, and urban gym rats, and the other filled with society's outcasts—the elderly poor, the substance-addicted, and the victims of mental illness.

When I go to the office to turn in Danny's keys, an elderly man is pleading with the director to give him a room, though he doesn't have enough money for the first month's rent. He insists that when his next social security check comes in, he will pay in full. He tells me he's just been kicked out by his wife

246

of sixty years. I offer my condolences, but he replies that he is delighted: "Living with her is unbearable, and it has been for years!"

The director has a soft heart so I suspect she gave him a room. But the conversation leaves me unsettled. I guess I assumed that if my marriage lasted for sixty years, I could count on being together "til death do us part." Well, sufficient unto the day are the anxieties thereof. I hand over the keys, then go back to my illegally-parked car and head toward home, where I once again try to jam Danny's belongings into the overstuffed utility room.

Timeout: Involuntary Commitment

A dramatic shift in the care of the mentally ill took place in the 1960's and 70's, when two assumptions seemed to gain near-universal acceptance: (1) Life in a mental hospital is nasty, poor, brutish and short (witness the 1975 movie *One Flew Over the Cuckoo's Nest*); (2) Holding mental patients in such facilities against their will is a violation of their civil rights. Hence, the burden of proof is on those seeking involuntary commitment to show that the person in question is either seriously dangerous (to self or others) or cannot function at all outside of an institution.

An extensive *Wikipedia* essay on involuntary hospitalization describes with admirable precision the effect of the major ruling on this issue:[45]

"In 1977, the U.S. Supreme Court ruled that involuntary hospitalization and/or treatment violates an individual's civil rights in *O'Connor v. Donaldson*. This ruling forced individual

---

[45] "Involuntary Commitment," in *Wikipedia: The Free Encyclopedia*, accessible at *en.wikipedia.org/wiki/Involuntary_commitment,* emphasis mine.

states to change their statutes. For example, *the individual must be exhibiting behavior that is a danger to himself or others in order to be held*, the hold must be for evaluation only, and a court order must be received for more than very short-term treatment or hospitalization (*typically no longer than 72 hours*). This ruling has severely limited involuntary treatment and hospitalization in the U.S."[46]

This 1977 decision precipitated the closing of countless mental hospitals in every state, with no provision in place for those who were being treated there. The result was a public health crisis of monumental proportions. Individual states scrambled to develop protocols consistent with the Supreme Court requirements.

In Massachusetts, the phrase "a danger to himself or others" is interpreted as "the likelihood of serious harm" vis-à-vis the person in question or the wider community. The law defines the likelihood criterion as follows: "(1) Substantial risk of physical harm to the person himself/herself as manifested by evidence of threats of, or attempts at, suicide or serious bodily harm; and/or (2) Substantial risk of physical harm to other persons as manifested by evidence of homicidal or other violent behavior, or evidence that others are placed in reasonable fear of violent behavior and serious physical harm to them; and/or (3) Very substantial risk of physical impairment or injury to the person himself/herself as manifested by evidence that such person's judgment is so affected that he/she is unable to protect

---

[46] The article refers at this point to M. L. Perlin, "The ADA and Persons with Mental Disabilities: Can Sanist Attitudes Be Undone?" *Journal of Law and Health* 8, 33-34.

himself/herself in the community and the reasonable provision of his/her protection is not available in the community."[47]

These conditions are heavily stacked against involuntary hospitalization, and most psychiatric facilities are so anxious to avoid lawsuits that they are reluctant to admit patients involuntarily if there's any doubt at all as to whether they fit the criteria. The result is that some doctors (since this is a doctor's decision) are willing to wash their hands of responsibility even for very psychotic individuals, unless they are (then and there) threatening to harm themselves or others. The third criterion, that the individual cannot effectively protect himself or herself in the community, is subject to widely varying interpretations, and since it would be difficult to defend in court, it has largely dropped out of the picture.

Given that mentally ill persons who are left untreated are often in danger themselves or likely to be a threat to others, some states interpret the Supreme Court's ruling more broadly. For example, "Oregon law allows a person to be treated for a mental illness against their will if they are experiencing an emotional disturbance and are imminently dangerous to themselves or others, or are unable to care for their basic needs.

To be committed, a person must meet the above standards in a court hearing where critical information is presented in the form of testimony in front of a judge and the person considered for

[47] Massachusetts General Laws, Chapter 123, Section 12 (b), accessible at www.malegislature.gov/Laws/GeneralLaws/PartI/TitleXVII/Chapter123/Section12.

commitment."[48] This law does not require that danger to self or others must be manifested in overt suicidal or homicidal behavior. Of course, even these criteria could be given such a strict interpretation in practice that the situation in Oregon would be identical to that in Massachusetts.

Several advocacy groups for persons with mental illness, including NAMI, have lobbied the Massachusetts legislature for years, hoping to revise the current involuntary admission statute into one that is more realistic and more humane. So far they have been unsuccessful. But as public awareness of mental illness as a brain disease continues to grow, there is hope that the courts will give parents and other relatives a chance at getting treatment for their loved ones before their illnesses drive them either to attack someone or attempt suicide.

The claim that mentally ill persons have the right to refuse treatment regardless of the circumstances obscures the reality that they are often in as much danger as a diabetic without insulin. Though an involuntary hospitalization might be as short as 72 hours, it can provide a person with a mental illness some measure of stability and safety during that time. This may be enough to allow them to recognize their need for further treatment. In many cases, people with mental illnesses refuse to take their medication because they haven't been taking their medication. They've become paranoid or oppositional or anxious and can't be persuaded to accept the only thing that will help them. When it's someone close to your heart, watching them disappear into psychosis is pure torture.

---

[48] "Involuntary Commitment," in Washington Country Government's web site at
www.co.washington.or.us/HHS/MentalHealth/GettingHelp/involuntary-committment.cfm.

17 Asylum

November 12, 2008

"In all circumstances, give thanks."[49] The Gospel reading for today is the story of the ten lepers who were miraculously cured by Jesus. Only one returns to thank him.

Danny is in the Arbour Hospital now, having been admitted on Friday. We are to meet with his "team" today to decide what to do tomorrow, as Danny has signed a request to be released following the mandatory three-business-day stay. What do I do for my son? His leprosy is of the mind and heart, and he doesn't even know how to ask for a cure. He fights against everyone, even those desperately trying to help him. But there's always hope that this time he will see things more clearly, and have the grace to accept the sad reality of his illness and the importance of taking the right medications in order to cope with it.

_____

[49] I Thessalonians 5:18.

252

This time is harder somehow, maybe because we've seen Danny do so well at times. It's like getting a glimpse of the person you know and love before the hard drive skips again and takes him away. None of the others in the family has been with Danny when he is suffering from so many psychotic symptoms, so they are just beginning to realize the seriousness of his illness. They are grieving for him; and for themselves.

In spite of everything, I'm encouraged by the people who have taken an interest in Danny. The hospital administrator, Mr. Arunde, has an office on the same floor as the clients, and he works with Danny on a daily basis, encouraging him, giving him clear expectations, listening, caring, putting an arm around his shoulder.

Since Mr. Arunde is Nigerian by birth, Danny feels a sense of solidarity with him. In conversation, I find that his education and work experience are in business, so he has every reason in the world to go for the money and stay far away from the frustrating and thankless task of caring for the least of these. But he actually seems to love the patients, and is constantly thinking of ways to improve their quality of life, in the hospital and beyond. When he learned that Danny likes to listen to rap music, he brought some CD's from home, apologizing that they weren't Danny's favorites. Then, since there was no CD player available on the floor, he bought one with his own money for Danny to use while he was there.

I'm humbled by this man's decision to live close to the patients, by his dedication and his desire to serve them. Once when I was visiting, a middle-aged, heavyset woman was lying across the floor in the middle of the hallway, creating an effective blockade. Nurses and orderlies tried in vain to get her to move, but their pleas were useless, and it would be no small task to lift her up bodily—a last resort, in any case.

Mr. Arunde came out of his office to see what the commotion was about. He stooped down and spoke quietly to the prostrate woman. Since I was nearby, I could overhear some of what he said. "I know you're frustrated about not receiving your medication, Roberta, but it just takes time to get to everyone. So we'll be ready for you in no time. Now, you know you can't just lie on the floor like this. Nobody can get by. Come on, let's get up." He reached out his hand, and Roberta grabbed hold of it and struggled to her feet. I wondered what his secret was. Reflecting on it later, I decided it was that Roberta knew he cared about her. He spoke to her as one person to another, not as a superior to an underling.

December 15, 2008

"You asked Our Lord to let you suffer a little for him. But when suffering comes in such a normal, human form—family difficulties and problems, or those thousand awkward things of ordinary life—you find it hard to see Christ behind it. Open your hands willingly to those nails . . . and your sorrow will be turned into joy."[50]

It was a bittersweet experience visiting Danny at the hospital on Thanksgiving. But all five of us were there, plate of turkey dinner in hand, so the family got to be together, whole again for an hour at least. Yesterday we visited *en masse* again— everyone but Joey, who had to work—and shared subs and sodas and hospital cafeteria cookies. It was almost festive. Danny moves to a new section of the hospital today—quieter,

---

[50] St. Josemaria Escriva, *Furrow* (New York: Scepter, 1986), 234.

and with more freedoms. He's grown more accustomed to this stage of his journey. So have we. But I long for the day when he will be free again and can begin to look for work and pick up some threads of ordinary life once more.

We're in the Advent season now, a time that is always consoling for me. Come, Lord Jesus. Come for all of us. Never leave us alone. Be our strength, our hope, our freedom, our joy.

December 26, 2008

Danny received a day pass to come home for Christmas yesterday, which was a great blessing for all of us. I picked him up at 10:00, armed with dress slacks, shirt, belt, and shoes (with shoestrings!) and a warm jacket to wear. We stopped at the Seven-Eleven for cigarettes, coffee, and donuts. Standing in the parking lot in 20-degree weather, cigarette and cup of hot coffee in hand, Danny's expression was one of utter bliss.

We met the others at the 11:00 mass, and even Alex came to church, mainly for my sake no doubt. Then home to turkey dinner and opening gifts and playing Christmas carols on the stereo. We were all so thankful just to be together. Danny had chosen gifts for each person in the family and given me some of his own money to purchase them. It had to be a joy for him to be able to give these things and not just to be on the receiving end.

We watched "Miracle on 34th Street" and the "Muppets Christmas Carol," but too soon it was time to head back to the hospital. Outside the front entrance, we stopped for a few minutes so Danny could get in one last cigarette. He hated to go back in, and we both spoke of our sadness at having the day come to an end. For those few hours, my son was just another young man, one of the crowd, dressed like everyone else, and home with his family for Christmas. He thanks me for coming and for bringing him home for the day, as if I could have done otherwise! We embrace, and hold each other for a long time, shedding tears of joy mingled with sorrow. Not for the first time; and not for the last.

January 15, 2009

"The largest single contributor to the excess death rate in individuals with schizophrenia is suicide. One review of studies done on this subject concluded that 'suicide is the number one cause of premature death among schizophrenics, with 10 to 13 percent killing themselves."[51]

A new start. Danny is transferred today to Lemuel Shattuck Hospital, a state hospital that is just five minutes by car from the Arbour. He called on Tuesday night to tell us he was leaving Arbour the next morning. It was the first time in months that he sounded happy—excited even. Things were *finally* moving forward! A few days or so at Shattuck, then on to the Fenwood Inn Residence where he would finally be a free man again. He was full of hope. Having spent some time with his friend Angela on Sunday, he was looking forward to being out of the hospital in time for her birthday in March. We spoke of the future in positive terms for a change, and I promised to visit him on Wednesday afternoon.

As it happened, I couldn't sleep Tuesday night. I stayed up until 5:00 a.m. finishing the footnotes and corrections on an essay I was supposed to have turned in to the editor a month ago. So when Danny called today at noon, I was in a deep sleep. The agitation in his voice was obvious. I tried to clear the fog from

[51] Torrey, *Surviving Schizophrenia*, 311.

my brain while I listened to his anguished account of the new scenario he is expected to sign on to.

Instead of a few days at the Shattuck as an inpatient, he's told it will be *at least* a two- to three-month stay before a bed opens up at Fenwood Inn. Worse, while at Arbour there were five or six smoking breaks a day, Shattuck requires several assessments before a patient can even go for a *non-smoking walk* with a staff member! If that goes well, he can eventually graduate to unsupervised smoking breaks, but at first he'll be limited to two of these per day. All we had been told at the Arbour was that Shattuck allowed smoking breaks—so this was a shock to Damian and me as well.

Cigarettes are such a source of consolation for patients with Danny's illness, a way to find calm and, as it happens, to treat some of the symptoms of schizophrenia[52]—not in the preferred way of course, but given its importance to them, perhaps the lesser of two evils. In the past, Danny has always refused nicotine patches or gum; for him, the process is part of the purpose. I can sympathize on that one—energy drinks are no substitute for sipping a hot cup of coffee in the morning.

[52] "Eighty per cent of people with schizophrenia smoke tobacco, according to research. 'That figure is concerning—it's more than 3 times the rate of the rest of the population,' according to Flinders Medical Centre's Professor of Clinical Pharmacology, Ann Crocker. . . 'The feedback is that it helps to temporarily relieve emotional and physical stress and facilitates feelings of well-being. Smoking may also be used to 'self-medicate' as nicotine releases dopamine in the brain—thereby reducing some of the negative symptoms of schizophrenia.'" Author undisclosed, "Most People with Schizophrenia Smoke Tobacco, Says Research," April 9, 2001, on the web page *myDr.com.au*. Available online at *www.mydr.com.au/mental-health/most-people-with-schizophrenia-smoke-tobacco-says-research#*.

On the phone, Danny is extremely upset—hurt, frustrated, and angry. He feels betrayed. I speak briefly with the admitting doctor on the phone, asking if my husband and I can meet with him that afternoon. Given the green light, we quickly shower and dress, then get out the map to find this new hospital—the seventh that Danny has visited.

Dr. Saverin meets us in the conference room, along with Danny and the nurse who is in charge of the floor that day. They confirm what our son has told us. The doctor fears that, given Danny's history of violence, he will become abusive—especially since he doesn't want to stay—which would delay his smoking privileges even further. I suspect Danny has already been at least verbally abusive, but no one raises the topic.

To my surprise, Damian comes to Danny's defense, explaining what a shock this is for him, and lobbying for some flexibility in the smoking policy. Danny is clearly disheartened at the prospect of starting from zero again, having to persuade a new panel of judges that he can stay calm, that he won't run away, that he will obey the regulations. Most of all, he dreads being in the hospital on Angela's birthday. He's just begun to develop a close relationship with her, and he wants to celebrate her birthday as her boyfriend, not as a mental patient.

The staff tells us a little more about the hospital and much of it is encouraging, but the bottom line stays the same. So I encourage Danny to sign in voluntarily, since that would likely lead to a shorter stay. He says he's afraid he'll go crazy just from the extended confinement. The floor nurse, who looks like a burly fishing-boat captain except for gentle blue eyes, perceives Danny's comment as a threat, and warns him that "going crazy" will only work against him here.

258

Again Danny begs to be discharged, but the doctor is adamant. "Why does it have to be this way?" he pleads. "Why is it always you against me? Why can't you be *for* me? Why won't you *help* me?" Dr. Saverin explains that he *is* trying to help, but that he has a responsibility not to release Danny until he believes he will be safe—with a place to live, a plan for ongoing treatment, and a commitment to stay away from drugs and alcohol. The nurse asks Danny if he's had a plan to stay clean and sober at any time during the last four years. Danny admits that, truth be told, he hasn't.

Eventually the doctor excuses himself and the nurse goes out to check the schedule. It's just the three of us again, looking glumly at one another across the conference table like brokers whose stock has just plummeted. Except that there's no bailout on the horizon—not for the patients in the state mental hospital. Danny puts his head in his hands and begins to weep, sobbing his heart out, a picture of utter despair. I come around the table, put my arm around him and my face next to his, and cry with him. "I'm so sorry, Son. I know this is so hard, and it's not fair. I'm just so sorry."

The nurse returns to announce that it's time for Danny's intake physical. So we try to pull ourselves together and get ready to leave. Danny hugs me close, and I have a brief moment to whisper in his ear, "Don't lose hope, Danny. God is still taking care of you. He's been there for you all along, and he's here too. He will make this work for your good—I know he will. I love you so much, Danny. I will always have your back, OK? Always." Danny nods, and maybe his expression eases a little. He and an orderly ride the elevator with us to the first floor. Then it's another good-bye. Why don't they get easier?

Damian's eyes are full of sorrow; he looks as close to tears as I've ever seen him. We've both gone through so many emotions in living with Danny's illness and the countless crises it provokes—fear, anger, despair, indifference, suspicion, sympathy, hostility, pity. Somehow none of them ever seems wholly appropriate. Recently I decided on the metaphor that fits Danny's journey best—Stations of the Cross. "Jesus falls the second time, and the third; is stripped of his garments, crowned with thorns, forced to carry his cross." Will I be there at the end? "Jesus dies; is taken down from the cross, and laid in the arms of his mother."

Back at home, Damian and I watch episodes of *Battlestar Galactica* until we can't keep our eyes open, trying to forget, to keep our minds off the image of our son, alone and broken-hearted. I fall asleep immediately but wake again around 2:00 and weep until I have no more tears. Why can't I take care of my son? Why can't I bring him home and keep him safe and shelter him with my love? But the reality is that I cannot. So, like every other night, and sometimes many times a day, I say, "O God, into your hands I commend my son." My own heart too. Don't let us go.

February 27, 2009

Today Danny is back in court. In November 2007, fifteen months ago, he set out to visit one of his friends in Jamaica Plain. There was just one catch—the friend's apartment is next door to the one where Danny lived before being forced out by a restraining order. He was walking down the main avenue when he ran into the initiator of that restraining order. Doug's expression was one a deer caught in the headlights. Danny's anger and frustration flashed to the surface: "Give me one reason why I shouldn't just beat you up right now." Doug managed to stammer, "You're not even supposed to be here! I'm calling the police."

260

Recognizing the precariousness of his position (the police station was just a block away), Danny hustled back to the T stop and jumped on the train before the police could find him. But the complaint gathered dust in their files until eventually they appeared at the YMCA in October with a warrant requiring Danny to appear in court.

The date was postponed when he was admitted to the hospital, but now that he is relatively stable and under the care of a psychiatric team, he must appear before a judge to answer for the violation of his probation. I've decided always to accompany Danny at his court appearances, since I want him to know that, whatever he has done, he will always be my precious son. As long as one person loves you, there is still hope for your future.

I arrive in the courtroom at 9:00 and Danny appears shortly after with a social worker from the hospital. We're joined by Mason, the public defender who has stood by Danny since his first arrest. His loyalty to my son is astonishing—one of those gifts that cannot be measured and can never be repaid. It's a relatively brief tango through the routine today, a mere rehearsal for the choreographed final performance. Everyone knows the steps by heart—judge, bailiff, lawyers, cops, even Danny and I. We stand and sit meekly on command, sans gum, cell phones, pencils, or reading material. Danny is given a hearing date of April 14th, a piece of paper, and some words of encouragement from Mason.

I offer to give Danny a ride back to the hospital, and in the car he tells me that Damian came to visit him on Ash Wednesday so (appropriately) he could go for a smoke and get some time outdoors. (Outdoor privileges are a new development this week, but for now they have to be supervised by a staff member or one of Danny's parents. It puts an added burden on us, knowing that his allotment of fresh air depends on the frequency of our visits.)

Later, Danny and Damian had a few moments of privacy in the TV room, and Danny stretched out on one of the battered sofas. He said his dad reached over and stroked his head for a few minutes, mussing his hair the way he used to do when the boys were small. Remembering that moment, Danny could barely keep back tears: "I guess he really does love me."

Sometimes I marvel at my husband. There are depths in him that I seem to have missed all these years. Maybe that's one of the rare gifts that come from unbearable suffering; the pain cuts so deeply that it reveals the innermost core of your soul. I know that, for Danny, this gesture of compassion was a healing balm on the wounds of his heart. How a father's love comforts us. It validates our pain somehow, as coming not from sentimentality or condescension, but from an objective perception of fact. "You have known great suffering. I see you. And I care."

March 22, 2009

"I go to prepare a place for you."[53]

Danny speaks excitedly about new opportunities at the Shattuck Hospital—computer classes, basketball night, job training. We will meet soon to start planning for his discharge. It's beginning to seem real to him, and he's far more realistic this time about the perils of life without walls—both excited and anxious. He tells me he wants to put together a team, as

---

[53] John 14:7

though it's a new concept to him. This has been our goal from the beginning, of course, ever since a young psychiatric intern at the MGH emergency room handed me a brochure about the FEPP program. It's a wonderful concept, and clearly the only workable solution to the vicious revolving-door cycle of mental illness.

But it is far easier to describe than to implement. Some providers want no part in a team, it turns out, and others clearly expect the client or his family to put a team together on their own. (Not likely!) Yet somehow here we are, three years after that morning at MGH, finally putting in place for Danny something like a team. I try to believe that it will actually happen, even though eddies of skepticism swirl in my mind.

Angela's birthday is approaching, and Danny uses some of his money to order a ring he found in a catalog—a small ruby nestled in a beautiful gold setting. I've ordered it for him and brought it in to the hospital so he can give it to Angela when she visits. They've talked by phone several times and she's been to see him once or twice. She seems to really care about him.

Just a few days before her birthday, she arrives at the Shattuck with her mother in tow (a little unusual, but Danny doesn't mind). They walk around the grounds for a while, and Danny tells her he'll be released soon—then they can go on a real date. Just as he's about to give her the ring, Angela announces that she's getting married. Danny is stunned. He doesn't know what to say. "You mean, to your old boyfriend?" "Yeah." "Oh. . . . so . . . when is the wedding?" "This weekend." "Wow. Really? Well, um, congratulations." "Thanks, Danny. I'm sorry I didn't tell you about it sooner. It was decided kind of suddenly." A few weeks later, he finds out that Angela was pregnant, which explains the hastily arranged wedding.

Angela leaves with her mother and Danny returns to his room, devastated and overwhelmed with grief. Now he's afraid he'll never find someone who will love him. Angela knew him when he was still in high school, before the illness shattered his dreams. There will never be anyone else like her, who knew him back then, and knows that, deep down, he's the same person he was at 16.

March 25, 2009

The discharge planning meeting convenes in the same conference room where we met in January. Those present include Danny, Dr. Saverin, a DMH case worker, a representative from Danny's outpatient team, Joey, and I.

The PACT team (Program for Assertive Community Treatment) will handle all aspects of Danny's treatment when he leaves the hospital, including visits with a psychiatrist, peer counseling, substance abuse counseling, medications (orally or by injection), vocational training, educational goals, housing, and so on. It sounds too good to be true, and probably is. Joey plans to find a two-bedroom apartment where he and Danny can live together. No other living arrangement has lasted more than three months, and Joey believes it's important for Danny to come home to family at night and have some semblance of a normal life.

It is unbelievably generous of Joey to want to provide a home for his brother, and everyone around the table marvels at his compassion. But we have our misgivings too, wondering what will happen to both of them if the apartment scenario doesn't work out. Dr. Saverin warns Joey of the obstacles to successfully caring for a relative with mental illness and multiple substance abuse problems. Joey is unreceptive to the implied conclusion that the shared apartment plan is doomed from the start. The doctor counters with a prediction, "There is a 75% chance that Danny will 'decompensate' within two months if he moves in with you." It's not an encouraging prospect. But Joey is skeptical about trying to predict social outcomes with mathematical precision. The meeting ends amid tensions all around.

My heart sides with Joey and Danny, who are convinced they can make the plan work, but my mind sides with Dr. Saverin and his thirty years of experience. He tells Joey that he himself would not try to care for one of his children if they were to become mentally ill. "When you're close to someone, you don't want to see them return to the hospital, so you don't require them to stay with their treatment plan until they've become seriously ill. And then it's much harder to restore them to the level of functioning they had before."

It sounds distressingly plausible. But maybe Joey and Danny will prove to be the exception to the rule. So, against the advice of virtually everyone else involved, I encourage them to give it a try. Without that shining possibility on the horizon, Danny's future looks utterly bleak, and I can't bring myself to take this last ray of hope away from him.

April 14, 2009

Danny's day in court has arrived, and the usual cast of characters is in place. I've been in this courthouse four times now, so it's almost comforting in its familiarity. I took public transit this time, and when I walk through the metal detector an x-ray of my purse reveals my cell phone. "You can't have that in here, Ma'am." "Oh. Well can you just hold onto it until I leave?" "No, we don't do that anymore. You'll have to take it back outside." "But I don't have anywhere to put it." "I'm sorry, but you can't have it in here. Please move aside, Ma'am, you're blocking the door." "Fine. But I don't see why you can't just keep it in a drawer for a while." Peeved silence from the guard.

I wander around outside, looking for a niche where I can hide the phone, but the courthouse steps and surrounding sidewalks are swept clean and devoid of decoration. Trying the side of the building, I find a tall wooden fence surrounding a few giant dumpsters. I balance the phone carefully on a ledge just inside the fence. Nobody finds it. I'm ridiculously pleased with my ingenuity. On my second trip through the turnstile, I'm phone-free. I give the woman at the desk a triumphant look. She glowers back, but we both know who won. Why does it matter so much to me?

Danny and his case worker arrive by cab from the hospital at 9:00, and his long-suffering lawyer arrives a few minutes later. We wait nervously for the judge to enter and start the proceedings. Doug, Danny's accuser, is absent, so we're hopeful that the case might simply be dismissed. At 9:30 the judge comes in at last, and Danny's case is the first to be called. But Judge Dimora decides to put off her decision for now, apparently wanting to consider the case in more detail. She handles the rest of the morning's cases the same way, rendering no decisions and directing everyone to report back after a recess for the second round.

It's 9:50 when Dimora departs with a pile of folders under her arm, and she doesn't return until 10:30. By this time, Doug has made it to court. Our hearts sink. Mason explains to Danny that he's in danger of being forced to plead guilty to two misdemeanors—violating a restraining order and making a threatening remark. This would give him a police record, of course, and make getting a job next to impossible. I double my prayers, not asking that Danny receive no punishment, but that he not be required to plead guilty.

When Danny's name is called, both Mason and the DA approach the bench to lobby the judge. Danny's lawyer comes away with a decision to continue the case without a finding and a one-year probation. If Danny complies with the terms of his probation, the case will be discharged on April 14, 2010 and he will not have a police record. It's as good an outcome as we could hope for under the circumstances. Danny is disappointed to have seven months added to his current probation time, which was set to end on September 13th, but we all know it could have been much worse. We're told that the judge's decision will be announced on the following round.

By the time we sit through the third and final call and get Danny set up with the probation department, it is after noon. He and I are granted some time for lunch, but required to be back at the hospital by 1:00. I've noticed that there's no relationship between human time and hospital time. Never mind that Danny has just been through a three-hour ordeal and punished for a remark he made 15 months ago to a man who should have been removed from his apartment long before things came to a head between them. Never mind that we've spent six months waiting to find out whether Danny's future is still visible on the horizon. We have forty minutes to eat lunch and make it back to the hospital.

The only place close enough to get something to eat this quickly is the employee lunchroom at an MBTA transportation building across from the courthouse. We mingle our relief and sadness with sandwiches and chips from the understaffed kitchen at the MBTA (no hamburgers; no hot food at all, actually). We have a view out the window of two large dumpsters teetering on the edge of a dusty, rubble-strewn parking lot. Too soon it's time for Danny to return to the routine of his weekdays at the Shattuck—groups, smoking break, groups, smoking break, dinner, smoking break . . . . I drive back to my parish for a meeting of a newly-formed support group where we try to find ways of connecting God with the illnesses that have made our lives unrecognizable to us. Sometimes it's easy to see them through the same lens. This isn't one of those times.

18 The Cost of Freedom

April 22, 2009

My goal in writing this journal is to tell Danny's story, though I
know that, in truth, I can only tell my version of that story.
Danny has spared me the details he doesn't want me to have
to live with. How he can live with them himself I have no idea.
In this chapter, I've decided to record a small part of my own
journey, perhaps because the Caring for the Soul group has
made me realize the importance of admitting one's own
helplessness—even, at times, one's despair.

I have been seeing a therapist for many years. At first, it was
because I was so distressed and fearful that I could hardly
breathe. It took some time for me to understand the source of
my dread, and longer still to learn how to live again. The
chronic illness that forced my early retirement from teaching
contributes to depression as well, so it's fortunate that I've
found a psychiatrist with significant expertise in psychopharmacology as well as the kind of personal warmth and
openness that make it easy to be honest.

Today, I wrote the following entry in my journal:

"I spoke with Dr. Hart this morning. She always has
encouraging things to say. I wish I had more of her strength,
her positive outlook, her coping ability. I told her I'm often sad,
though not about anything specific, and that sometimes I'd just
like to give up, go to a remote cabin in the woods, or take a bus
to heaven—even purgatory! Dr. Hart tells me it might be selfish
to take such a negative view, because there are people who
need me, and because the world always needs people who
care. OK, point taken. I just wish I had more enthusiasm for the
journey.

Dr. Hart wouldn't want to go on the bus, she says. She wants
to stay and see how things turn out. I guess I lack that kind of
curiosity about the future. Partly it's because I'm afraid of what
it holds. But it's also because I've come to see how little I can
do to affect it for the better (or even for the worse). God takes
care of his world and everyone in it, with or without us. I can't
be any less dispensable than my friends who have already
gone home. But, as Dr. Hart says, I can focus on what I have,
and on the beauty and love and genuine goodness there is,
existing side by side with the grief and pain.

It is the Easter season after all. The great season of paradox,
with defeat and desolation crashing up against victory and
jubilation. In the *Summa Theologica*, St. Thomas Aquinas
replies to the question: "Whether Christ's body ought to have
risen with its scars?" His answer is yes, citing Venerable
Bede's commentary on Luke 24:40: "Christ kept his scars, not
from inability to heal them, but to wear them as an everlasting
trophy of his victory," and the opinion of St. Augustine:
"Perhaps in that kingdom we shall see on the bodies of the
martyrs the traces of the wounds which they bore for Christ's

name: because it will not be a deformity, but a dignity in them; and a certain beauty will shine in them."[54]

April 30, 2009

"Take care that you do not despise one of these little ones; for, I tell you, their angels continually behold the face of my Father in heaven."[55]

We are all little ones. Our Lord still has hopes for each one, and still has need of us. Every patient in the hospital, every prisoner in the penitentiary, every addict on the street, is accompanied by a glorious being who gazes on the face of God night and day, pleading for grace and mercy, for one more chance. Not only that, but our Lord himself goes in search of each one, as he tells his disciples in the next breath. "Will not a shepherd leave ninety-nine sheep on the hillside to go in search of one stray?" He searches still, not only among the mountain passes, but in the streets and alleys of the city, in bars and brothels, hoping that, over the din of their desires and desperation, those he loves will hear his voice.

When the boys were small, I used to tuck them into bed and sing for a little while as they settled into sleep. Most of the songs I knew by heart were hymns and choruses I learned as a child. One of Danny's favorites was "The Ninety-and-Nine,"[56]

---

[54] St. Thomas' comments are found in the *Summa Theologica* III, Q. 54, a. 4. Augustine's remark is in *The City of God* XXII.19.

[55] Matthew 18:10

[56] Words of this hymn are by Elizabeth C. Clephane, 1868. Music by Ira D. Sankey, *Sacred Songs and Solos*, 1874.

e parable of the shepherd who searches for that
... lost sheep. He climbs over mountains with rocks and sharp
thorns that rend his hands and leave drops of blood along the
way. Finally, when all seems lost, "Out in the desert he heard
its cry; sick and helpless and ready to die."

Danny would stop me every time at those words: "Don't say
'ready to die,' Mom. Don't say that!" He couldn't bear for the
lamb to be so close to death, even though the next verse
records the triumphant cry of the shepherd echoing all the way
to heaven: "Rejoice! I have found my sheep!" I used to wonder
what it was in the heart of my little boy that made him tremble,
even though the story had a happy ending. But now I'm the one
afraid for the life of my son as he wanders in the wilderness
where his symptoms have driven him. Don't say "ready to die."

May 6, 2009

I spent yesterday with Danny, learning about the program for
psychiatric rehabilitation at Boston University, a center that
offers courses for college credit to students with mental
illnesses who are trying to get their lives back on track. Danny's
case worker at the hospital has paved the way for him to start
classes this summer. His tuition will be covered by the
Massachusetts Rehabilitation Commission and he's looking
forward to being a student again.

Afterwards, we picked up some things to make life at the
hospital more bearable—Gatorade, granola bars, gum, and a
few bags of candy, plus T-shirts and gym shorts for the warmer
weather and a new pair of Nike sneakers. We are together for
six hours, and still Danny holds onto me when I hug him good-

bye. "Mom, please don't go yet. Stay with me." But I can't stay. I try to be encouraging, reminding him that his dad will be visiting tomorrow and Joey will come by later in the week. But I know that's not much consolation when he has to spend so many hours of every day alone.

Not long after I arrived home, Danny called with great excitement to say that he'll be discharged next week. *Next week*?! I feel a wave of panic, one I quickly try to suppress. It seems so sudden, even though we've been waiting for this day for six months. It has to be a monumental shift in a person's life to go from a routine that is set in cement and enforced by a host of personnel from doctors to orderlies, to days with hours of unoccupied time and no one telling you how to fill it. There will be groups, of course, the ubiquitous partial program that runs from nine to noon on weekdays, and Danny will spend an hour or two at Boston University on Wednesday and Thursday afternoons. The rest is just "open."

It's odd how little a person can be prepared for open space from within a closed environment. Danny is at maximum privileges status now, but even so he has never spent more than an hour on his own outside the hospital grounds. When he has a pass of six or eight hours it's always with my husband or me. Joey can also take responsibility for his brother, but his work and study schedule make even brief visits difficult, and six or eight hours in a row is unthinkable for him. With us, Danny's free time is still supervised, of course, and planned for maximum attention to the things he wants or needs.

All of that changes in the deceptively simple move from one floor to another at the hospital, to the DMH shelter called Fenwood Inn. It sounds so rustic; you expect a large fireplace and a veranda, but what you get is a bunk with seven other guys in a cluttered room with a horrendous smell (not all the clients have "personal hygiene skills"), and a pint-sized locker for your gear. Up at 6:00 am every day with no access to your room until after 4:30 pm.

There will be a new team to get used to—psychiatrist, nurse, social worker, and counselor. Danny is still making the transition from some of his oral medications to injectible versions of the same. It's not a seamless process, as his symptoms have sometimes returned in the absence of a steady dose of the meds. All of this combines to create a knot of anxiety in my stomach. But the system grinds on, relentless in its machinations, and as bewildering when it works as when it doesn't. Doors open and shut, people appear and disappear, according to a plan known only to the Almighty.

May 28, 2009

"Comfort ye, comfort ye my people, saith your God. Speak ye comfortably to Jerusalem, and cry unto her, that her warfare is accomplished, that her iniquity is pardoned: for she hath received of the Lord's hand double for all her sins."[57]

I wonder what kind of warfare this passage refers to. Maybe it's every kind. No more fears, dangers, cares, or sorrows, no more tears or broken hearts, no more despair, no more guilt or punishment. Our enemies without and within, all made subject to Christ the King.

Today I'm feeling a little sorry for myself. I'm worn out and discouraged, in need of a friend to understand and console me, but there is none. Still, is it such a negative thing to have no human being to lean on today? Perhaps not. If our Lord thinks

---

[57] Isaiah 40:1-2, King James Version.

of me always, with infinite love and tenderness, then he will give my soul whatever consolations it needs. I keep trying to put everything in his hands, and trust him to take care of them. The second part is harder than the first, since not to trust is to keep a hand on them myself, just in case . . .

Danny will be "free" soon, but what does that word mean? He'll never be free of this illness, of the specter that haunts him always—sometimes very near, sometimes farther away. Outside the hospital and 21 now, he is free to drink and seek out drugs, free to provoke a fight, free to refuse his medications, free to sink into psychosis again. Even so, I want that freedom for him and I know he chooses it too. Life without it is so constrained as to seem almost no life at all.

It's different for those who need the safety and structure of the hospital, whose quality of life is better inside than outside. They accept the negatives in exchange for the care and protection that make it possible for them to live and to reach their potential. But to be confined indoors for weeks and months against one's will, believing it's not absolutely necessary, is a terrible burden. It feeds a person's distrust of himself: "Am I more impaired, more 'crazy' than I realize? Am I unfit to mingle with the rest of society?" And especially, "Why am I so *alone*?"

Since Danny became ill, my favorite scripture has been Psalm 130:1: "Out of the depths I cry to you, O Lord. Lord, hear my voice." The depths and the darkness take many forms. They can appear across our path like bottomless crevasses, filing us with dread. Who will hear a cry from those depths save God alone? That is why I must learn to trust him. In the unbearable agonies, he is all I have.

June 4, 2009

I am 54 today. It hardly seems possible to be poised like this on the brink of official senior status. My husband and I are on our way to Minneapolis for a conference, where we will reunite with friends of thirty years. Good friends are such a gift. I hope they'll feel the warmth of our love for them, and that it will stay with them after we're gone.

Today I read in the Gospels the parable of the workers in the vineyard. I think as I grow older I'm comforted by the part that used to make me indignant, where those hired late in the day receive the same wages as those who began in the early morning. Maybe it means there is mercy yet for those of us who, though we set out early, could have accomplished so much more.

Danny was discharged from the Shattuck Hospital on Thursday, a week ago today. He's had a rocky start, but things are settling now into something resembling a routine. Friday morning, before the day had really begun at Fenwood Inn, two women got into a bloody fight outside the nurse's station. Danny was the only one strong enough to keep the larger woman from beating the smaller one senseless, so he entered the fray and finally got the two separated. The Fenwood Inn staff were grateful for his intervention in that situation. Sadly, on Sunday he got into some altercations of his own, with one fight on the subway leading to a brush with transit security. They ran a background check but made no arrests. We're already holding our collective breath, waiting for the next crisis—hoping it will never happen, but knowing the odds are against us.

Damian and I appear in court, just two days before Danny's release, to apply for a Rogers Guardianship. This document enables us to oversee his treatment plan and psychiatric medications, but not to make decisions about his housing, finances, etc. Danny was not required to attend and chose not to, which made the experience easier on us. The guardianship was granted, and we emerge from the courthouse wondering whether it will actually help us get treatment for our son when he doesn't think he needs it.

I'm told that now I can requisition Danny's medical records, especially the discharge notes, and that I should compile a short version of these for the next time he goes into a hospital (or gets arrested). In fact, I should make several copies. In other words, don't be fooled into thinking that this is the end of the journey. It's a battle that will last a lifetime. I'm still not sure I want to read the medical records myself. So many dark nights of the soul will be recorded there, and brought back to mind. No wonder Alcoholics Anonymous preaches "one day at a time."

When I begin the collection process, I will need to write to twelve hospitals, four outpatient programs, and countless doctors, all since Danny's journey began in April 2006. Still, I feel I shouldn't complain. Many others can tell a similar story, and usually their stories are much worse than mine. One of the women in my NAMI Caring and Sharing group has a daughter who suffered her first psychotic break at the age of 12. Now she is 34, and in those twenty-two years she has been in 65 hospitals.

When Danny first became ill, numerous friends and mental health professionals warned us that "the mental health system is broken." They might have put it more strongly—cruel, inhuman, inscrutable, horrifying—a Sartrean hell from which there really is no exit.

There is only one factor preventing the mental health system from grinding to a complete halt—the thousands of doctors, therapists, nurses, social workers, administrators, and hospital staff who refuse to let the whole sorry mess stand in their way. Against all odds, they bring concern and energy and expertise to serving those with diseases of the brain that remain exasperatingly mysterious, and that undermine the agency and ability of those afflicted either to fight against them or to overcome the stigma attached to them.

For their efforts, mental health workers in Massachusetts are rewarded with massive cuts in the Department of Mental Health budget. "In January 2009, the administration laid off roughly 100 Department of Mental Health case workers and 20 administrative staffers, part of more than $9 million in budget cuts to the agency. Roughly 3,000 clients lost their case managers and were shifted to the remaining 350."[58] Danny is one of those who were "shifted" to new case managers, twice in the last six months.

One local paper reports: "Most community-based services were affected or eliminated, including the Support, Education and Employment Program, which provided supervision to thousands of residents. The alliance [NAMI] estimates 3,600 people had reductions in services and 2,600 people were completely without day services."[59]

I'm often puzzled by the benign language used to describe the recent assault and battery on the DMH budget. In the article

---

[58] Jim O'Sullivan, "Senate Prez Vows to Restore Money to Mental Health Budget," *GateHouse News Service*, February 10, 2010.
[59]Rosemary D'Amour, "Mental Health Advocates Rally against Budget Cuts," *Daily News Tribune*, April 23, 2009.

just quoted, we read that "community-based services [like the PACT team] were affected or eliminated" and that thousands of clients of DMH experienced "reductions in services."

Mental illness isn't even mentioned. One could easily get the impression that we're talking about raising electricity rates or scheduling fewer garbage pickups. The truth is that we are cutting the lifelines of *thousands* of people with brain disorders, effectively evicting them, not just from warm places to stay on winter days, but from critical health care services, communities of friendship, and opportunities for meaningful work. Some will survive, some will get sicker, and some will die. Let the politicians speak in euphemisms, if they must, but the press should speak the truth.

Adding insult to injury, Massachusetts' governor is pushing for a further 20% cut in the DMH budget for in-patient facilities in the coming fiscal year. Whenever the economy falters, it's so tempting to shortchange the homeless and the mentally ill, citizens who are massively unlikely to organize and fight for themselves. Never mind that these are also our neighbors, our brothers and sisters in the human family, or that they could easily be our own family members, friends, or colleagues. We know that if we take up their cause we will, to some extent, share the stigma that falls upon them.

Without groups like NAMI and supporters like state senate president Therese Murray, my son and thousands like him would simply disappear from the collective public conscience, especially when money is at stake. I find it both miraculous and deeply moving that so many capable mental health workers stay at their posts in spite of overwhelming case loads and underwhelming public support. They are my heroes, and while I have no way to repay them, I at least want to acknowledge them and offer my heartfelt thanks to each one.

19 Respite

August 23, 2009

Day of jubilation! Joey has found a two-bedroom apartment right in our neighborhood that he and Danny can afford to rent together, and today is moving day! For the first time in over four years, Danny will live in his own home. We have a small U-Haul truck, and decide to go by Joey's apartment first, since he has some furniture and kitchen equipment that will take up most of the room.

When we arrive at the hospital, the boys head into Fenwood Inn to gather Danny's things. They return lugging the odious black trash bags. I could live quite happily for the rest of my life without seeing a black trash bag ever again. The PACT team officially takes over Danny's treatment today, and their help turns out to be the key to his transition back to the community.

Damian comes to the new apartment to help with the unloading. There are some tight moments, but eventually we manage to shove every item of furniture up the stairs to the second floor apartment. The decor dates from the 1950's, but the place is clean and spacious, with lots of windows and the coveted hookups for internet and cable TV. Danny strolls through the place a few times, looking like a prince in his palace. His expression is one of pure delight, coupled with a hint of disbelief that this could actually be happening. My husband and I leave the rest of the unpacking to our young men and return home, feeling a mixture of relief and hope and trepidation.

August 24, 2009

Today I make yet another appearance in court to ask that the Rogers Guardianship be made "permanent" (i.e., that it be extended for a year's time). The PACT team suggests that only one person act as the official guardian, so I have signed on for that role. Damian will not have to appear today; I'm glad he at least can be spared this time around. Our car is in the shop receiving a new clutch (the third in three years!) so we have a rental car which is due back by noon.

Rather than drive into downtown, I plan to park on a street near the train station, but as I look for an open place at the curb, I remember that the rental car doesn't have a local parking sticker. Fortunately, there's a small shopping center nearby which is almost completely deserted at 8:30 on this Monday morning, so I park in an out-of-the-way area where I won't take up any premium spaces. I notice there is a four-hour parking limit, but I expect to be back in plenty of time.

While riding the train, I glance around at the other passengers, wondering if they can sense my nervousness. I fervently wish I were just heading to work like they are, casually reading the morning paper or chatting with the regulars on the inbound commute. Right now I would give anything for just an ordinary day, of the kind I used to complain about as devoid of excitement.

Emerging onto the street from a station unfamiliar to me, I look around anxiously for the courthouse. It's hard to miss. The Brooke Courthouse is a disturbingly bulky building, brooding over a tangled crossroads of major urban thoroughfares. I've arrived early, but there's already a long line waiting for the ritual *pas de deux* with the metal detectors—keys and phone here, purse to the right, and *do-si-do* with the wand. At least we're allowed to keep our cell phones.

The interior of the courthouse looks recently renovated. The fresh decor is certainly a step up from the sorry accommodations at the other courts I've had the occasion to visit. But no need to think about that right now. There is no discernible directional help on the first floor, but after standing around for a few minutes with a bewildered expression, I'm directed to an information office on the second floor where I can learn where the Rogers case is being heard.

Another woman, dressed in a gray tailored suit and with a leather briefcase in hand, follows me to the information office— it turns out we are looking for the same courtroom. We're told we are in the wrong place, and instructed to go to an office on the fourth floor instead. Back in the elevator, I notice a man in the corner with a Rolex watch and the mandatory leather briefcase. I'm pretty sure I recognize him, so I say, "Good morning! You look familiar."

He seems a bit startled. I don't feel very threatening, but who knows? "Well, I spend a lot of time in courthouses," he offers. "Yes, that must be where I've seen you. Where is your home base?" "Well, usually it's the court in Jamaica Plain." "Oh, that must be it!" I reply. "I've been there several times." Suddenly aware of the woman attorney next to me, I add: "Not for myself, I mean—for my kids." Too late I realize this doesn't help.

Now the prim lawyer and I are joined at the hip and she is clearly unhappy about it. After a prolonged search of the fourth floor, we find the designated office and . . . wrong again. We are to appear in *Probate* Court, which is back down on the second floor. Sensing my companion's growing discomfort, I decide to take the stairs. Eventually I find out where to appear and am relieved to see that it's still a few minutes before 9:00, the witching hour here in judgment land.

In keeping with the updated interior, the courtroom is well-appointed. Even here, however, surrounded by the relative luxury of wood paneling, freshly-painted walls, and stain-free carpeting, my palms grow damp as I absorb the atmosphere of foreboding that permeates the pews of the benchwarmers. In the open area between the railing and the bench, lawyers lounge in soft leather chairs, allowed to shuffle their papers, type on their Blackberries, and whisper to each other. In that airy zone, just a few feet away, the ambience is completely different. Attorneys and clerks exchange greetings, crack jokes, and stroll around with confidence, obviously at ease on their own turf. I envy them. Every time.

The judge, a weary-eyed middle-aged woman, finally arrives at 9:45 to greet a full house of prosecutors and their respective targets. Her comically gigantic desk sits at least twenty feet away from *les miserables* and is raised high above the fray. Facing this imposing pedestal of gravitas, one feels called before the gods on Mt. Olympus, and afraid that the outcome might be correspondingly arbitrary. I have seen hardened gang members, pierced and tattooed thugs, even night-club bouncers, turn into stammering little boys before this seeming wheel of fortune, close to tears, and desperate for mercy.

I know how they feel, small and vulnerable and naked before the blindfolded eyes of Lady Justice. I can't imagine how my son endured his first court appearance in boxers, socks, and hospital gown, wrists and ankles shackled, having been beaten, starved, frozen, and humiliated for the past 48 hours. He didn't have a prayer. Or maybe that's all he did have.

We are called into the game one by one, in alphabetical order. M comes mercifully early in the queue today. Danny is not present and his attorney is not contesting our petition, yet I feel wholly inadequate, standing awkwardly at the railing facing the judge. (Hands at one's side? Clasped? Open in supplication?) When I speak, my voice wavers. The DMH lawyer, familiar from Danny's commitment hearing, stands next to me and presents a more coherent version of our case. The decision is favorable, the forms are completed, and we are free to go.

Outside the courtroom, I greet both lawyers and thank them. The DMH lawyer tells me she is leaving for another assignment, and introduces me to the attorney who will take her place. I want to cry. I feel that we've been through so much together, though I know these hearings are just routine for her. Anyway, I give her a hug and wish her well, sincerely hoping I will never have the opportunity to get to know her replacement.

I feel absurdly grateful to emerge from the solemn atmosphere of the courthouse into the fresh air. But part of me stays behind with the others in the judgment hall, as they await their own moment of relief or anguish. Needing to debrief, I make some phone calls to family members, but nobody picks up. Reluctantly, I descend into the darkness of the subway station and return to the shopping center parking lot to retrieve my rental car.

I arrive at 11:45, pleased to see that I'm well under the four-hour limit. But the car is nowhere to be found. Assuming it must have been stolen, I call the local police. They give me the

number of what must be the stolen-car department. No word
there regarding a car matching the description I give—neither
in the records of the stolen nor in those of the towed. Finally,
they offer me the number of a local towing company . . . just in
case.

I now look more closely at the signs posted in the parking lot.
Below the four-hour rule, there is a lengthier notice in small
letters: "Anyone leaving the property will be subject to towing."
How could they possibly know who leaves the lot, I wonder,
especially when it's as deserted at it was this morning? I find
later that there are hidden cameras covering the entire parking
lot and, no doubt, hidden watchers of the cameras. Big Brother
is alive and well and living in my town. I dutifully call the towing
company and, yes, my car resides in their lot. By now it is
noon, so the car will be returned after the deadline. I offer a
prayer for an hour's clemency at the rental office.

It will cost $112 dollars *in cash* (this is repeated three times) to
liberate the car. After a trip to the ATM and a hot and tearful
walk to Bert's Towing, I appear before a greasy, dust-covered
desk, cash in hand. Bert seems busy. I wait. When at last he
looks up from his papers, he nearly leaps out of his chair:
"Jesus!" It seems the typical, er, customer announces his or
her presence with high-decibel profanity. I sympathize with that
approach myself, but am still too close to tears to speak at all.
When I return the car to the rental company and glance at the
receipt, I can't help noticing that the weekend rental charge is
less than the towing cost. Still, Damian (thankfully) understands
about the whole sorry episode, and even tries to console me.
Compared to the more common crises in our lives, he reminds
me, this is a blip on the radar.

August 27, 2009

Today is Danny's initial appointment with his new probation officer, Georgia. The first order of business is to go to the clinic that will handle the drug testing. During the pre-enrollment interview at the clinic, I learn that Danny had access to pills from other patients while at the Shattuck Hospital and Fenwood Inn. Anything and everything—uppers, downers, painkillers, narcotics, opiates. The going rate was a dollar a pill, but sometimes they could be had for free. He says he tried all of the above at various times, sometimes without even knowing what he was taking. Oddly, I seem to be the only one in the room shocked by this revelation.

At that time, Danny relied heavily on marijuana—to relax, to recharge, to calm down, to pep up—apparently it's an all-purpose remedy. He is told to return the next day for the actual "intake." The first scheduled tox screen won't take place until the following Monday. This elaborate process strikes me as completely futile, since Danny's probation ends in two weeks on September 11th (an unfortunate date, but one doesn't get to choose). After the intake interview, we drive through downtown traffic again and make our way to Danny's appointment with his probation officer.

The probation department has moved to a new location and is now housed in a non-descript, one-floor office building that looks like a first-grader's drawing—a plain beige rectangle with the bare minimum of small square windows. Still, it's a vast improvement over the previous location, a massive structure that loomed over its surroundings like a vulture in waiting. As one reporter described it, "On any list of eyesores, [this] high-rise is likely to score near the top. It has been called a 'triumph of Stalinist architecture,' a 'hideous monument to concrete,' 'the city's sore thumb' and numerous epithets that cannot be repeated."

When we arrive at the probation counter, we're told Georgia is not in her office. But given the relative urgency of seeing her today, we're told to find her in one of the courtrooms down the hall. Sure enough, there she is, in the safe zone behind the railing, chatting with the clerks and the bailiff, positively brimming with playful energy and bonhomie. It's a full ten minutes before she notices us.

The three of us then step into the hallway for a brief consultation. The upshot is that Georgia will await the result of Monday's tox screen. If it's negative, she will petition the court to discharge Danny from probation and forgive the court costs he's accumulated while in the hospital. If the test is positive, she will turn Danny over to the judge for violating the terms of his probation.

We're to return on September 11th, the putative end of Danny's probation—two and a half years after his case was decided. On that very day, he must face the prospect of a yet longer probation, or something worse. Sometimes the court system is cruel beyond belief. It also happens that neither Georgia nor the public defender who has always been there for Danny will be able to appear on the 11th. Another probation officer, unknown to us, will present the case for or against Danny. On the other side, it will just be Danny and me. In a way, that sums up his whole story. His story and mine.

September 11, 2009

I pick Danny up around 8:15 to make the trip to the courthouse. Both of us are apprehensive, wondering whether he'll be brought before a judge and what will happen if he is. We try not to think about it, stopping by Dunkin Donuts for coffee before this dreaded appointment with fate. When we arrive, Danny is reluctant to go inside, smoking a couple of cigarettes first and wearing out the sidewalk with fretful pacing. Finally, bracing ourselves for the worst, we enter through the security gate and arrive at the counter of the probation office with fear and trembling. Is it a sickness unto death? Only time will tell.

The supervisor of the probation department, familiar to us from past "dealings," approaches us with a jovial expression on his face. What does it portend? He explains that Georgia is absent today, but he has gone ahead and put the paperwork through, so Danny is all set. "Wait. What? You mean this is the end of his probation?" "That's right. I just sent a note to the judge that your probation has been discharged. You're free to go, and you will have no criminal record from this incident. Congratulations."

Danny and I stare at each other in disbelief. How could it be true? We've spent the last two weeks in dark foreboding, and then today it's just no big deal. That's it. We nearly sprint out of the courthouse and into the beautiful fall day, laughing and hugging each other, and trying to take in the magnitude of it all. It's been two and a half years that felt like two and a half decades. Recovering our appetites, we head to the best breakfast cafe in the neighborhood for a celebratory feast of French toast and omelets. They never tasted so good.

October 2009

Danny's psychotic symptoms continue to bother him on a daily basis. He can cope well enough when they stay on the back burner, but when they force their way to the surface he grows extremely anxious and frustrated; he can't carry on a conversation or even watch TV. Sometimes he turns up the volume on his stereo because it helps to drown out the voices.

"What do the voices say?" I ask, wondering why I haven't asked before. "Well, they usually don't tell me I'm gay any more, or that nobody cares about me, or that I might as well kill myself. But they're just annoying. Yesterday, one kept saying my name over and over, 'Danny, Danny, Danny, Danny, Danny . . .' I told him to shut up, but he wouldn't. So finally I said, 'Look, if you don't shut the f*** up I'm going to choke you to death.' The voice was quiet for a few minutes, and then it said, 'Why would you do that to me?'" Danny and I laugh together at that one. He confides, "You know, Mom, sometimes I laugh because of something like that and people think it's weird. But if I tried to explain, they would think I'm really crazy."

Danny has stopped smoking marijuana and is faithful about taking his medications, two giant steps on the road to recovery. Even so, he is sometimes filled with anxiety or distracted by the voices. Recently he said, "Mom, when I wake up in the morning I never know where I am. It takes a while to figure it out. It's like I have to start over every time." What must it be like to live inside his mind, to do battle against the forces of darkness every day, trying to hang onto some semblance of normalcy?

Danny is quieter now, and the familiar sadness returns to his eyes. "I can't even find a girlfriend, Mom. Girls don't like me—I don't know how to talk to them. Sometimes at a party they come up and talk to me for a few minutes, but then they just get nervous and walk away. How am I ever going to find somebody who loves me?"

My heart aches for him. "You will one day, Danny. Just try to be patient, OK? Keep working on becoming as well as you can be. One of these days, a girl will come along who thinks you're wonderful." As with so many other things, I try to keep my head up and encourage Danny to do the same, even when both of us are suffering on the inside. I rarely share these conversations with others, even my husband. It would feel like multiplying the sorrow for no reason. We don't have any answers for Danny, and there is nothing we can do to give him the things he so desperately needs—friendship, love, meaningful work, a sense of purpose, a clear mind. But God can do what we cannot. So I pray, many times a day, and offer what I can for his healing and peace, begging God to hold our hands and help us keep walking.

November 9, 2009

I sit in the waiting room of Lily's therapist, waiting for her to resurface. Life is too hard for everyone right now. Lily had a difficult day at school, with a biology midterm and makeup exams in calculus and psychology. Calculus didn't go as well as she had hoped, and she's counting on good grades this term to help her get into the colleges she wants to attend. Other sorrows enter in too, no doubt, but I don't know what they are. Instead of listening to her and drawing her out, I've been doing the talking—sharing my worries about Danny and my frustrations with her dad—bad idea anyway, as I already know.

She must feel that her hardships and sorrows are small compared to Danny's or those of the rest of us, so I don't think she expects me to care as much as I should about how she is doing. Instead I pay a therapist to listen to her as a mother should listen, while I sit in the waiting room absorbed in my own problems and projects.

How will I live with myself if I lose the confidence of this child, so dear to my heart and so deserving of love? She is beautiful of soul, like gold tried in the fire, and I'm afraid of not being a mother who is worthy of her. Please, Lord, give me more grace.

November 25, 2009

It's the day before Thanksgiving and I have many things for which to be thankful. Danny and Joey are still living together in their apartment, in spite of some speed bumps along the way. Alex is continuing with his classes at the state university and seems genuinely happy for the first time in years. Lily, our baby, graduates from high school in June, and is busy applying to colleges and, of course, spending every waking minute with her friends. Damian and I have known some peace and a sense of normalcy for the past few months, and are beginning to recover our strength and our hope.

February 3, 2010

When I think back on Danny's childhood, one of the qualities that stands out most vividly is the sensitivity and empathy he had for those who were suffering. From an early age, he would notice whenever I was sad or discouraged, and come to tell me how much he loved me, trying to cheer me up.

When he was in second grade, his teacher called me in to say that Danny was being disruptive in class and she couldn't figure out why. He was a good student and seemed to have a lot of friends. Eventually, she recognized a pattern—whenever she scolded the boy sitting next to him, Danny would immediately start acting up so as to draw her attention away from the other boy. That was Danny. For all his energy and impishness, he always felt sad at the suffering of others.

I've just returned from a trip to the Midwest to attend the funeral of the man who was my mentor in graduate school. Over the thirty years since, he became one of my most cherished friends, and Damian and our children knew him well. I was grateful for the concern and sympathy expressed by each one.

291

But my youngest son entered into my grief with all his heart, calling and texting while I was away to tell me how sorry he was for my loss. Today, when he couldn't reach me by phone, Danny left this message:

"Hi Mom. I hope you're doing OK. I know you're probably still down about your friend, but life goes on for the good ones. He'll be missed, but everybody has to say good-bye at some point. I was talking with my friend last night and he said death is the most powerful thing in life, because it defines life in so many ways—we're always moving closer to it. I agreed that it does define life in a sense, and maybe gives it its final meaning.

But I said birth is a more powerful force. Even when death comes to people who have lived pretty bad lives, it's still sad, because you shouldn't take pleasure in their death, and it's especially sad if they didn't have a chance to repent. It's sad when good people die too, because they were so good and you really miss them. But whenever a baby opens his eyes, there's always hope, because he's so young and innocent. Anyway, I hope that helps a little bit. I love you, Mom."

It does help. And it reminds me what kind of man my son is. How ironic that this one, who has suffered so much and has every reason to shake his fist at the world, should be for me the champion of hope.

20 An Ending

"Comradeship and serious joy are not interludes in our travel; rather our travels are interludes in comradeship and joy, which through God shall endure forever. The inn does not point to the road; the road points to the inn."[60]

I wish I could say that this is the happy conclusion of Danny's story, that he will go from strength to strength, and that his illness will remain in check for the rest of his life. As I write, Danny's 24th birthday approaches—it is July 2011. He and Joey were booted from their apartment at the end of February, leaving Danny homeless again for five weeks. DMH then placed him in one of their downtown shelters, but in early September he was robbed and beaten by four gang members who hang out near the shelter. He was kicked in the head so many times that he nearly lost an eye. A few weeks later, DMH switched Danny with a resident of the Fenwood Inn shelter, so he ended up where he began just a year before.

Fed up with shelter life, Danny used some of his savings to move into an apartment with three other tenants—students

---

[60] G.K. Chesterton, *Charles Dickens* (1906), ch. 12. Accessed online at: www.online-literature.com/chesterton/charlesdickens/12.

293

who had no knowledge of his illness. The Fenwood Inn staff seemed to be caught off guard, even though Danny had told them of his plans, so there was no treatment plan in place. In just two weeks, Danny had a psychotic break and was hospitalized for a week. The landlord refused to return any of the 2 ½ months' rent he had paid at move-in, even though the apartment was re-rented within a few days.

When Danny was discharged, he stayed with Joey in the tiny garden apartment he had just rented in Cambridge. Eventually, the management discovered the arrangement and forced Danny to leave. He continues to stay on the street (in warmer weather), or more often with various friends made during his travels through the social services labyrinth that we laughingly call a system.

He is said to be at the top of the list at a local housing authority, though this has been true for several months now. We continue to hold out hope, awaiting the public housing voucher that would give Danny a permanent place to live—his own home.

A short stay at the MGH inpatient psychiatric unit convinced him to give up street drugs for good. The doctor ordered an MRI and compared it to the one taken in 2006 on Danny's first visit to the Psych ER. It was obvious that there had been additional damage to his brain, and the doctor warned that if he didn't quit "smoking up," within a few years he would barely be able to function. Once off marijuana, Danny turned instead to his prescribed medications for treating his symptoms. He's now very much aware that, for him, they are the difference between health and disaster.

The medications help to control Danny's symptoms, but only to a certain extent and only some of the time. It's still hard for him to focus and stay calm enough to watch TV for long or sit through an entire movie. But he is taking a night class at ⌐ ⌐. ⌐ and it's going very well. Though it will take time, he plans to finish his bachelor's degree, possibly in mathematics, and go on to teach at the high school level, following the example of his mentor Mr. Cole.

As for his social life, Danny's efforts to reconnect with high school friends meet with little success, and making new friends is even harder. I continue to hope, with him and for him, that he will find a girlfriend who is understanding of his illness and able to love him through the hard times—someone who sees into his soul, and finds the kind, intelligent, loving, thoughtful person he truly is.

Though these are not impossible dreams, there is certainly no guarantee that they will be realized. Every person with a mental illness has ups and downs, and there is no way of telling how deep the downs will be. I've tried to tell the truth in these pages, and the truth is sometimes painful.

On the other hand, while this may seem strange, I've learned so many important lessons during the years of Danny's illness that I look back with gratitude as well as sadness. Those who walk this way will know what I mean. And perhaps, in spite of our differences, everyone who suffers walks this way.

Life's hardships bring with them the opportunity to grow in the virtues we find so hard to acquire any other way. While my own progress is slow, I would like to list some of the qualities that stand out to me in friends and relatives who live daily in the shadow of mental illness, whether their own or that of someone they love.

Humility: Withholding assumptions about others; readiness to revise opinions; focusing more on others than on oneself

Compassion: Looking with kindness on the homeless and imprisoned, so many of whom suffer from mental illness, neglect, and alienation from family and friends

Vision: Seeing beyond the odd behaviors or unnerving silences of those afflicted with mental illness into the unique and irreplaceable people they are

Abandonment: Leaving everyone in God's hands; trusting him with the past, the present, and the future—what is trivial and what is essential

Trust: Willingness to lean on others and let go of the illusion of self-sufficiency

Receptivity: Being wholly present in the moment and listening actively; letting each person know that he or she is worthy of time and attention

Hope: Never giving up, and never writing off the future; lifting others up; looking for signs of growth and moments of grace

Many of these virtues are also goals of the spiritual life, but they are the secret of serenity for everyone, especially for all who suffer.

My faith runs through this story as it runs through my life—the only thread strong enough to hold my heart and soul together. Without God, who brings redemption and healing even out of sorrow and pain, this journey would be more than I could bear. But I know our Lord holds Danny in his hands, loving him with infinite tenderness, and that only he can give my son what I want for him more than anything else—everlasting life in the house of the Father.

Like Chesterton, I believe all our lives are only a prelude to the joy and love and companionship we were made for. We just have to choose them.

To hope is not to deny the darkness and pain—it's to believe they don't have the last word. My desire is that everyone who reads this book will renew their determination to promote effective and humane help for those who live will mental illness.

For all who bear such a burden—especially for my son—may you never lose sight of how important you are to this world, and how much you have to give. I truly believe that one day, for you too, your wounds will be your glory.

FOR MY SON

All smiles and teases
Sprockets and springs
Sparks flying
Never mind the crash
And roll, just
Jump the gap, shields up
It's X-Man at the ready

All heart and honor
Fierce as a friend
Unflinching
First into the breach
Full-throttle
Side by side, guns cocked
No man left behind

All high adventure
Caution be damned
Bike-jousting
Dodging cars, slam
Hard to soar
In glory, laughing
Even when you land

All question marks
Bruises and scars
Blind-sided
Weary, war-ravaged
Brought down
Behind enemy lines
Naked to the soul

All but abandoned
Still standing
Head high
Look fate in the eye
Daring to be
Hold hope in both hands
It's this man at the ready   *ALM*

FIGHTING MAD

ABOUT THE AUTHOR

Ana Miranda (a pen name) holds a PhD in a discipline in the humanities, and has taught at several universities in the Midwest and the eastern seaboard. She and her family have lived in the Boston area since 1999 and are still trying to learn the native language of "New English."

Ana writes and lectures within her academic specialty and is an internationally acclaimed speaker on topics of special interest to women. She is an active member of the National Alliance on Mental Illness, and helped to found a support group for people of faith who suffer from mental illness, in their own lives or the lives of those they love.

This is her first book, undertaken as a labor of love, with the desire that others who are on this same journey will find here a measure of understanding, encouragement, and hope.

CPSIA information can be obtained at www.ICGtesting.com
Printed in the USA
LVOW12s1138081213

364392LV00018B/570/P

9 781463 579135